Formulating American Indian Policy in New York State, 1970-1986

Formulating American Indian Policy in New York State, 1970-1986

Laurence M. Hauptman

State University of New York Press

E
78
N7
H36
1988

Published by
State University of New York Press, Albany

Printed in the United States of America

For information, address State University of New York Press, State University
Plaza, Albany, N.Y., 12246

Library of Congress Cataloging-in-Publication Data

Hauptman, Laurence M.
    Formulating American Indian policy in New York State, 1970–1986.

    Bibliography: p.
    Includes index.
    1. Indians of North America—New York (State)   2. Indians of North
America—Government relations—1934–   . I. Title.
E78.N7H36   1988   974.7'00497   87–18102
ISBN 0–88706–754–9
ISBN 0–88706–755–7 (pbk.)

10 9 8 7 6 5 4 3 2 1

For my mother and father
and to the memory of
Pauline Lay Seneca (1902–1986)

Contents

▼▼▼▼▼▼▼▼▼

PREFACE

▼▼▼▼▼▼▼▼▼

Scholars have extensively studied federal American Indian policies and policymaking but few researchers have focused on state administration. Despite the importance of state-Indian relations, most of the existing studies are historical surveys of American Indian populations of a particular state which tell little if anything about the formulation of state governmental policies.[1] The present study grows out of my earlier research on the Iroquois Indians in the twentieth century that led to the publication of *The Iroquois and the New Deal* (1981) and *The Iroquois Struggle for Survival: World War II to Red Power* (1986).[2] In these previous monographs, I consciously attempted to provide Iroquois-centered analyses of shifts in federal Indian policies and chose to base my conclusions on my analysis of documents in government and private archives as well as on interviews and fieldwork in Iroquois communities. In sharp contrast, *Formulating American Indian Policies in New York State: A Public Policy Study* has an Albany-centered focus, although I retained a similar methodological approach by continuing to do archival research as well as interviewing and fieldwork.

In 1985–1986, I was a senior fellow at the Nelson A. Rockefeller Institute of Government in Albany where I studied New York State-Iroquois relations. Out of this research came a lengthy report submitted in September 1986 to the governor of New York State and to American Indian nations.[3] The present study, no longer a report, is an expanded and revised analysis of state Indian policymaking up to January 1987. This book is a descriptive analysis of how New York State government formulates American Indian policies both at the statewide and agency levels. I have not attempted to draw theoretical assumptions or offer exhaustive comparisons with other states. My major objective is to present a base, rather than provide "all" the answers or even cover every state agency's involvement with American Indian communities. I hope to prevent policymakers from "going around the same rock again."

In my experience, state politicians and administrators have been unaware of past policies and the implications of these policies for both the American Indians and the government itself. When politicians and administrators leave office, they take with them their individual experiences learned on the job, leaving their successors to make the same mistakes. Writing about the making of Canadian Indian policies, the eminent anthropologist Sally Weaver of Waterloo University has explained this problem by insisting that, as a consequence, "the collective experience is not synthesized and lessons from even the recent past remained unlearned." She added: "Thus, policies promoted as innovative often arouse a strong sense of *deja vu* in Indians and long-standing government employees."[4]

Although the New York State-American Indian relationship is in some ways unique, this case study has relevance and application to other states. State-Indian relations in New York and elsewhere have had a long and stormy history. State governments from New York to California have had similar sources of conflict with American Indian nations. These sore points include Indian land loss and land claims; state criminal and civil jurisdiction; the lack of state services; overlapping federal and state responsibilities; state powers of taxation; tribal v. state sovereignty; unprotected Indian burial sites; and the limited American Indian employment in state governments. Stephen L. Pevar, staff counsel of the American Civil Liberties Union Indian Rights Committee, has succinctly observed: "Every Indian reservation is located within the boundaries of a state. This is a fact of life which many state and tribal officials would just as soon forget."[5] Consequently, American Indian nations from the 1780s onward often turned to their "Great Father" in Washington, D.C. in attempting to seek redress from state actions. To further emphasize the importance of state-Indian relationships, Congress has awarded some states, including New York, civil and criminal jurisdiction over its American Indian populations.[6]

New York State has a government-to-government relationship with nine American Indian nations: the Iroquois—the Cayuga, Mohawk, Oneida, Onondaga, Seneca Nation, the Tonawanda Band of Seneca and the Tuscaroras; and the Long Island Algonkians—the Poospatuck and Shinnecock. All but two—the Poospatuck and Shinnecock—are also federally recognized Indian nations. The state ranks tenth in size of native populations in the country. There are over 38,000 American Indians residing in New York State, which includes ten reservations, specially leased parcels of land in the environs of Plattsburgh called Ganienkeh, and five major urban Indian communities—Buffalo, New York City, Niagara

Falls, Rochester, and Syracuse. There are also Indian populations in New York who are recognized neither by state nor federal governments, most notably the Ramapo Indians of Orange and Rockland Counties. In contrast to New York State's non-recognition of the Ramapos, New Jersey has a government-to-government relationship with the Ramapo Indians. In addition, perhaps as many as half of the American Indian populations of New York State are from other other states or from Canada, having relocated here in search of better economic opportunities.[7]

New York has three coordinated statewide policies toward American Indians; furthermore, several but not most of the numerous state agencies also establish policy initiatives towards Indians. Since 1970, state policy has been (1) to protect New York State's land base as well as its counties and its agencies in American Indian land claims litigations and/or land controversies such as the Seneca-Salamanca lease dispute; and (2) to mediate any and all conflicts through negotiations, rather than through the courts, with any Indian, official representative, or self-proclaimed leader in order to avoid bloodshed. Both of these statewide policies intersect with and affect each other. One other policy is also apparent, namely (3) the historical assertions by New York State of jurisdiction in Indian civil and criminal matters, which resulted from the passage of congressional legislation in 1948 and 1950. This latter policy is somewhat played down today, except on the tax issue, because of state concerns about the need to mitigate open conflict with and prevent further litigation by the Iroquois.[8]

Outside of an opening chapter which provides historical background to the more contemporary relationship of New York State and American Indian nations, this longitudinal study has the starting date of 1970, the year of the last major state investigation of Indian affairs. In 1967, New York State held a major constitutional convention. Spurred on by the atmosphere of legislative and civil rights reform of the time as well as the fact that the Indian Law had not been examined in toto since 1909, the New York State legislature authorized the Assembly Standing Committee on Governmental Operations chaired by Joseph Reilly, to form the Subcommittee on Indian Affairs. The subcommittee was administered on a day-to-day basis by chief staffer John Hudacs and issued a fifty-three page report in 1971.[9]

This present study concludes with numerous recommendations based on the descriptive portrait of state policy operations provided in this book. The underlying theme of *Formulating American Indian Policies in New York State: A Public Policy Study* is that Albany officials will not succeed in improving Indian conditions or services or attracting more American Indians to governmental employment because of the overall distrust by native populations of state intentions caused by the continued impasse on all American Indian land claims. The lack of trust by American Indians of New York State officials and their policies is as true today as it was in 1971 and is the major problem in American Indian-New York State relations. According to the Subcommittee on Indian Affairs' report in 1971.

> It is imperative that open and honest communication be initiated between the Indian tribes and the State. Indians need access to government to express their needs and to discover what resources are available. The Subcommittee on Indian Affairs has attempted to establish a basis of trust upon which communication can begin. The Indian tends to be suspicious of any governmental aid to assist him in helping himself. It should be noted that there is a hesitancy among certain groups of Indians to engage in the white man's political world. Often groups of Indians will refuse to vote for fear of partaking in the white man's world and thereby, in their minds, jeopardizing the status of the reservation land. This deep overriding suspicion of termination of the reservation is a difficult obstacle to overcome. . . [10]

The deep suspicion which pervades American Indian-New York State relations today is largely based on land issues, the Oneida, Cayuga, Mohawk and Stockbridge-Munsee land claims, and the Seneca-Salamanca lease controversy, which will be given considerable attention in this book. The primacy of Iroquois-New York State relations in contrast to Long Island Algonkian-New York State relations is, in part, because of the serious nature of Iroquois land issues. New York State officials must focus their energies on settling one or more of these outstanding land issues since continued inertia prevents real progress in almost all other areas of New York State-Indian relations. Despite state officials' admissions of clouded land titles to parts of its present territory and two Oneida Indian legal victories in the United States Supreme Court since 1974, no land title has been transferred to Indian hands. This fact is in stark contrast to Indian land settlements in other states, including Connecticut, Maine, Massachusetts, and Rhode Island.[11]

Recognizing the importance of land issues to building trust with the American Indians, the Assembly Subcommittee on Indian Affairs spent considerable time hearing testimony on the subject. On November 18, 1970, the subcommittee held a special hearing in Syracuse devoted to exploring the circumstances surrounding the extensive and serious land claims made by the Oneidas. Although the subcommittee's report indicated that no state action on the Oneida land claim be taken until the conclusion of the Oneidas' proceedings before the federal Indian Claims Commission, eventually concluded in 1973, the Subcommittee on Indian Affairs recommended: "On the basis of testimony given at the Subcommittee's hearing on the issue the Oneida Nation of Indians appear to merit an opportunity to have their land claims heard and just determined."[12] The subcommittee's report also boldly advocated the drafting of a New York State constitutional amendment "to provide that reservation lands be exempt from the eminent domain of the state" in order "to preserve the remaining lands of the Indian community and to allay the Indian fear of further land loss."[13]

New York State government will not succeed in developing a much-needed formalized structure—"Indian Office," or a "Division of Indian Affairs"—for planning purposes, for conflict resolution, and for facilitation of services until land issues are first addressed and settled. Nor will large numbers of Indian people seek employment in New York State government until the adversarial relationship between the state and its Indians ends and trust is established. A new state office will be built on sand if these outstanding land issues are not resolved. Future confrontations between Indian communities and state agencies could be expected if these open sores fester.

New York State's long delay in sitting down and *seriously* negotiating with the recognized leadership of Indian nations has already produced results unfavorable to settlement. Today many Indians, hardened by beliefs that no improvement in Indian-state relations will ever occur, cynically "manipulate the system," either for individual gain, for the media value of embarrassing state officials, and/or for political advantages in tribal in-fighting.[14] Further delay in the land settlement process will exacerbate the problems in New York State-American Indian relations, weakening the chances of future progress.

Although the author takes credit/blame for his conclusions, he should like to thank the following for their helpful comments about the manuscript: Christopher Lavin of *Rochester Times-Union* and the Gannett News Service; Dr. John W. Kalas, Vice-President of the Research Foundation of SUNY; Mr. A. Keith Smiley of Mohonk Mountain House, New Paltz, New York; Mr. George Abrams of Salamanca, New York; Ms. Jeanne Marie Jemison, Surrogate of the Seneca Nation of Indians; Dr. Hazel V. Dean-John, Associate in the Native American Indian Education Unit of the New York State Department of Education; Dr. William N. Fenton, Emeritus Research Professor of Anthropology, SUNY/Albany; Dr. Jack Campisi, Visiting Professor of Anthropology at Wellesley College; Dr. William Starna, Chairman of the Department of Anthropology at SUNY/Oneonta; Dr. Christopher Vecsey, Professor of Religion at Colgate University; Mr. David Jaman of Gardiner, New York; Dr. William T. Hagan, Distinguished Professor of History at SUNY/Fredonia; and Mr. George Hamell, Exhibit Curator at the New York State Museum. I should also like to thank Mr. William Evans and Mr. William Gorman of the

New York State Archives and Mr. James Corsaro of the Manuscript Division of the New York State Library for their help in locating valuable sources. Mrs. Susan Jaman helped put this manuscript into final form with her impeccable word processing. My greatest acknowledgment goes out to my wife, daughter, and son, who had to bear with me during this most difficult research and incessant daily traveling to Albany.

Laurence M. Hauptman
New Paltz, New York
March 15, 1987

EASTERN IROQUOIS
SETTLEMENTS

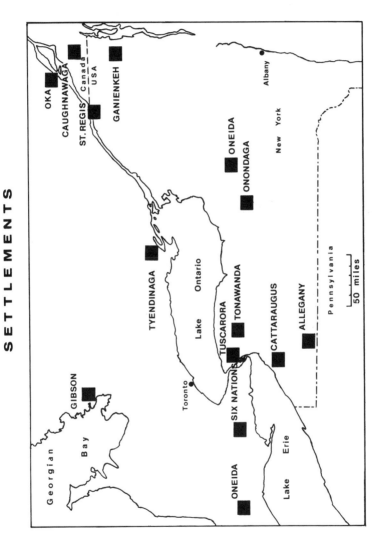

Credit Line: Jo Margaret Mano, cartographer.

WESTERN IROQUOIS
SETTLEMENTS

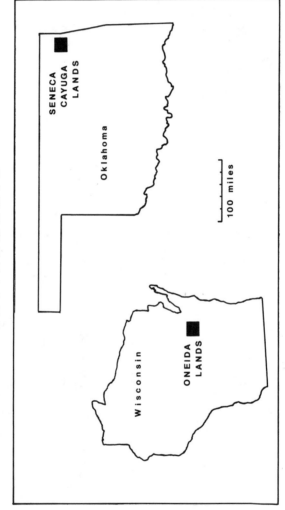

SENECA CAYUGA LANDS

Oklahoma

100 miles

Wisconsin

ONEIDA LANDS

Credit Line: Jo Margaret Mano, cartographer.

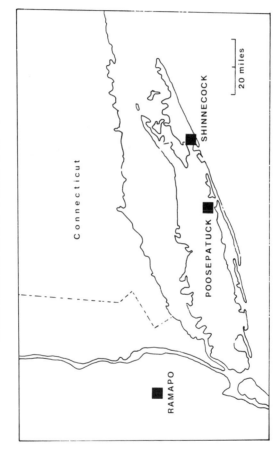

INDIAN SETTLEMENTS
Southern New York State

Connecticut

RAMAPO

POOSEPATUCK

SHINNECOCK

20 miles

Credit Line: Jo Margaret Mano, cartographer.

PART I

The Structure of New York State's
American Indian Policies

1

▼▼▼▼

New York State American Indian Policies in Historical Perspective, 1777-1950

> These Indian people have been kept as "wards" or children long enough. They should now be educated to be men, not Indians, and it is the earnest belief of the committee that when the suggestions made, or at least the more important of them are accomplished facts and the Indians of the State are absorbed into the great mass of the American people, then, and not before, will the "Indian problem" be solved.
>
> —*New York Legislature, Assembly.* Report of the Special Committee to Investigate the Indian Problem of the State of New York Appointed by the Assembly of 1888. *Albany, N.Y., 1889*

Writing in an article in the *Columbia Law Review* in 1922, Justice Cuthbert W. Pound of the New York Court of Appeals focused on Indian affairs in New York State, concluding: "Three sovereignties are thus contending over the Indians—the Indian nations, the United States and the State of New York—none of which exercises such jurisdiction in a full sense."[1] New York officials have repeatedly attempted to expand the state's sovereignty over Indian affairs since the state's founding in 1777; in the process, they have often clashed and/or impinged upon federal and Indian national sovereignties. Consequently, while state politicians and reformers frequently referred to the so-called "Indian problem" as being in dire need of a solution, the Indians have historically perceived Albany policy and policymakers as their main problem.

Since 1777, American Indian-New York State relations have centered on land and jurisdictional questions.[2] Although state policies were at times protective and often obsessively paternalistic in approach, one can conclude that more frequently than not New York State American Indian policies were designed to get at the Indian land base. The documentary record is clear about that fact. For example, in 1856, the comptroller of New York State, going against federal law, announced in a public notice that substantial lands from the Cattaraugus Indian Reservation were about to be sold to pay off alleged tax delinquencies.[3] In 1871, a joint resolution was passed by members of the New York State Senate and Assembly calling for the federal government to provide relief for the white people of Salamanca who had made leases with the Seneca Nation of Indians. The resolution stated:

> Resolved (if the Senate concur), that the Senators from this State in Congress be instructed and the Representatives be requested to presume the passage of some act as the formation of a treaty with the Seneca Nation of Indians, whereby title may be obtained to the whole or a portion of the Allegany Reservation, or such relief secured for white settlers as the circumstances demand.[4]

One-hundred-fourteen years later, white Salamancans and their legislators in Albany are still petitioning Washington for similar relief.[5] Moreover, every New York State legislative investigation of Indian affairs from 1888 to 1945, with one notable exception, championed the idea of state jurisdiction over the Indians in order to absorb them into the body politic. Frequently, the major voices heard at these hearings belonged to the non-Indian legislative chairman or counsel, usually a white man from an area bordering a reservation, or to those who, more often than not, opposed tribal custom and the tribal land system.[6]

To be sure, the state government was not the only problem that the Indians faced. America's definition of progress led the federal government to make treaties for Iroquois lands which were made through bribery and coercion.[7] Washington policymakers from 1790 onward regulated trade and land sales between Indians and the state or land companies; however, more often than not, the "Great Father" in Washington ignored its own laws and its trust responsibilities to Indian nations.[8] Moreover, culturally myopic federal policymakers and ardent true-believing missionaries often rubbed Indian sensibilities the wrong way. American Indian internal divisions only contributed to the weakening of resistance and often facilitated the land transfer process.

The years immediately after the American Revolution were the decisive period in the history of the Iroquois Indians. In the decade and a half following the conflict, the Iroquois lost over 95 percent of their lands as a result of unprecedented white pressures on their vast and rich estate. Although the religious and cultural forms of Iroquois life and reverence for tradition continued, the military power of the individual nations— Mohawk, Oneida, Onondaga, Cayuga, Seneca, and Tuscarora—as well as that of its ancient league were gone forever.

Indeed the American Revolution was an internal and disastrous civil war in Iroquoia as it was for all of British North America. The Oneidas and Tuscaroras proved invaluable to the patriot cause. The vast majority of the other four Iroquois nations joined the British in their war out of Niagara. Despite choosing sides, their allegiance to America or to Great Britain made little difference in their eventual treatment by their white neighbors, and friend sometimes fared worse than foe in the postwar treaties.[9]

Just as the Iroquois became entangled, much to their disservice, in the war of brothers between the colonists and Great Britain, the Indians became the victims of a battle within the American polity from 1774 onward. The contest between federal authority and states' rights and between states over each's claims to western lands became major outside factors shaping the Iroquois world in the decade and a half after the war. The most prominent statesmen of the Revolutionary era fought major battles over these two issues.

Through the early part of New York State history, the state's policymakers dealing with Indian affairs and their federal counterparts were speculators in western lands. Historian Reginald Horsman has correctly observed that these land speculators were on both sides of the national control-states' rights debate: "Those speculators who hoped to profit by state-granted lands opposed cession to the central government, whereas the speculators who had not gained recognition by the state governments pressed enthusiastically for the land cessions, hoping to gain a more favorable hearing from Congress."[10] Those advocates of the states' rights position over Indian affairs in New York included the most famous and powerful families, such as the Clintons and Livingstons, who stood to benefit most by Indian land title extinguishment.

Significantly, state calls for assumption of jurisdiction over the Indians were tied to land issues from the first. Congressman James Duane, an advocate in Congress for New York State control, insisted on this point from 1778 onward.[11]

According to historian Barbara Graymont, New York State Indian policy in the American Revolution era was based on extinguishing "any claim of the United States Congress to sovereignty over Indian affairs in the State of New York," on extinguishing "the title of the Indians to the soil"; and on extinguishing the sovereignty of the Six Nations. Even before the end of the war, these policies had been set in motion.[12] As early as October 23, 1779, the New York State legislature designated the governor and four commissioners to look out for New York's interests at the future peace negotiations with the Indians.[13] In the same month, John Jay, later to serve as governor of New York during key Iroquois negotiations of the 1790s, wrote to Governor Clinton. Fearing Virginia's claims to western lands and the extension of federal authority over Iroquois lands conquered by the Continental Army during the Sullivan-Clinton campaign, Jay urged Clinton to quickly have New York State assert its claim to this area. According to Jay:

> Since the successes of General Sullivan against the six [sic] Nations, some People have affected to speak [sic] of that Country as a conquered one, and I should not be surprized [sic] if they should next proceed to insist that it belongs to the united [sic] States, by whose Arms it was won from independent Nations in the Course and by the Fortune of War.
>
> Would it not be proper for New York to establish Posts in that Country, *and in every respect treat it as their own.* In my opinion our State has had too much Forbearance about these matters. Virginia, who has Claims and Rights under much the same circumstances, manages differently [emphasis mine].[14]

It is also clear that Duane and Jay were working in tandem to secure New York State control over these Iroquois lands. Governor George Clinton as well as Duane and Jay believed that the Congress had no right to interfere in New York affairs, which included state efforts at negotiating and extinguishing Indian title.[15]

Five months before the preliminary articles of peace were signed in 1783, the New York State legislature moved to expropriate Iroquois country, except for lands occupied by Oneidas and Tuscaroras, for military bounty lands. By March 1783, the New York State legislature empowered the Council of Appointment to appoint three Indian commissioners who would, in conjunction with the governor, have control of Indian affairs, and secure the rights of the Oneidas and Tuscaroras for their loyal service in the American Revolution. One of the three appointed New York Indian commissioners was Major Peter Schuyler, who, through the Genesee Company of Adventurers, attempted in the 1780s to evade New York State's constitutional provision against private individuals conducting land negotiations with the Indians without a license.[16]

The federal-state jurisdiction question soon came to the fore when Congress called into question New York State's determination to use Iroquois country for military bounty lands. Nevertheless, the New York State legislature continued to assert the state's sovereignty in Indian affairs within its own borders. State officials such as Governor Clinton, who had depended on federal support during the American Revolution, now refused to cooperate with Congress on Indian matters. Importantly, the year 1784 marked two major negotiations with the Iroquois—one an inconclusive state negotiation; the second, the federal-Iroquois Treaty of Fort Stanwix. It is important to note that while the federal treaty negotiations were being conducted, sentries were posted to keep the New York Indian Commissioners Peter Schuyler and Peter Rykman away.[17] The federal commissioners later reported to Congress about the "great inconveniences from the conduct of the Governor of this state, in attempting to frustrate the treaty, and the consequent licentiousness of some of its citizens. . . ."[18]

Despite federal guarantees to protect the Oneidas and Tuscaroras at Fort Stanwix in 1784, the New York State legislature, proposing to speed up white settlement, passed two laws in 1784 and 1785 to facilitate the "settlement of the waste and unappropriate lands" in the state, and set up procedures to advertise and distribute Indian lands, even before the state had bought title.[19] Previously, state officials had pointed out to the Indians that they were going to be treated fairly and the Indians' land base would be respected. Governor George Clinton had addressed the Indians at Fort Schuyler (Stanwix) on September 4, 1784:

> Brethren, we have been informed that some designing persons have endeavored to persuade you that we mean to take away your lands. This is not true. You must not believe it. We have no claim on your lands; its just extent will ever remain secured to you. It is therefore, the object of our present meeting to have metes and bounds thereof, precisely ascertained in all its parts, in order to prevent any intrusions thereupon.[20]

Clinton gave further assurances, indicating that in order to prevent Indian-white disputes and conflict, the New York State Constitution provision forbidding Indian land sales to individuals without legislative permission would be enforced.[21]

In reality, New York officials built a rising empire state on profits from Indian land cessions. The Oneidas are a case in point. Between 1785 and 1838, these Indians lost their lands in New York State through a series of thirty-one "treaties," despite being on the patriot side during the American Revolution, provisions in the New York State and U.S. Constitutions, and congressional acts and federal treaty guarantees. Jack Campisi, a prominent ethnohistorian, has described how land loss occurred:

> The [Oneida] factionalism permitted the New York State representatives to bargain one group against another, appealing to the vanity and desire for gain on the part of individual Oneidas. The state legislature, which had guaranteed protection against speculators, was dominated by the most unscrupulous land barons in America, the Hudson Valley aristocracy. What they really sought to protect were their rights to exploit. The trusted advisors of the Oneidas, men like Kirkland, Penn, Penet, and Eleazer Williams, were in the pay of the land companies and were anxious themselves to receive rich estates. Finally, as the supposed danger of an Indian uprising in New York State subsided, the federal government lost its need to placate the Indians.[22]

Taking advantage of an internal Oneida dispute between Good Peter and Beech Tree, New York State officials made the first of these state "treaties" in 1785 at Fort Herkimer, obtaining a huge land cession between the Chenango and Unadilla Rivers, as far south as the Great Bend in the Susquehanna River and the Pennsylvania border for $11,500 in goods and money to the Indians. This Oneida cession was the first in a series of post-Revolutionary negotiations that state officials made with separate Iroquois nations, especially the Cayugas and Onondagas.

In open defiance of congressional intent from 1783 onward, New York State continued to deal with the Indians as it pleased. While the federal government was attempting to keep the Iroquois at peace and from joining an Indian war in the Ohio country through federal treaty-making in the decade from Stanwix (1784) to Canandaigua (1794), New York State had designs on territorial aggrandizement. In this period, the Iroquois status changed from independent or collective sovereignties on a large, viable agricultural land base tied to the religious ritual cycle, to being dependent peoples boxed in on island reservations. Instead of the ancient Covenant Chain that bound Indian and white as equal partners, the Indian's world and power shrunk. Land "purchased" by state "treaty" from Oneidas for fifty cents an acre was sold for seven to ten times its original purchasing price. Meanwhile, the state was encouraging the settlement of the central portion of the state. Madison County, which had less than 1,000 settlers in 1800, had 39,000 by 1830. With the development of the Erie Canal, the Indians in central and western New York soon found themselves surrounded by whites who coveted their lands. By the 1830s and 1840s, railroads further added to the rush for the fertile lands.[23]

While New York State was encouraging Indian land title extinguishment by flouting federal laws, the federal government itself was facilitating land transfer and extinguishing Indian land titles from the Treaty of Fort Stanwix (1784) to the Treaty of Buffalo Creek (1838). Federal attempts to reduce the Indian land base also furthered the objectives of private land speculators and land companies such as the Ogden Land Company. Urged on by the New York congressional delegation and special landed interests in Congress, these treaties substantially reduced the Indians' estate and contributed to Indian removal to the West.[24] Federal efforts at removing Indians from New York continued through the Civil War era. All too frequently, the long established federal trust responsibility to the Indians of New York State was ignored and suffered from neglect. Hence, the sovereignty of Indian nations in New York shrank because of state and federal policymakers' constant infringement on the tribal realm.

The reduction of Indian sovereignty was also manifest in state statutory law. The New York State legislature first became involved in Indian statutory law in 1813, with regulations banning the cutting of lumber on tribal lands. In 1821, the New York State legislature transferred the enforcement of the 1813 law to county district attorneys. By 1835, the legislature, without federal approval, began permitting as well as ratifying leases made by non-Indians on the Allegany Indian Reservation. By 1840 and 1841, New York State attempted to tax lands from which the Senecas had agreed to be removed by the Treaty of 1838.[25] The United States Supreme Court struck this statute down:

> Until the Indians have sold their lands, and removed from them in pursuance of the treaty stipulations, they are . . . entitled to the undisturbed enjoyment of them . . . we must say, regarding these reservations as wholly exempt from state taxation . . . the exercise of this authority over them in an unwarrantable interference.[26]

The State of New York became increasingly involved in providing for the educational and social welfare needs of American Indians in the mid-nineteenth century. In 1846, the state legislature provided $1,200 for the erection and operation of school houses on the Allegany and Cattaraugus Indian Reservations. Within three decades, state supported Indian schools were in operation from Southampton, Long Island to Salamanca under the aegis of the State Superintendent of Public Instruction. In 1855, the state legislature passed a bill to establish and maintain the Thomas Asylum for Orphan and Destitute Indian Children. With the creation of the New York State Board of Charities, children at the Thomas Asylum as well as Indian needy as a whole became the charge of this state agency.

The New York State Board of Charities evolved into the New York State Department of Social Services and became the lead state agency involved in Indian affairs over the past one-hundred-twenty years.[27]

Throughout the end of the nineteenth century and early twentieth century, the New York State legislature also conducted a series of major investigations into what its members considered the "Indian problem." American Indians in New York State and elsewhere were faced with a prevailing white societal attitude that sought to absorb native peoples into American society through a four-pronged formula of forced assimilation. This so-called Americanization process included (1) the Christianizing activities of missionaries on reservations in order to stamp out "paganism"; (2) the exposure of the Indian to white Americans' ways through compulsory education and boarding schools such as Carlisle, Hampton, and Lincoln Institutes; (3) the break-up of tribal lands and allotment to individual Indians to instill personal initiative, allegedly required by the free enterprise system; and finally, in return for accepting land-in-severalty, (4) the "rewarding" of Indians with United States citizenship. These premises, strange as they may seem today, were advocated even by such prominent reform groups as the Indian Rights Association, the Women's National Indian Association, the Lake Mohonk Conferences of Friends of the Indian, and the United States Board of Indian Commissioners. Exhibiting a Social Darwinist bias and advocating a similar paternalistic approach, these reformers believed that responsible men of affairs owed an obligation to what they considered "weaker races." Behind these attitudes was the seldom-challenged assumption that it was possible to kill the Indian but save the man.[28]

The New York State legislature in 1855 began its first probe of the "Indian problem." This first committee emphasized the needs of "civilizing" the Indian and educating him into the ways of the white man.[29] In 1882, Dr. C. N. Sims, the chancellor of Syracuse University, headed an official commission "to inquire into the morals and social condition of the Onondagas." Sims concluded by "blaming the victim," indicating that there were few enterprising individuals on the reservation and that the major problem was "the general indolence of the Indians."[30]

One of the most significant New York State legislative investigations of Indian affairs occurred in 1888 and was chaired by Assemblyman J. S. Whipple of Salamanca. This special committee and its report of 1889 has bred resentment among the Iroquois toward New York State government even to the present day.[31] Iroquois family life, customs, land claims, lifestyle, and religious practices and traditions were held in contempt by the assembly committee and used to emphasize the "need for the changes in landed patterns and tribal governments." The report concluded that the

"Indian problem" could be solved only by ending the Indians' separate status, giving them full citizenship and absorbing them "into the great mass of the American people." The committee's findings cited disgruntled and/or deposed Indian leaders such as Albert Cusick or so-called Indian experts such as Chancellor Sims to back up its case. Without question, the report had its harshest words for the Onondagas since both missionaries and state officials apparently were most frustrated in dealing with their conservatism and resistance to change. With no understanding of cultural relativism, the report condemned the traditional governmental leadership on the reservation as "corrupt and vicious," characterized the religious practices as "depraved, immoral, and superstitious, and described the social and industrial state as chronic barbarism." It insisted: "Their present condition is infamously vile and detestable, and just so long will there remain upon the fair name of the Empire State a stain of no small magnitude." The Whipple Report maintained that reservation lands, especially Onondaga, Allegany, and Cattaraugus, be allotted in severalty among tribal members with suitable restrictions as to alienation of lands to whites and protection from judgments and debts. It urged the extension of state laws and jurisdiction over the Indians and their absorption into citizenship. Finally, the report concluded: "These Indian people have been kept as 'wards' or children long enough. They should now be educated to be men, not Indians, in order to finally and once and for all solve the 'Indian problem'."[32]

In 1900, Governor Theodore Roosevelt of New York appointed a five-member commission to once again investigate the state's "Indian problem." Since the commission was composed of noted national reformers of Indian policy, its report advocated a different direction on jurisdiction but, nevertheless, had an assimilationist focus similar to the Whipple Report. In appointing the commission, Roosevelt elaborated on what he expected them to do:

My desire is that you should take up the whole Indian question as it affects this state. In the brief time all that can be done by you is, I fear, to sketch the general lines along which it is necessary to work, and the first steps to be taken either by the Legislature or the Executive, or both. I think that all true friends of civilization are agreed that as rapidly as possible the reservations should be broken up, and the property divided so as to substitute individual for tribe ownership, and have the Indian given full rights of citizenship.[33]

The commission held two two-day meetings in Philadelphia and in New York City. No first-hand inspections were made of Indian reservations since three members of the committee had been "more or less familiar with the reservations from personal inspection, and most of them . . . had a previous acquaintance with the subject." Citing the recommendations of previous commissions, administrators, and reformers, the commissioners' report blamed the lack of progress on the Indians' status as an *"imperium in imperio,"* a foreign country within the State of New York. They decried the resulting isolation which perpetuates "a condition of things repugnant to Christian civilization" such as "barbarous feasts and ceremonies." Although hastily prepared since Roosevelt's gubernatorial term was to end on December 31, 1900, the commission's report, nevertheless, was specific in its policy recommendations. It urged that "so far as legally possible, all jurisdiction over the Indians should be relegated to the National Government"; that "steps be taken for the allotment of their lands in severalty" under the provisions of the Dawes Act; and that they "be admitted to the full rights of American citizenship."[34]

Other state legislative investigations of the "Indian problem" followed in 1905 and 1914 with conclusions similar to those expressed in the Whipple Report.[35] Jurisdictional transfer was the main concern of the New York State Constitutional Convention of 1915. The convention drafted an amendment, later rejected by the voters, abolishing Indian courts, transferring jurisdiction to state courts, and extending state laws to the Indians except as otherwise provided by the treaties of this state and the United States Constitution and treaties with the Indians. Instead of proposing allotment, the report of the convention's Committee on Relations to the Indians stated that the amendment was "not intended to affect, nor can it in any way affect, the tribal lands of the Indians," because they could be disposed of only with federal consent.[36] Despite this statement, New York State continued through the 1970s not to acknowledge that it was necessary for it to receive prior federal approval in land transactions with Indians.[37]

Federal-state tension over jurisdiction continued well into the twentieth century. The federal government provided little monetary aid to the Iroquois until the New Deal. By the 1930s, the New York Agency of the BIA paid and distributed annuities under federal-Iroquois treaties, collected rentals on leases, provided educational loans and scholarship programs beyond state schools, administered special federal work relief programs such as the New Deal's Indian Civilian Conservation Corps, and made special investigations and prepared annual reports to Washington. New York State, through the Department of Social Services in Buffalo, administered the Thomas Indian School, almost all social welfare and work relief programs, as well as payment of state annuity moneys to the Mohawks, Onondagas, and the scattered Cayugas. The New York State Department of Health was in charge of administering to the health needs of reservation Indians. In the educational realm, the chief of the Special Schools Bureau of the state Education Department administered district schools on the reservations and worked with public schools which some Indians attended in towns adjacent to the reservation; beyond high school, the state provided aid for students attending state normal schools and colleges. The state Department of Highways financed the construction and maintenance of highways on the reservations. With the expansion of federal government services to the Iroquois in the 1930s and the change from a federal operating budget of the New York Agency of a few thousand dollars, the ambiguities between state and federal jurisdiction became more accentuated.[38]

New York State legislators and representatives in Congress, inspired largely by assimilationist goals, myopic philanthropy, a need for legal order, or less-than-noble motives of land and resource acquisition, sought increasing control over Indian affairs in the last quarter of the nineteenth century and into the mid-twentieth century. At the time of the Whipple Committee and again in 1906, 1915, 1930, and 1940, legislators attempted to effect this change. The Iroquois waged a major battle, especially in 1930, to fight off state jurisdiction. Even though the jurisdiction bill of 1930, one introduced by influential conservative Republican Congressman Bertram Snell of Potsdam, had provided for a formal recognition of property rights guaranteed by treaties, the Six Nations, suspicious of non-Indian motives, feared it as a "contravention of treaty rights" and an effort that would subject them to the uncontrollable whims of state politics.[39] According to Chief Clinton Rickard:

> In 1930 a serious threat faced our Six Nations people in the form of the Snell Bill in Congress, which would give control of our Six Nations to New York State. We Indians have always feared being under the thumb of the state rather than continuing our relationship with the federal government because it is a well-known fact that those white people who live closest to Indians are always the most prejudiced against them and the most desirous of obtaining their lands. We have always had a better chance of obtaining justice from Washington than from the state or local government. Also, in turning us over to the state, the federal government would be downgrading our significance as a people and ignoring the fact that our treaties are with the United States.[40]

While New York State was seeking to gain jurisdictional control over the Indians during the interwar period, the Iroquois were undergoing a period of cultural and religious revitalization which spilled over as new attempts at seeking justice from the governments of Canada and the United States, as well as New York State. On March 3, 1920, the United States Circuit Court of Appeals for the Second Circuit, in *United States v. Boylan,* an ejectment proceeding involving the removal of Indians living on a thirty-two acre tract of land, the Oneida homeland, and the partition of it to non-Indians, found that these Indians were a federally recognized tribe and that New York State courts had no jurisdiction in disposing of the Indians' property without the consent of the United States.[41] This hard-won Indian victory gave the Iroquois hopes for other victories in the courts.

In August 1920, the Everett Commission, a New York State Assembly committee formed in 1919 to examine "the history, the affairs and transactions had by the people of the state of New York with the Indian tribes resident in the state and to report to the legislature the status of the American Indian residing in said state of New York" began holding hearings. After nineteen months that included on-site inspections of Iroquois reservations in Canada and the United States, Chairman Edward A. Everett of Potsdam issued a report in 1922, which reflected largely his opinion and that of the commission's stenographer, Lulu G. Stillman. The report concluded that the Iroquois as Six Nations were legally entitled to six million acres of New York State, having been illegally dispossessed of their title after the Treaty of Fort Stanwix in 1784. This report, however unrepresentative of the commission, helped revive the Iroquois efforts to recover lands through legal means. The Everett Report, never published, was generally buried by New York State officials. Today, Indians in the state point to the report, and to official reactions to it, as "proof" of New York's effort to prevent native peoples from achieving justice.[42]

The Everett Report resulted in the Indians bringing a test case, a class action suit, on behalf of the Iroquois Confederacy. James Deere, a Mohawk, entered an ejectment proceeding against the Saint Lawrence River Power Company, a subsidiary of ALCOA, and seventeen other occupants of a one-mile-square parcel of land. In October of 1927, the United States District Court dismissed the Deere case because of what it insisted was the court's lack of jurisdiction.[43] The Iroquois would have to wait over forty years before they would get their second chance in court.

The Everett Report was more the exception than the rule. Few New York State policymakers took the Indians' land claims assertions seriously until 1974. What state policymakers focused on from the late 1920s until 1950 was the continued quest for New York criminal and civil jurisdiction over Indians. At a time when Indian hopes of a restored land base were being opposed by New York State officials (except Assemblyman Everett), these same state officials were pursuing the goal of federal jurisdictional transfer to New York.

In January of 1942, the United States Circuit Court of Appeals for the Second Circuit of New York handed down *United States v. Forness, et al.*, one of the most momentous decisions affecting Iroquois peoples in their history. The case involved a five-year legal brouhaha between the Seneca

Nation and delinquent non-Indian leaseholders on Indian lands in the City of Salamanca, a city of mostly non-Indians which is almost entirely on the Allegany Reservation of the Seneca Nation. The federal court ruled against Fred and Jessie Forness, the operators of a large garage in the city, who, along with over 800 non-Indian leaseholders at Salamanca, were delinquent in their payments to the Seneca Nation. The United States Department of Justice brought the test case on behalf of the Senecas to determine if the Indians had the right to cancel Forness's and other federally authorized leases because of non-payment. The Fornesses had not paid rent on property in the central business district for eleven years, and were a total of forty-four dollars in arrears on a ridiculously undervalued lease of four dollars per year. The Circuit Court of Appeals also questioned a New York State law that provided for the acceptance of a tender of payment of rent in arrears, even within six months after execution of judgment. This provision in state law had allowed the Fornesses to pay after the cancellation of their lease. The lower federal district court had previously refused to apply the state law but had rendered judgment for the Fornesses anyway on the grounds that his tender of payment prevented forfeiture of his lease. In the higher court's decision, Justice Jerome Frank clearly stated that "state law cannot be invoked to limit the rights in land granted by the United States to the Indians, because . . . state law does not apply to the Indians *except so far as the United States has given its consent* [emphasis mine]."[44]

Alarmed by the implications of the Forness decision, especially in challenging concurrent jurisdiction of the state and federal governments in Indian matters, the New York State legislature, under pressure from those with interests in the southwestern part of the state, created the Joint Legislative Committee on Indian Affairs on March 8, 1943, to deal with the "more or less continuous state of confusion" about state authority over Indian reservations.[45] The joint legislative committee's intentions were made clear by its make-up and by the way it operated in its first year. Like the earlier Whipple Committee of 1888–89, the 1943 committee was dominated by New Yorkers from the southwestern corner of the state. Although the committee's membership consisted of nine legislators, including ones from Brooklyn, Manhattan, Binghamton, and Rochester, its chairman, William H. Mackenzie, its vice chairman, George H. Pierce, and its most important voice and chief counsel, Leighton Wade, were from southwestern New York. Wade was from Olean, as was State Senator Pierce, while Assemblyman Mackenzie represented Allegany County. A fourth committee member, Leo P. Noonan, represented Cattaraugus County. The committee quickly scheduled nine hearings throughout the state in 1943, with the first in the series to be held at Salamanca in

August of that year. As in the past, the state legislature's committee loaded its witnesses in favor of its position to transfer federal jurisdiction to the state.[46]

After its closing hearing in October 1943, the joint legislative committee issued a report in February 1944 that focused almost entirely on the Salamanca lease controversy and the questions of jurisdiction. The report recounted the history of the leases and emphasized the lack of state jurisdiction over reservation Indians as a result of the Forness decision, which it characterized as a "reproach" both to the state and the nation. It recommended that Congress take appropriate legislative action and that the Indian tribes, the Bureau of Indian Affairs, and New York State officials hold a conference to deal with the dispute. The report suggested that there were two alternatives: an increased recognition of state jurisdiction or that the federal government assume the state's annual burden of 400,000 dollars by taking over education, health, highway, and social services to reservation Indians. The language of the report was loaded in favor of transfer of jurisdiction. The report failed to mention that highways and bridges maintained on reservations were used by all the state's peoples or that they were not built or maintained for the special use of the Indians.[47] Another section of the report was entitled the "Ogden Land Company Title." The report concluded about the Ogden's preemptive claim: "The existence of this claim is a *continuing obstacle to purchase* [emphasis added] by the City of Salamanca of the 3,570 acres of reservation land occupied by the municipality."[48] The old Iroquois fear, that state legislative "reform" meant new threats to their dwindling land base and that state efforts to solve the "Indian problem" by jurisdictional transfer were actually less-than-nobly motivated, seemed to be confirmed in the Indians' minds.

Jurisdiction and leasing seemed to be separate issues and were viewed by policymakers as unrelated; nevertheless, the Indians never viewed them as entirely distinct largely because in the past those New Yorkers who pushed for jurisdictional changes were so often the same attorneys or legislators who represented non-Indians in their legal struggle against the Iroquois. It is important in this regard to remember that the Snell Bill of 1930 had been drafted by Henry Manley, the assistant attorney general of New York State. Later, in the early 1940s, Manley was one of the attorneys for the Fornesses and other Salamanca lessees in their legal appeals to stop the Senecas from initiating eviction proceedings. In the 1950s, Manley worked on behalf of the New York State Power Authority in its successful fight to condemn Tuscarora lands for a reservoir.[49]

On March 15, 1945, the Joint Legislative Committee on Indian Affairs issued its report on jurisdiction. The report included two draft bills, which recommended congressional approval of transferring criminal and civil jurisdiction to New York State, and offered to cooperate with Congress in securing these laws. The report concluded that committee members seriously doubted that an "overwhelming majority" of the Indians on the reservations would ever unite in favor of these bills and stated that "the moving force to accomplish these reforms must come from without." The only Iroquois government to endorse the proposed bills were the elected chiefs under state charter at Tonawanda. In a vaguely worded statement, the report claimed that letters "were received from other individual Indians, residents of reservations in various parts of the State, expressing complete approval of the proposed legislation." The report, after recounting a January 4, 1945 conference at Albany with various Indian groups, discounted Indian opposition as based merely on "pride in the Indian tradition and a resentment against outside interference" and "deep-rooted suspicion of the white man" based justifiably on "the exploitation of Indian property rights during an earlier but unforgotten era."[50]

As a result of the lobbying of New York State officials and support of powerful Senator Hugh A. Butler of Nebraska, the Congress passed the criminal jurisdictional transfer bill which was signed into law on July 1, 1948. Within twenty-six months, Congress tranferred civil jurisdiction over Indians to New York State. Despite overwhelming criticism by Indians of these moves, both of the bills passed overwhelmingly.[51] In a remarkable document, the Tonawanda Seneca traditional government sent an elaborate legal brief to President Truman condemning New York for not settling Indian land claims, while, at the same time, interfering in Indian lives. They claimed that the state discriminated against Indians; did little for Indian educational and medical needs or for reservation road improvements; treated Indians as merely charity cases; and collaborated with vested interests, especially public utilities involved in power development and private corporations involved in mineral extraction, to keep the Indians divided and economically deprived.[52]

In sum, the historic interplay of federal, state, and Indian sovereignties from 1777 to 1950 had shaped the Indian world. State and federal projects of the 1950s and early 1960s were to further restrict Indian sovereignty and reduce the Indian land base in New York State. The New York State Power Authority, the St. Lawrence Seaway Development Authority, and the Army Corps of Engineers were to have their day and Iroquois lands were once again to be seen as sacrifice areas in America's definition of progress. Since the "jurisdictional question" had largely been resolved in 1948 and 1950, although not to the Indians' liking, land issues once again came to the fore, serving as the backdrop of New York State-Indian relations after 1950.

2
▼▼▼

Indian Land Issues:
At Odds With The "Family
of New York"

The aforementioned meeting and lack of response of your people, lead less militant people [than the Indians at Moss Lake] to sometimes entertain the thoughts that only the "heavies" that carry rifles and take over buildings and properties, at the loss of lives, are the people who receive the most attention and are the better taken care of. Perhaps this [militancy] is the attitude that has to be adopted by all the New York States Tribes to receive equal time at what we feel are important issues for all concerned.

*—Mohawk (Akwesasne) Tribal Council
Letter to Governor Hugh Carey,
March 14, 1977*

Land issues are without question the backdrop to contemporary American Indian-New York State relations. They influence attitudes as well as strategies on both sides, they color as well poison the air, and most importantly, they prevent real progress in so many other areas affecting the state's relationship to the Indians. Land issues shape how contemporary American Indians view the outside world; they also determine many of the official decisions made in Albany relative to Indian communities. The State of New York and American Indians discuss and come into conflict in other important areas such as over the custody of wampum housed in the New York State Museum, taxation issues, hunting and fishing rights, the sanctity of Indian burial sites, and jurisdiction; however, the key issue in understanding the present uneasy relationship between the Iroquois and New York State is land. The Indians' remembrance of land loss, even as recent as two decades ago, produces constant distrust of outsiders, marks Albany as the "enemy's capital," and retards certain positive responses made by some progressive state officials and their agencies. It also contributes to internal tribal differences and fractionated Indian political behavior about the strategies to use in Indian-state negotiations.

To many of the Iroquois, their federal treaties with the United States government put them above the legislative actions of any one state. They trace the source of their sovereignty to the period 1784–1794 and define their world as far different and distinct from other Indian nations. This is based upon four historical factors: the long-established practice of colonial governments and their rulers in England, France, and Holland to negotiate with tribal representatives of the Iroquois Confederacy in council, and the three major treaties consummated after the American Revolution—Fort Stanwix (1784), Jay (1794), and Canandaigua (1794). To the Iroquois, these treaties guaranteed individual national and/or collective Iroquois sovereign status as well as free passage and unrestricted trade for Indians across the international boundary between the United States and Canada, a border seen by these Indians as non-existent and artificially created by whites.[1] Nevertheless, in 1948 and 1950, the United States Congress awarded New York State criminal and civil jurisdiction over Indian affairs. Despite the passage of these important acts, which became the model for Public Law 280 applied in other states, the Iroquois Indians have steadfastly rejected the idea, however real in American law, that they are subject to the laws of a state, especially one that had earlier dispossessed them.[2] Moreover, the Iroquois also have had the persistent belief that the ability of outsiders to tax them, still a real issue, is the first step toward the loss of their lands. Their elders also take exception to any reference to them as "New York Indians."[3]

The Iroquois in New York, Oklahoma, Wisconsin, and Canada have been viewed as being distinct from each other in their culture, history, and institutions ever since the late eighteenth and first half of the nineteenth centuries. Indeed, they are six separate nations historically— Mohawk, Oneida, Onondaga, Cayuga, Tuscarora, and Seneca—who occupy fifteen separate settlements today. Each of these Indian nations has beliefs in its individual tribal sovereignty and many, though not all, have a collective belief in a body called a league. At the present, two Iroquois leagues continue to function, one centered at Onondaga near Syracuse, New York, and the other at the Six Nations Reserve near Brantford, Ontario. Despite this second supralevel affirmation of Iroquois sovereignty, governmental officials in Albany as well as Washington, D.C. and Ottawa historically have recognized Iroquois sovereignty only in the existence of individual tribal or band governments, in certain tribal judicial authorities, such as the Peacemakers' Court of the Seneca Nation, and in the acceptance of some features of Indian customary law. The continuous rejection by the United States and Canada of the idea of collective sovereignty of the Six Nations Confederacy has frequently motivated many Iroquois League supporters to protest against policymakers and their policies.

Much of the Iroquois' focus, as individual nations or as a collective body, since the American Revolution has been to protect their shrinking land base, especially from New York State. Consequently, most Iroquois in New York see themselves as citizens of their own Indian nations; do not choose to participate or vote in local, county, state, or American national elections; rarely lobby or even visit the state capital; and refer to the New York State Indian law, volume 25 of McKinney's *Consolidated Laws of New York State*, as "that Black Book." In the high-powered lobbying and political world of Albany, this conscious Indian separation is an anomaly, which reduces the Indians' ability to affect change in areas where the state is willing to accede, namely, in areas unrelated to Indian land rights.[4]

The present generation of leadership in each of the Iroquois communities reached political maturity during a period of severe trauma as a result of land loss from the late 1940s to the mid-1960s.[5] This fact is especially important in understanding Indian perceptions of state and federal officials as well as their renewed push for land rights from the mid-1960s onward. The Iroquois, in the twenty-year period after World War II, lost significant acreage in five of their reservation communities, beginning with a dam project at Onondaga in the late 1940s. The St. Lawrence Seaway project in the 1950s led to the expropriation of approximately 1,300 acres of Caughnawaga Mohawk land near Montreal as well as 130 acres of St. Regis (Akwesasne) Mohawk land near Massena; it also weakened economic self-sufficiency by destroying the Indian fishing and cattle industries along the St. Lawrence River, in part because of increased industrialization and resulting pollution of the air and waters. The Kinzua Dam, which opened only twenty years ago, pushed by Pennsylvania interests and the Army Corps of Engineers, flooded the entire Cornplanter Tract, the last Indian lands in Pennsylvania, and over 9,000 acres of the lands of the Seneca Nation. The New York State Power Authority's Niagara Power Project, completed in 1961, condemned one-eighth or 560 acres of the Tuscarora Indian Reservation near Lewiston, New York, in a plan for a massive reservoir conceived of by master-builder Robert Moses.

In the process of condemnation, expropriation, and removal, the Iroquois Indians' psyche was also affected. Destroying the Old Cold Spring Longhouse and taking the Cornplanter Heirs from a source of their medicine and spirituality, the Allegheny River, and placing them in more crowded communities in two ranch-style housing developments with far different spatial relationships produced nightmares and lifelong tragic memories. These travesties occurred at a time when Indian land needs were becoming acute on the reservations.

One important sidelight not generally recognized was that Cayugas, outsiders without land rights on the Cattaraugus Indian Reservation, and Oneidas, outsiders without land rights at the Onondaga Indian Reservation, were in some ways more affected by states and federal policies than the nations directly involved in dealing with governmental officials. Every time there is a land crisis on these two reservations, as in the Kinzua and Onondaga dam crises, land pressures intensify and Indians with no reservation land rights such as the Cayugas and Oneidas are increasingly seen as outsiders or as "Indians who came to dinner and stayed two hundred years." Hence, it is no coincidence that these two landless Indian nations in New York are at the forefront of Indian claims litigation.

Today, the main issue affecting Iroquois-New York State relations is the claims of various Indian nations to sizeable tracts of land. These claims assertions are not new, despite popular belief, but have been maintained by Iroquois people for nearly two hundred years. Land claims have been the subject of countless council meetings and their settlement was the stuff of family hopes during times of economic and political despair. Moreover, the Iroquois have over the years inculcated in their children the righteousness of their land claims and a belief in the eventual favorable conclusion of this agonizing process.

Despite their meaning to the Iroquois, settlements of these claims have received little priority and have been purposely ignored by state officials. Although there is the outward insistence by Albany policymakers of a willingness to negotiate and settle these Indian land claims, the opposite is true. A public policy study submitted to the Governor's Office in August, 1987, further substantiates this conclusion. According to this study prepared by William A. Starna, Senior Fellow of the Nelson A. Rockefeller Institute of Government: "However, information derived from additional interviews clearly points to a conscious decision not to negotiate having been made at the level of the Executive Department prior to the bringing of the suit by the Stockbridge-Munsees." (1986). Starna added: "Thus, although the state asserts its interest in negotiating settlements rather than litigating them, and one high official in the Executive (Department) contends that it is 'more advantageous to enter into claims settlements without litigation,' the exact opposite has been true."[6]

The major claims of the Cayugas, Mohawks, and Oneidas as well as the non-Iroquois Stockbridge-Munsees affect the present and future of much of the central and northern regions of the state. The Oneidas in their pursuit of their two-centuries-old claim have been most successful in overturning American legal precedents, winning two favorable decisions in the United States Supreme Court; though, despite their success in litigation, they have not yet received any land or financial compensation from New York.

Much of the Indian legal argument in the land claims cases centers around New York State violations of the Indian Trade and Intercourse Acts of 1790 and 1793. The 1790 act regulated trade with the Indians and prohibited the unauthorized purchase of land on all land sales not approved by the federal government. The 1793 act tightened federal control over Indian policy by adding a section requiring the presence and approval of a federal commissioner when the states intended to extinguish Indian land rights. From this act onward, as Jack Campisi has correctly observed, the process of ratification of so-called state treaties, i.e., land transactions, was "the same as with any federal treaty."[7]

In November 1970, before a special hearing of Chairman Reilly's New York State Subcommittee on Indian Affairs, George Shattuck, at that time the attorney for the Oneidas, explained how these Indians were systematically dispossessed by state violations of the Trade and Intercourse Acts. Although the state recognized the need for a federal commissioner's presence at land negotiations and purchase later in 1798, no federal commissioner was present at the 1795 Oneida-New York State "treaty" or at twenty-four of the twenty-six "treaties" made after 1798. According to Shattuck: "If you simply dismissed the Oneida argument as a 'clever legal technicality to go back 200 years', you would ignore these Indians' longstanding pleas for justice."[8] Shattuck then described how the Indians had been locked out of state and federal courts. Without special enabling legislation allowing for the suit, the Indians would be ignored again. Shattuck argued:

> So the State has done a very great job, they take away the land fraudulently from people who couldn't even sign their full names, then they conveniently make the law that says, 'We are sorry we have got your land, but you are not a person or a corporation or an entity which can bring a lawsuit to get it back, and furthermore the State has sovereign immunity and you can't sue us anyway.' So they were just locked out, they were just locked out, they had no recourse.[9]

Shattuck then insisted that the federal remedy was not satisfactory either since the Oneidas could only bring a monetary action before the Indian Claims Commission against the United States for breach of fiduciary responsibility in allowing the state illegally to take Indian lands. Shattuck also pointed out that a potential Oneida victory in the federal Indian Claims Commission would also not allow interest on the 175 years of damages which the Oneidas claimed.[10]

Unable to convince the federal or state governments of the seriousness of the claim, Shattuck in 1970 filed a test case in federal court. He sued

Oneida and Madison Counties, challenging the validity of the Oneida-New York State "treaty" of 1795 and seeking trespass damages for a two-year period, 1968 and 1969. By suing the two counties and not New York directly, Shattuck attempted to circumvent the previous federal legal restrictions against such an action. Hence, the case revolved around whether the federal courts had jurisdiction in this matter.

William L. Burke, the attorney for the two counties, supported by the New York State attorney general's office, argued that the federal courts had no jurisdiction in the matter. Burke, joined by Assistant Attorney General of New York State Jeremiah Jochnowitz, also emphasized the legal theory of laches, namely that the Indians had not brought "timely suit" but had waited 175 years to do so. Subsequently, the United States District Court for the Northern District of New York and the United Court of Appeals for the Second Circuit dismissed the action, deciding that the Oneidas' complaint had indeed not raised a question under federal law as Burke and Jochnowitz had argued in their first contention.[11]

Nevertheless, Oneida hopes were soon raised when the United States Supreme Court agreed to hear the case. In his arguments in November 1973 before the high court, Shattuck reiterated the long-held Oneida position that the 1795 New York State treaty was executed in violation of the Constitution, three federal treaties, and the Trade and Intercourse Acts. Using archeological, historical, and linguistic expert findings, Shattuck insisted that the Oneidas bringing suit were federally recognized successors in interest to the Oneidas of the 1790s and those of the pre-contact period. The Oneidas were not, as Shattuck observed, complaining of mere technical failures to comply with the letter of the law. In his exhibits, Shattuck showed that federal officials had always responded to the Oneidas by denying the merit of the claims and discouraged legal action. They were wrongly advised after 1920 that they had no federal tribal status in New York; that Congress would retroactively ratify any illegal land sales even if they won in court; and, even before the jurisdiction bills of 1948 and 1950, that they were under state jurisdiction, which precluded any federal action of redress. Since the Indian nations were also barred from New York state courts, the Oneidas were in effect denied a legal forum. Thus, Shattuck argued, as their guardian, the United States had a constitutional, treaty, and congressional responsibility to provide the Oneidas with their day in court by allowing them to sue in federal courts.[12]

The Supreme Court rendered its decision on January 21, 1974. In a unanimous decision with eight justices participating, the court sustained the Oneidas' position and remanded the case back to the lower federal courts. In this landmark decision, by holding that the Trade and Intercourse Acts were applicable to the original thirteen states including New

York, the Supreme Court opened up the federal courts to the Oneidas as well as to other Indians seeking to get back land in these states. No longer would they be stymied by jurisdictional barriers. According to Justice Byron White's written opinion: "The rudimentary propositions that Indian title is a matter of federal law and can be extinguished only with federal consent apply in all of the States, including the original 13." White added that controversy arises under the laws of the United States sufficient to invoke the jurisdiction of federal courts and reversed the earlier federal court determinations, remanding the case for further proceedings to the federal District Court for the Northern District of New York.[13]

In the decade since the Supreme Court ruling of 1974, the Oneidas have squabbled amongst themselves and with other Iroquois about the direction of the claim. Separate feuding groups have brought actions and counteractions that have drained energies and delayed a final settlement of any legal doings. They have been divided over who should be parties to the claim, who should lead the action, what is the role of the Six Nations' Confederacy council at Onondaga in the suit, whether land or money or both are the goals, and even who are the rightful heirs in interest to the thirty-two acres of remaining Oneida lands in New York. Although there is internal discord, all Oneidas are united in believing that they were wronged by the State of New York.[14]

Despite these continuing divisions, the Oneidas, on March 4, 1985, won another legal battle in the United States Supreme Court. In a five-to-four decision, in a test case argued by Arlinda Locklear, an attorney for the Oneidas, involving fewer than 900 acres of the extensive Oneida tribal land claim, the court held that Oneida and Madison Counties were liable for damages—fair rental value for two years, 1968 and 1969—for unlawful seizure of Indian ancestral lands. Associate Justice Lewis F. Powell, Jr., who wrote the majority opinion, insisted that the Indians' common law right to sue is firmly established and that Congress did not intend to impose a deadline on the filing of such suits. Since the counties had firmly maintained that the Indians had not made a timely effort to sue and thus had forfeited their legal rights, the decision nullified the major non-Indian argument and opened the door for further Oneida litigation involving their lost lands. The court also suggested that, because of the tremendous economic implications of the case, Congress should help settle the New York Indian claims as it had done in Connecticut, Maine, and Rhode Island.[15]

New York State officials were stunned by both of these decisions. For years they had minimized or denied the issues, even though they had admitted in an earlier court and in legislative reports that the state title to formerly Indian-held lands was clouded.[16] It is clear that state officials underestimated the Indians' ability to bring suit and now are faced with overwhelming political opposition to settlement on the Indians' terms by state agencies, county legislatures, farm groups, wine growers, school districts, church groups, as well as many individual landholders in the claims area.[17]

When a Cayuga Indian land settlement bill in 1980 restoring a 5,400 acre Indian land base was defeated by less that two dozen votes in the House of Representatives, the Indians, angered by this setback, brought legal suit for 64,000 acres of land. This litigation, along with six million acres of land tied up in the Oneida suit and 12–14,000 acres in the Mohawk action, put economic pressure on the state by making it difficult at best for corporations, counties, individuals, institutions, and municipalities to secure bank loans, federal grants, and home mortgages. It also intensified already existing anti-Indian feelings and led, in 1982, to the so-called "Ancient Indian Land Claims Bill," introduced by Representative Gary Lee and Senators Alfonse D'Amato and Strom Thurmond. This bill called for a federal monetary formula and the extinguishment of all Indian land claims six months after passage; however, the bill died in committee.[18] During the summer of 1986, state officials continued to claim that Cayuga negotiations were still under way, with federal, state, county, and Cayuga representatives at the table; however, in reality, no meetings of the principals were being held and no new piece of federal legislation had been introduced or even drafted!

Besides these four major land claims, New York State-American Indian land relations are and have been seriously affected by the problem of the Salamanca leases.[19] Although this is not a land claims issue, Albany bureaucrats and legislators, southwestern New York politicians, and their constituents attempt to tie this lease issue to other problems that the state has with the Iroquois.[20] The City of Salamanca and its environs are almost entirely on the Allegany Indian Reservation of the Seneca Nation of Indians. Founded with the coming of the railroad in the mid-nineteenth century, this city is composed of thousands of non-Indians who live and work on land leased from the Senecas. Salamanca's residents have ninety-nine year leases with the Seneca Nation formally confirmed by Congress in the years from 1875 to 1892. Most of these approximately 3,000 leases run out in 1991!

For the last decade, the lease negotiations have made little progress because of Seneca memories of past bigotry and current racial tensions in Salamanca, the persistent attempts by non-Indian residents of the city to get Washington or Albany to dispossess, allot, or buy out the Senecas' land interest, and the volatile world of Seneca Nation politics. In 1902, Congressman Edward B. Vreeland from Salamanca expressed his motives for urging allotment legislation on the Senecas: "I represent 8,000 people who live upon these reservations; who hold ninety-nine year leases from these Indians, and want to get a title to their lands."[21] In November 1985, at a congressional hearing initiated by then Congressman Stanley Lundine focusing on the Salamanca-Seneca lease stalemate, the city's attorney indicated to members of the House Committee on Interior and Insular Affairs that Congress's original intent in giving ninety-nine year leases was to give what he claimed was "tantamount title" to the non-Indian citizens of Salamanca. He then urged Congress to "buy the City from the Seneca Nation of Indians."[22] Although in the past (through 1969) New York State policymakers of Indian affairs directly intervened on behalf of the southwestern New York interests and not the Senecas, state Indian policymakers have openly shied clear of direct involvement, insisting it to be a federal matter.[23] Nevertheless, southwestern New Yorkers make their concerns known in Albany through Assemblyman Daniel Walsh, the Democratic Majority Leader until his recent resignation, and State Senator Jess Present, two powerful voices who cannot be completely ignored by those in Indian policy formulation.[24]

New York State officials, both openly and by inference, confirm today the importance of land issues, fear the implications of Indian claims litigation such as those by the Oneidas, and bemoan the constant unresolvability of the Seneca-Salamanca lease disputes. The ever-present issues of land, especially the Oneida and Cayuga claims, led a prime mover of state Indian policy in the Department of State to deny there is even an American Indian policy emanating out of Albany for fear that an historian might affect the tense negotiations.[25] They also led the powerful Democratic Majority Leader of the New York State Assembly to label his current relationship with the Seneca Nation as "adversarial" and another powerful Republican state senator to describe the Seneca-Salamanca lease dispute as his "albatross" that just won't go away.[26] Land issues also affect agency responses to American Indian concerns, including the delivery of health and educational services to the Iroquois.[27] Moreover, unresolved land issues affect the ability of municipalities, counties, and the state to sell bonds. A 1986 New York State prospectus for a $3.5 billion bond offer devoted two pages to potential state and county liability in the event of successful Indian litigation and/or settlement in the Oneida, Cayuga, and Mohawk claims cases.[28]

Land issues influence the state's relationship with the American Indians in many other ways. Although a formalized "Indian office" has been suggested on numerous occasions. Many American Indians themselves have been critical of the idea in part because the state has not settled outstanding issues, most significantly those involving land.[29] Because of the litigational nature of Indian-state relations, key figures in state Indian policies are non-Indian attorneys, who have been long familiar with Indian land issues: Robert Batson, Gerald C. Crotty, and Mario M. Cuomo. Other important figures in state Indian policy are Evan Davis, the governor's counsel, and Henrik Dullea, the director of State Operations. As of late 1986, Batson headed the "desk," as it is called, at the Department of State, working to devise statewide strategies and solve the day-to-day land and jurisdictional problems brought to it by other agencies. Referred to by legislators and staffers for the governor as the state's "Indian expert," despite the presence in Buffalo of an Indian with seventeen years of administrative experience in policy matters, Batson serves as a major policymaker on land issues and works close with the governor's office, the Department of Law, and the New York State legislature.[30] As the designated "expert" since his legal work on the Moss Lake agreement of 1977–1978, Batson's job is to separate out extraneous issues from the real issues of land claims. He represents the governor at discussions with federal officials in Washington and at national meetings on state Indian affairs, is a personal envoy of the governor at land negotiations to settle Indian claims, and cooperates with the Department of Law, the governor's counsel, and agency counsels in legal controversies affecting New York State-Indian relations. He also is in direct communication with Howard Rowley of Rochester Gas and Electric Company who serves as a mediator in conflict areas, ranging from the sales tax issue to Iroquois land claims.[31]

Another key to New York State-Indian negotiations is Gerald C. Crotty, who now serves as Governor Mario Cuomo's secretary/chief of staff. Mr. Crotty, a thirty-six year old "whiz kid" in New York State government, is from a Buffalo-based politically-connected family. His father was head of the Erie County Democratic Party and ran for attorney general of New York State in the 1950s. His brother Peter is counsel to the State Facilities Development Corporation while another brother Paul was finance commissioner of New York City. Since 1979, Gerald C. Crotty has quickly moved up the administrative ladder from assistant counsel to counsel to his present position as number-two man in the governor's office. Before coming to Albany, he worked with the New York City law firm of Hawkins, Delafield and Wood where he focused on municipal and constitutional law, securities law, as well as municipal and public finance. His earlier work included defending the state of Maine against American Indian land claims. During his work on the Maine Indian land claims case, Crotty insists that he read every legal decision involving Indian land tenure and drew up the argument for the Maine Mortgage Bank that "the State did not have to give any lands back to the Indians." In 1979, when he was brought into New York State government as assistant counsel to

Governor Hugh Carey, Crotty turned some of his attention to New York land claims issues, especially those of the Cayuga Indians, as well as to the mediation of the siege between rival Mohawk groups at the St. Regis (Akwesasne) Reservation. Crotty considers his work at mediating the Mohawk confrontation and achieving a peaceful settlement "one of the greatest senses of accomplishment" he has had in working in state government. "Meditation is the key. Saving lives is more important than issues, law or history. We'll negotiate with anyone if they are capable of doing some damage." In the end, "we managed to convince the 'traditionals' that the only way to solve the crisis was to have one of their chiefs run for office."[32]

In contrast, Crotty is frustrated and on the defensive when he talks about the unresolved Indian land issues in the state. Having given assurances to Representative Morris Udall, chairman of the House Committee on Interior and Insular Affairs, that there was wide support for a Cayuga settlement bill, the Carey administration found the state's congressional delegation bolting after the bill reached the floor of the House of Representatives. Because of the lobbying of New York Representative Gary Lee, the bill was subsequently defeated in 1980. Crotty's explanations about why there has been little if any movement since 1980 are revealing. He insists that the new Cuomo administration had to slowly adjust to the new responsibilities of leadership, that the Indian land claims issues are immensely complicated, that there are "still legislators with Indian-hating attitudes," and that the Indians cannot agree amongst themselves and/or are unwilling to compromise. On one hand, he suggests that it is "possible to buy a land settlement from the Reagan White House" since "we are willing to give land" to a future settlement; on the other hand, he maintains that New York State is not only worried about the existing outstanding land issues but that "there's the potential for other land claims being filed in the future—Shinnecock, Seneca, etc.," which prevents a quick land claims settlement. In order to improve the administration of Indian affairs, Crotty insisted in July 1986 that an Indian office/division be created in the Department of State and that Batson be made its director. Although there are other personnel in the governor's office who have had experience in dealing with Indian issues, such as Dr. Henrik Dullea and Jeff Cohen, Crotty and the governor himself have had the longest involvement in this area.[33]

Governor Mario M. Cuomo has had a decade of experience in negotiating with the Iroquois since the Moss Lake crisis of the mid-1970s and is at the top of the hierarchical pyramid of decision-making with respect to American Indians. As a mediator from his early days in resolving the Forest Hills housing crisis in the early 1970s, he brings both an awareness of the importance of conflict resolution and a key understanding of ethnicity. Because of his personal style of leadership, which is far different from his predecessor in the governor's office, Cuomo is more directly involved in policies and decision-making.[34]

Cuomo's involvement in this area began in August 1976, when he was appointed as Governor Carey's special representative at the Moss Lake (Ganienkeh) crisis negotiations. At the time, Cuomo was secretary of state. Because of a two-year stand-off situation and the inability of Commissioner Ogden Reid, then commissioner of the New York State Department of Environmental Conservation, to resolve this crisis, Cuomo entered the negotiations, joining Howard Rowley and Scott Buckheit of the American Arbitration Association in efforts at mediation.[35]

Moss Lake was a major event in contemporary state-Indian relations. The incident started in May 1974, when a group of Mohawks, mostly Caughnawagas, took over an abandoned Girl Scout camp at Moss Lake in the Adirondacks. This occupation had been preceded by an earlier temporary seizure of property by Mohawks led by Standing Arrow near Fort Hunter in 1957 and 1958.[36] Claiming aboriginal occupancy of the land in 1974, even though the particular tract was clearly in historic Oneida-claimed territory and in the Adirondack State Park, these Mohawks managed to bring the entire state Indian machinery to a halt. The 612-acre site at Moss Lake had been purchased in August 1973 by New York State, which had plans to clear the land of all structures in order to restore it to a wilderness state. The New York State Department of Environmental Conservation (DEC), which had jurisdiction over the site, and the then Governor Malcolm Wilson, feared an armed confrontation during a gubernatorial election year and did not immediately try to remove the Indians; however, DEC commissioner, James Biggane, urged Attorney General Louis Lefkowitz to initiate legal proceedings. Initial state actions for summary judgment against the Indians were dismissed. Moreover, a group of non-Indian residents (COPCA) of the area on their own commenced ejectment proceedings against the Indians and were granted a judgment in September 1975; nevertheless, the court decision was deferred pending the outcome of negotiations between state officials and Indians at Moss Lake.[37] To complicate matters further, the federally- and state-recognized Mohawk Tribal Council at the St. Regis (Akwesasne) Reservation condemned the Indians' takeover and called for the assertion of state jurisdiction to remove the Indians from Moss Lake.[38]

In May 1977, New York State officials and the Indians at Moss Lake reached a settlement. The Indians were given use, not land title, of two parcels of state lands in Clinton County, one at Miner Lake in the Town of Altona and the other at the Macomb Reforestation Area. In order to avoid the restrictions of the federal Indian Trade and Intercourse Act of 1790, the Turtle Island Trust was created with Maytag Foundation money in order to facilitate the transfer of state lands. Other complications arose, namely questions related to an access road, the Indians' delay in vacating Moss Lake, and the fact that state officials had not consulted with Clinton County legislators before the settlement was inked and announced to the media. It is significant to note that although numerous private individuals and state officials were involved in this process from 1974 to 1978, Secretary of State Cuomo is largely credited with the settlement and preventing what Governor Carey feared and called "an Attica in the Adirondacks."[39]

The Moss Lake crisis, which occurred five months after the first favorable Oneida decision in the United States Supreme Court, has cast a long shadow on state Indian policy down to the present. The crisis also had far-reaching results and mostly not positive ones. It helped destroy the position of Director of Indian Services, who was blamed for the crisis, and with it, by 1977, the Interdepartmental Committee on Indian Affairs; it led to the emergence of Cuomo, Batson, and Rowley in Indian policy mediation and formulation; it intensified Indian-Indian conflict in New York State; it delayed state negotiations with those Indian groups seeking more peaceful methods of land acquisition; it resulted in two shootings including the wounding of a nine-year-old girl; and it brought Governor Carey, as well as Secretary Cuomo and the New York State legislative leadership into a political war.[40]

Cuomo's role at Moss Lake reveals much about how New York State officials make Indian policies. From his earliest involvement in the crisis beginning in August 1976, Cuomo realized the importance of a separate Division of Native American Affairs for coordination purposes and for conflict-resolution objectives.[41] Yet, his basic focus was not to create a permanent structure to resolve longstanding problems with tribal governments, but only to look at the immediate in order to mitigate the potential for armed conflict and bloodshed.[42]

Throughout the crisis, Cuomo and other state officials revealed a limited understanding of American Indian communities, their culture, history, leadership and legal status. They failed to make use of the expertise of legislative staffers working for the subcommittee on Indian Affairs as well as Indians employed in state government. In order to keep peace, Cuomo bypassed, thereby insulting, the recognized Mohawk Indian tribal council in favor of those with rifles and/or those who claimed official tribal leadership positions in the negotiating process, resulting in the undermining of tribal leadership. Moreover, one Seneca Indian activist, who had been previously repudiated by the Seneca traditional Council of Chiefs at the Tonawanda Reservation, ended up at the Moss Lake negotiating table.[43] Cuomo also went against one hundred nine-two years of state Indian policies by negotiating with the Six Nations Confederacy Council at Onondaga, a body that had never been formally given a political recognition by the State of New York. Only when negotiations failed to proceed as swiftly as Cuomo envisioned, did the then secretary of state shift his style to a hard-line approach, insisting that the state would pursue legal ejectment proceedings against the Indians.[44]

The Moss Lake agreement of 1977 reflects much about state officials' thinking on American Indians and their land claims. Secretary Cuomo carefully spelled out the parameters of the Moss Lake agreement to the chiefs of the Mohawk Nation and to the chiefs of the Six Nations of the Iroquois Confederacy by insisting that the accord "will not have any legal effect upon any of the legal claims or rights of the Six Nations Confederacy or the Mohawk Nation under any of the treaties made by the Six Nations." Cuomo added that there "is nothing about this resolution that is legally binding in any way on the Six Nations, the Mohawk Nation, the People of Ganienkeh, or the State of New York." Significantly, the future governor concluded: "Naturally, the State does not concede that the claims of the Six Nations are valid, but the State is committed to resolving all such matters in a legal and peaceful way."[45]

In 1980, Robert B. Goldman prepared a study for the Ford Foundation on conflict resolution in which Mario Cuomo's efforts and style were lauded in two separate chapters. In one of the chapters prepared by Richard Kwartler, Cuomo and Howard Rowley's roles at Moss Lake receive attention. In a most revealing passage, Kwartler quotes Cuomo about the final Moss Lake settlement:

> The Mohawk settlement has moved us toward a realization that the way to resolve these things is not by letting them go to court because if the Indian goes to court and wins then the court will say that the land belongs to the Indians. *If the land belongs to the Indians, the court will not actually deliver the land to the Indians because the legislative process will then intervene to say that's an absurd result*—for example, to give the whole City of Saratoga to the Indians. We must find a different process—conflict resolution without litigation, a process of negotiation.[46] [Emphasis mine.]

Thus, at Moss Lake proper legal redress and justice for American Indians took a back seat in Cuomo's mind to what he considered the hard-boiled "realities" of the political process. It is also clear that historical and legal realities, as well as the settlement of longstanding land claims also took a back seat to state policymakers' efforts at assuaging a small group of activist American Indians who were potentially dangerous, threatening, and capable of generating negative publicity to the state and its leadership. Having minimized Indian matters for so long, state officials were also extremely ignorant of the Indian world with which they were coming into contact, a fact that is as true today as it was in 1974–1977. This negative assessment is further confirmed by the Starna study of 1987. Starna found only one person employed at the higher echelons of government who had any understanding, albeit superficial, of Indian communities, their history and their culture.[47]

Today, Ganienkeh, the relocated Moss Lake community under the 1977 agreement, is virtually abandoned, with its original "leaders" scattered as far away as California.[48] This community is a testimony to a bankrupt state Indian policy that looks to "immediate fixes" rather than to permanent improvement, such as a major land claims settlement. Although the threat of violence did force the governor's office to support some needed legislation for American Indians, which may or may not have passed without the Moss Lake takeover, the actions of state officials did not help foster trust in the long run, since they further alienated several Indian councils, delayed and weakened efforts at major Indian land settlements, and gave further impetus to a negative type of Indian politics based on media exploitation and confrontational activism.

3

▼▼▼

THAT ELUSIVE INDIAN OFFICE

"At the present time, there is no workable mechanism to deal with Indian affairs in New York State government."

—Maurice Hinchey,
Assemblyman,
February 25, 1986

According to the national president of the Governors' Interstate Council on Indian Affairs, thirty-nine states of the Union have an "Indian office." These "Indian offices" vary considerably, ranging from a formal commission of three to twenty-four members to states with only a governmental liaison and/or contact person for Indian nations. New York State is included in the thirty-nine states with an "Indian office," even though it has one of the least developed administrative structures for Indian affairs in the United States.[1] In actuality, New York State's day-to-day administrative structure for Indian affairs as of late 1986 includes only an "Indian Affairs Specialist" in the Department of Social Services working out of a bureau-level office in Buffalo and an associate counsel in the Department of State in Albany who keeps the governor informed on various issues, most notably Indian land claims litigation. There is also a Native American Indian Education Unit in the New York State Department of Education which employs two educators, one at the associate level, as well as a Superintendent of the Tonawanda Indian Community House who is an employee of the New York State Department of Social Services and who reports to the Indian affairs specialist. The four personnel from the Departments of Social Services and Education, all of whom are Iroquois, are overworked but extremely dedicated people who help build bridges to Indian communities. They get too little recognition for their efforts and are often unfairly labeled by some in their own Indian communities as "State Indians." Often they are forced to take or share the blame because of less-than-sensitive actions and policies by others in their agencies, by other departments, by the New York State legislature, and/or by the governor's office. They are also put in the awkward position of attempting to explain bureaucratic regulations of state agencies, the shifting winds of politics in the state capital, as well as the rationale for new policy directives to rural isolated native populations who have largely negative preconceptions about state actions and motives.[2]

Importantly, under Chairman Joseph Lisa's leadership, the assembly subcommittee from 1970 to 1977 urged an expanded approach to New York State American Indian policies and services. Its 1971 final report, largely drawn up by John Hudacs, now the New York State labor commissioner, recommended the creation of a three-member Commission on Indian Affairs as well as a statewide Indian Advisory Council "to assist the Commission in considering problems, programs and legislation relating to Indians and Indian reservations in New York State." Each Indian nation within the state would choose its representatives to the advisory council who would attend all meetings of the Commission on Indian Affairs; these representatives would be compensated for expenses of attending commission meetings. The report of 1971 urged that the Interdepartmental Committee on Indian Affairs, which was composed of representatives from ten state agencies servicing Indian communities and which was created by Governor Thomas Dewey in 1952, be restructured in order to improve state services for American Indians; however, this Interdepartmental Committee, which was chaired by a director of Indian Services, went out of existence during the Moss Lake crisis.[3] The assembly subcommittee report also made a most important recommendation about the New York State legislature, one that was not heeded. It called for the creation of two subcommittees on Indian affairs within each house, which would sit jointly and periodically meet with the Indian nations "in order to open and maintain avenues of trust and communication with the Indian populace."[4]

Despite Hudacs' subsequent move to the governor's office in 1975 and the resurrection over the last decade of this plan and other modifications and variations on it, there has been a "hiatus" in developing a truly improved structure for state services. Although most New Yorkers, including those in the capital district, view Indians as being people west of the Mississippi, other eastern states, such as Florida, North Carolina, and Michigan are far more progressive than New York in providing state services to its "first Americans." Indeed, the 1986 version of the "new" initiative proposed by Governor Cuomo provided substantially less money and less hiring of personnel than two earlier attempts to upgrade the administration of Indian policies and services planned in the mid-1970s during New York State's budget crisis![5]

In the mid-1970s, the impetus for a new Indian office/division came directly from the Assembly Subcommittee on Indian Affairs. After the firing of the Director of Indian Services in 1975, Joseph Lisa, chairman of the subcommittee, wrote Governor Carey, insisting that the director be retained "until an adequate replacement can be found for his position or a re-evaluation is made of the present administering structure."[6] Soon after, Fernando (Fred) DiMaggio, Lisa's chief staffer on the subcommittee, helped draw up "A Reorganization Proposal for New York State's Administration of Indian Services." This plan called for the abolition of the Interdepartmental Committee on Indian Affairs, but the retention of the position of director of Indian Services, and the addition of four new positions—"Coordinator of State and Federal Programs" and three "Field Representatives." The reorganization would cost the state $150,000 per year. It also called for an Albany office and two branch offices at Syracuse and Buffalo. In order to facilitate communication with American Indian communities, the proposal advocated the establishment of a Native American Advisory Committee and the creation of an "Indian desk" at each agency serving Native American communities.[7]

In conjunction with this effort, Hudacs, by then a program analyst in the governor's office, prepared an alternate proposal. Allied to Lisa and DiMaggio because of his past work on the subcommittee, Hudacs drew up a memorandum entitled "Suggestions for Improving New York State Indian Affairs" and sent it to Governor Carey in the late summer of 1975. Hudacs unequivocally stated that there was an urgent need to create an administrative device that had the support of the state's Native Americans and which had proper state funding. Hudacs recommended the hiring of three new full-time positions, instead of four, and the creation of two offices, instead of three, eliminating the Syracuse branch office, thus reducing the cost of the overall proposal to $130,000. As in the Lisa-DiMaggio plan, Hudacs advocated the establishment of an "Advisory Council" but specified that it be composed of one representative from each of the tribes recognized by New York State as well as representatives from urban Indian communities. The number of members on the advisory council would be set by the director of the Indian office "but the selection should be left to the Indian constituents themselves." In contrast to the Lisa-DiMaggio plan, Hudacs recommended the restructuring but not the abolition of the Interdepartmental Committee on Indian Affairs. In order to raise Indian services to priority status, he insisted that the committee consist of the "head of each agency or a permanent high level designee who will provide strong leadership in that agency." Each agency involved in Indian services to Indian communities should also "designate one middle management level employee as a liaison officer" who should service as "that agency's contact for day-to-day operational matters involving Native Americans." According to this Hudacs plan, an Office of Native American Affairs should be established in the Department of State by Executive

Order. Importantly, the director of this new office "should have extensive credentials" in matters dealing with minority groups or affirmative action plans and "should preferably be a New York State Native American."[8] Hudacs concluded:

> It is important that any proposal for recognizing the delivery of services to the State's Indian population be brought to their attention for discussion before it is implemented. The same concern should be evident when considering candidates for the positions created within any organizational structure such as the Office of Native American Affairs. Recommendations for candidates from the State's Indian population should be solicited.
> If the office is to be effective, it must not only employ individuals who are sensitive to the needs of the Indian community but it must also be recognized as an organization created in conjunction with the population it is directed to service.[9]

In 1979, as a result of a major crisis and confrontational situation in which the New York State Police and governor's office personnel stood between two rival Mohawk groups fighting it out for political control of the St. Regis (Akwesasne) Reservation, state officials drafted two new proposals for the reorganization of Indian policy administration. Once again, the threat of violence by Indians prompted official attention in Albany. In a most revealing memorandum, Mario Cuomo, then lieutenant governor, wrote Governor Carey on November 5, 1979:

> As Secretary of State, I served, as you know, as representative for the State on Indian matters. During that time I became aware of the need for (1) a clear and identifiable focal point for Indian affairs at the State level, and (2) land claim negotiations. As Secretary of State, I filled both functions. Serving as Lieutenant Governor has provided me with a new perspective on the matter; namely, that the functions are distinct and of a continuing nature. I think, each should be institutionalized in the body of State government.
> I recommend you establish an Office of Indian Affairs in the Executive Department for the purpose of reorganizing the state's administration of Indian services. The Interdepartmental Committee on Indian Affairs should be continued and a new Native Americans Advisory Committee established. The Office of Native American Affairs would be primarily a coordinating entity. A Native American "desk" should be established in each State agency serving native Americans, e.g., Social Services, Eduction, Health, Commerce, etc.
> I believe this can be done with little if any extra cost.
> I urge you take this action as soon as possible.[10]

The document reveals that Cuomo in 1979 believed that Indian policy administration should be given additional priority, that Indian land claims and social services be distinctly separated from each other, and that consultation with American Indians was essential to success in this reorganization. This Cuomo plan has never been implemented and the governor's key staffers as late as July 1986 were pushing the state's Indian land claims "expert" as the potential director of an Indian office serving native communities. They have dismissed the need for the resurrection of the Indepartmental Committee on Indian and have never mentioned the idea of a Native Americans Advisory Committee. Moreover, staffers such as Gerald Crotty in the Governor's office in 1986 cynically equate the improvement of state services to Indian communities with leverage in Indian land claims negotiations.[11]

A second proposal was prepared by Marilyn Schiff of the governor's office in late November 1979. In two separate memoranda, Schiff outlined why the "Office of Indian Affairs" should be located in the Department of State. She persuasively argued for the move because of the Department of State's involvement in Indian affairs since 1976 and because of the logic of placing it in an agency that houses the state's community services and planning functions. Schiff specified that the "Office should not deal with the additional minorities, who actually have separate problems" and suggested that negotiations "and trouble-shooting [the present roles of Robert Batson and Howard Rowley] should be handled independently because of their short term nature. Perhaps it is timely to return the bulk of this responsibility to the Attorney General's Office, where it properly and historically belongs." Schiff documented the weaknesses of continuing the machinery of Indian Affairs under the Social Service law, and retaining the position of Director of Indian Social Services in the Department of Social Services. She also recommended, as Hudacs and Cuomo had previously, the retention of the Interdepartmental Committee on Indian Affairs. In her proposal, Schiff recommended an allocation of $100,000 for the new office by the hiring of a deputy secretary of state specifically to supervise Indian Affairs, and the employment of one research assistant and secretary. Although Schiff recognized the need for raising the priority of Indian affairs in New York State government by giving it "Deputy Secretary" status, her plan was far less elaborate than three of the four previous proposals.[12]

After the diffusion of the crisis at the St. Regis (Akwesasne) Reservation, Governor Carey proposed the creation of the New York State Division of Native American Services. In a press release dated April 2, 1981, Carey announced that he was sending a bill to the legislature which "would centralize the State's Native American affairs in one agency and help assure that State and Federal programs and policies provide the maximum benefit. It would also establish a strengthened line of communication between the State and its Native American population." The bill also recommended an appropriation of $125,000 for the Department of State in order to make it the coordinating agency in Indian affairs. It also recommended that each agency involved in providing services to Native Americans be required "to designate a Native American program officer."[13] This bill, and several variations of it, were met with strong opposition in the New York State Senate.[14] Importantly, many Indians, though not all, have also opposed this administrative reorganization plan because they distrust new state initiatives because of New York's failure to settle any outstanding Indian land issues.[15]

As a result of this legislative impasse, Governor Cuomo took a new political direction. In 1984, he announced his intention of restructuring Indian policy administration, but did not specify the means of achieving it:

> Native Americans must be encouraged to participate in our governmental process. At present, responsibilities for Indian affairs are scattered across several departments and agencies, needlessly complicating relations between our government and Native Americans in our state. I will propose creation of a Native American Services Office within the Department of State to consolidate functions dealing with Indian affairs and to improve our government's responsiveness to the needs of our Indian population.[16]

By January 1986, Cuomo had concluded that an executive order approach was the only politically feasible means of achieving the creation of this new office. Thus his "Message to the Legislature" on January 8, 1986 contained the following words on Indian administration:

> The Indian tribes and nations located throughout the State each have authority for self-government within their territories. The State has long provided services to help meet the health, educational, social and physical needs of Native Americans. However, the State has no ongoing mechanism in place to ensure that the needs of Native Americans are met or to see that relations between the various State agencies and the nine recognized Indian tribes and nations within our borders are handled appropriately. Accordingly, I will promulgate an Executive Order that will assign specific responsibility for coordinating State services and programs which affect Indians to the Department of State. All State agencies will be directed to work with the Secretary of State in fulfilling this important responsibility.[17]

In the same message, Governor Cuomo announced that he would recommend new funding for state historic sites, including Ganondagan, the first state-managed American Indian historic site.[18] Despite the obvious importance of land issues to New York State-American Indian relations, the governor never referred to it in this nor had he in his three previous "State of the State" messages.[19] Subsequently, the governor's office prepared an executive order, which was to be funded at $57,000, assigning the secretary of state of New York primary responsibility for "coordinating state services and programs which affect American Indians." The secretary of state would be given the power "to advise and assist" the governor in developing American Indian programs; to "identify, coordinate and compile information on existing state programs and activities"; "to assist Indian leaders and other Indian people in obtaining services"; "to investigate specific complaints concerning the delivery of services"; "to work with state agencies to assure that services to which American Indians are entitled are in fact provided"; and to assist in conflict resolution of disputes between state agencies and Indian nations. In order to facilitate this executive order, all state agencies were "directed to work in a spirit of cooperation with the goals and aspirations of American Indian governments," to cooperate with the secretary of state, and to designate an agency "liaison to respond to the requests of the Secretary pursuant to this Executive Order."[20] Although this executive order was supposed to be formally promulgated in September 1986, the governor's office, for no apparent reason, has tabled the initiative, and, at present, the director of State Operations is apparently in charge of coordinating Indian relations.

To be sure, the governor's office is not altogether responsible for the failure of leadership in Indian affairs. The New York State legislature, which was responsible for exposing the horrendous conditions and poor state services to American Indians in the early 1970s, has now shifted away from looking systematically at "Indian Issues." The Assembly Subcommittee on Indian Affairs, which existed from 1970 to 1977, was truly an extraordinary experiment for the state. Prior to 1970, the New York State legislature, especially through its Joint Legislative Committee on Indian Affairs which existed from 1943 to 1964, was seen by Indian people as "the enemy," largely because of the activities of its chief counsel, Leighton Wade of Olean.[21] Before that, the state legislature in 1888 and 1906 had urged an end to the separate Indian status by breaking up the reservation system through allotment. In 1922, when, during a legislative investigation, Assemblyman Edward Everett found grounds for Indian land claims against New York State, the legislature (and the governor's office) quickly buried the report.[22]

In sharp contrast, the Assembly Subcommittee on Indian Affairs of 1970–1971 conducted the most responsive legislative investigation into Indian affairs ever held in New York State. It held numerous evening and weekend meetings around the state and on each reservation to accommodate the special needs of Indian working people. Established to seek revisions in the Indian law which had not been updated since 1909, the assembly subcommittee went beyond its mandate and suggested revisions in the Education and Conservation Law to service Indian needs. It is no exaggeration to state that almost all of the legislation on Indian affairs over the past fifteen years had its origins in testimony and the reports of the subcommittee.

Since 1977, the New York State legislature has had no operating subcommittee focusing specifically on the legal complexities of New York State-Indian relations and the needs of native peoples. With the defeat of Chairman Lisa in November 1976, the state legislature lost its major advocate on Indian affairs and the subcommittee soon went out of existence.[23] Despite the insistence of several legislators in both houses on both sides of the political spectrum that Indian interests are being served, they, admit nevertheless, that few, if any, Indians have come to their office to lobby.[24] Indeed, James Donovan, the powerful chairman of the Senate's Education Committee, readily admitted that he had not seen "an Indian delegation in his office in at least six years."[25] It is important to note that this same legislator, a vocal critic of the governor, still harbors ill-will toward Cuomo for what Donovan claims was "the Carey administration's mishandling of the Moss Lake situation."[26]

In contrast, lobbyists for New York State title insurance companies, the New York State Farm Bureau, the New York State Winegrowers Association and the New York State Association of Counties frequently push their legislative agendas that include resistance to a favorable Indian land settlement. Consequently, it is not surprising that legislation allocating state moneys for counties' legal defense against Indian land claims has been introduced and passed in recent years, an amount which totals over $150,000 for 1986–1987.[27] It is also not surprising that the Assembly's Standing Committee on Governmental Operations, the same committee whose subcommittee was so active in promoting Indians' interests, has changed its "Indian focus," insisting in its annual report for 1980:

> The Committee will continue to actively monitor the negotiations and court proceedings involving the various Indian Land Claims in New York State. The Committee is particularly concerned with the inability of local representatives to accomplish out of court settlements. This failure to avoid costly litigation is severely detrimental not only to the taxpayers of a particular locality but also to the citizens of the State as a whole.[28]

Despite the lack of a formal structure for Indian policy in the state legislature since 1977, the primary responsibility for the failure of leadership must be placed on the shoulders of two governors and their key policy advisors. Cuomo announced a "new day" in state-Indian relations at the conclusion of the Moss Lake crisis in 1977; however, Indian services, as of late 1986, have almost the same limited priority in state government that they had a decade ago. When he announced his intention to seek reelection for governor, Cuomo issued a one hundred forty-six page summary of his accomplishments during his first three years as governor of New York State. Nowhere in the *Three-Year Report* dated January 1986 were American Indians mentioned. Although there were references to programs that have an impact on American Indian life, such as aquaculture development, Indian affairs were distinctly missing from Cuomo's extensive list of achievements in office.[29]

New York State's Indian policies should not evolve because of fears of armed confrontation with angry Indian dissidents but should be carefully planned in conjunction with responsible representatives from the state's Indian communities. No longer will the governor's office rhetoric about the imminent creation of an Office/Division of Native American Services or of an imminent Indian land settlement be sufficient, especially after more than a decade of false starts and broken promises in each of these two areas.[30] Today, New York Indian policies are affected by the baggage of two centuries of state neglect and malfeasance and by officials' ignorance of American Indians and their communities. For too long, state policies have been designed "to control and to manage, rather than to improve," the delivery of services to American Indian communities.[31] By examining state agencies and their policies/non-policies toward American Indians, that designation becomes even more apparent.

PART II

**New York State Operations
and American Indians**

4
▼▼▼

"The Other": The American Indian and New York State Agencies

> Perhaps you should title your study "THE OTHER" since that's the way New York State government often categorizes American Indians.
>
> —*Rosa Castillo-Kesper,*
> *New York State Department of State,*
> *May 5, 1986*

The three chapters in Part II focus on New York State operations *vis-à-vis* American Indians. The first of these chapters analyzes in general terms how state agencies, offices, and divisions perceive American Indians, their communities, and their concerns. In the second of these chapters, the analysis concentrates on the two departments with the longest experience providing services to American Indian communities in the state, namely the Departments of Education and Social Services. In the third of these chapters, the report analyzes how land issues affect agency responses to American Indians. A caveat, however, is in order. Because of the extensive nature and bureaucratic maze of New York State operations, this report does not attempt to document and/or analyze every program and funding area that bears on American Indian communities, since services to American Indians are often not separately classified as "Indian."[1] Hence, the three chapters in this section of the report are intended to provide a general picture of state agency, office and division approaches to American Indians.

New York State government, with few exceptions, has largely ignored native populations. Although there have been improvements, the small size of the American Indian population and the Indians' conscious separation from the Albany political world of lobbying have resulted in minimal efforts by most state agencies to address problems. This lack of response is also conditioned by the tremendous ignorance by state officials of Ameri-

45

can Indians. Through archival research in agency files and interviews with key personnel in New York State government, it is apparent that many agency employees involved with native communities appear to know too little about the historical and legal status that separates the Indians from the rest of the "family of New York." Consequently, American Indians are merely categorized with other racial minorities, are separately classified in the "other" category, or are not even considered at all by many state agencies.

New York State agencies have varying awarenesses of American Indians, their communities, their concerns, and their needs. State agency responses vary from having no programs specifically geared to American Indian populations to those agencies which have made a dramatic turnaround in their program directions over the last decade and a half. Much of the limited knowledge about native peoples comes largely from the few hardworking and dedicated American Indians and their personal friends working in state government.

Unfortunately, the ranks of Indians in the state government are small. As of December 1986, there were only 379 American Indians and Alaska Natives out of 181,000 state employees.[2] This statistic is also misleading since the civil service definition of "American Indian/Alaska Native" is the following: "A person having origins in any of the original peoples of North America and who maintains tribal affiliation or community recognition."[3] The inclusion of the words "community recognition" makes the designation so vague that it is generally meaningless. Does it mean Indian or non-Indian communities? Besides this dilemma, the definition includes native peoples from out-of-state.

Consequently, no one really knows how many Iroquois and Algonkians native to the state are employed by New York State government. This problem directly affects Indian-New York State relations since native peoples from other areas of the country often have different perceptions and concerns than Native Americans from New York. For instance, American Indians from Oklahoma talk of "dual citizenship"—in their Indian nation and in the United States. Most Iroquois view themselves solely as citizens of their Indian nations, although the United States and New York recognize them as American citizens as well. Significantly, many American Indians from other areas are more participatory in the outside non-Indian process than the Iroquois. Nevertheless, the New York State Department of Civil Service definition is a vast improvement over six years ago when three definitions of "Indian" were employed by state agencies![4]

The composition of the New York State agency work force also has a direct impact on American Indian services in the state. As of June 1986, the New York State Department of State, the agency assigned the lead responsibility by Governor Cuomo for coordinating state Indian operations on January 8, 1986, had no native employees.[5] The question arises then about how an agency with a governor's mandate to perform a specific function can operate effectively without "bridges" to the communities it is supposed to serve. Even more incredible, the "desk" at the Department of State, an agency that serves as the "advocate for the poor" and local government functions, was manned as of 1986 by an attorney (Batson) whose special expertise is defending New York State *against* Indian land interests.[6]

Other agencies have their own limitations when dealing with American Indian communities. The New York State Division of Human Rights also has no American Indian employees. The chairperson of the Division of Human Rights' Native American Affirmation Action Committee had, four months after the State-of-the-State address, no knowledge of its content relative to American Indians and was unaware of the specific designation of the Department of State in coordinating Indian policies. He was also not familiar with the governor's plans for an executive order, or that there was a "desk" at the Department of State to deal with problems which arose related to Indian legal matters.[7]

Based on the most current published figures, the following state agencies, offices, and divisions also have no American Indian employees: Banking, Bridge Authority, Energy Research and Development Authority, Civil Service Public Employment Relations Board, Financial Control Board, Housing Finance Agency, Insurance, Investigations Commission, Labor Relations Board, Law, Public Service, and Teachers' Retirement System. There were also no American Indian employees in the following divisions of the Executive Department's Executive Chamber: Adirondack Park Agency, Executive Advisory Commission on the Administration of Justice, Division of the Budget, Office of Business Permits, Commission on Cable Television, Council on Children and Families, Consumer Protection Board, Commission of Correction, Division of Criminal Justice Services, Board of Elections, Office of Employee Relations, Board of Equalization and Assessment, Governor's Judicial Nominating Committee, Division of Housing and Community Renewal, Human Rights Appeal Board, Joint Labor-Management Committee, State Liquor Authority, Division of Parole, Division of Probation, Permanent Commission on Public Employee Pension and Retirement Systems, Commission on Quality of Care for the Mentally Disabled, Racing and Wagering Board, the Saint Lawrence-Eastern Ontario Commission, Board of Social Welfare, and the Energy Office.[8] As of May 1986, a total of eight American Indians and only one born and raised on an Indian reservation and/or urban community in New York are employed as full-time faculty members on the sixty-four campuses of the State University of New York![9] Moreover, approximately seventy-five percent of all American Indians employed by the state held positions in four agencies: Office of Mental Health, Department of Transportation, Office of Mental Retardation and Developmental Disabilities, and the Department of Parks, Recreation and Historic Preservation.[10]

State agencies also have many other real problems that hinder their delivery of services to Indian populations. Without doubt, there is also a lack of statistical data defining the conditions and problems Indians face on and off reservation Indian communities. For example, the Department of Corrections cannot ascertain how many Indians are incarcerated in New York State even though the department has statistics relative to Blacks and Hispanics and can even determine how many kosher meals are provided. American Indians are classified in the "other" category. It is significant to note that the department has no special policies relative to or provisions for Indian religious practices, unlike other minorities. Because of security factors, the department also restricts the right of Indians to wear their hair in a traditional manner, thus also impinging on Indian cultural sensitivities.[11]

The problem of statistical data also affects the responses of other agencies. The Departments of Labor and Commerce have no statistical breakdown and/or estimates about Indian unemployment. Significantly, in these two departments, American Indians are also classified in the "other" category.[12] Furthermore, the Department of Audit and Control has no separate category for Indian reservations.[13] The Department of Social Services, one of the most improved areas of state Indian policies in the last decade and a half, has public assistance figures for Indian reservations, but these statistics also include non-Indians, and non-New York State Native Americans residing on reservations. They have no accurate figures for off-reservation Indians living in Buffalo, Niagara Falls, Rochester, and Syracuse; moreover, ethnicity and race statistics for New York City are not available because of a recent court order blocking disclosure.[14]

As of May 1986, the Office of Mental Health (OMH) has not done a needs assessment study of Indian patient characteristics required for proper planning of treatment, despite the fact that because they collect data by race and ethnicity they have a separate patient category for American Indian/Alaska Native. OMH has no centralized agency Indian policy and has not attempted to make culturally relevant outpatient services available for American Indians. Although five minority demonstration projects have been established and training manuals and program design concepts are being written, published, and distributed for black, Hispanic, and Asian populations, no OMH state-wide efforts for American Indians have been undertaken.[15] Moreover, OMH's *Five Year Comprehensive Plan: Mental Health Services, 1985–1990* maintains that its current minority demonstration programs were "a necessary first step in addressing minority needs and in obtaining essential information regarding patient characteristics, service requirements and treatment success." However, nowhere in the five-year planning study are American Indian populations and their special needs mentioned.[16]

The Division of Alcoholism and Alcohol Abuse (DAAA) programs have similar limitations. As of 1986, the DAAA has not prepared training manuals or developed program design concepts focusing on the special needs of American Indian alcoholics. DAAA's *Five-Year Comprehensive Plan for Alcoholism Services in New York State, 1984–1989* does not mention American Indian populations and their community problems. The agency funding for Indian services is totally inadequate to meet the severe need and such treatment facilities as there are include trailers that barely meet state and federal standards.

Nevertheless, unlike OMH, DAAA administrators have begun to listen to Indian criticism of earlier agency policies and contracting procedures. For example, they have worked well in recent years with the Mohawk Nation's experimental program at Partridge House where they have learned about Mohawk life and special needs in counselling from Donald Richmond, the director of the center. DAAA also has a Mohawk on staff in Albany working in the area of program administration. In addition, DAAA's coordinator of the Northeastern Regional Office also has taken advantage of special funding for alcoholism-related services to American Indians through a combined multi-county—Franklin, Essex, Clinton—DAAA program.[17]

State administrators, both at the agency level in Albany or at regional headquarters, are often too quick "to blame the victim."[18] The baggage of centuries of distrust, a theme of this report, hinders state efforts at data collection. American Indians do refuse to cooperate and collaborate in data retrieval efforts, which does prevent improvement and even delivery of state services. A good example from one agency illustrates this fact. The Department of Health, unlike its counterparts in other states such as North Carolina, has no up-to-date dental and medical statistics for Indian populations, except compilations of the number of clinical visits, neonatal and mortality data, and an incomplete and outdated report on Seneca Nation health care.[19] The department is well aware of this problem. In June 1983, Elma Patterson, Indian Affairs Specialist in the Department of Social Services, requested information on health data in order to complete a survey for the American Indian Health Care Association. Because much of the information requested was "not available at the present time," Karen Kalaijian, a longtime advocate of improved Indian health care in the department, requested that "appropriate Bureaus" . . . "consider the feasibility of modifying existing surveillance systems to enable us to better define the health status of this population group in the future."[20]

Although the New York State Department of Health contracts out Indian medical and dental clinical services, has increased its funding for Indians by ten-fold in a decade, and has done major scientific studies requested by Indian nations in its laboratories, the Department of Health is burdened by Indian memories of the agency's lack of response to Indian health care prior to 1975.[21] Despite Governor Cuomo's statement in his State-of-the-State message of January 8, 1986, that New York State "has long provided services to help meet the health . . . needs of Native Americans,"[22] Indian health care in New York until the mid-1970s could be better described as "scandalous." Policymakers at the commissioner's level were totally misinformed about the Indians' status and even casually insisted that the Indians of New York State were not federally recognized nations and hence were the sole purview of state health agency initiatives. At other times, commissioners, such as David Axelrod, have claimed incorrectly that the state had no special responsibility since "technically speaking, the Six Nations are not within the State of New York and are by virtue of their treaty with the U.S. government the direct responsibility of the federal government, not the state government."[23] Meanwhile New York State operated outdated, archaic, and inferior health facilities described in the Assembly Subcommittee report of 1971. Worried about the adequacy of facilities and services in 1977, William Leavy, now executive deputy director of public health in the department, pointed out the agency's inaction in assessing and improving Indian health care delivery: "I am concerned that the legislative report of 1971 [Assembly Subcommittee on Indian Affairs] has been left somewhat unanswered and I am also concerned that we develop a rational basis for budgeting Indian health funds over the coming years."[24] Indian health care in New York was also characterized in one study prepared in 1972–1973, but published in *Clinical Pediatrics* in 1977, as being worse than the ghetto areas of Rochester and New York City. Furthermore, a Harvard University Public Health Study prepared in 1975 with the cooperation of the Seneca Nation documented among other things that Indian infant mortality rates were well over twice the national average.[25]

The Department of Health assumed supervisory control of Indian health services in 1955 when medical services were transferred from the Department of Social Services following a recommendation by the New York State Interdepartmental Committee on Indian Affairs. Federal involvement in Indian health concerns in New York State dates to the nineteenth century; however, nearly all of the limited health services provided to Indians before 1955 were administered by the New York State Board of Charities, now the Department of Social Services. The philosophy of Indian health and medical delivery in New York State at the time of transfer in the mid-1950s was succinctly put by the director of local health services of the New York State Department of Health: ". . . the long term objectives of the health and medical program for Indians residing on the reservations was to assist them in achieving complete social and economic integration and the eventual elimination of any special projects of programs on their behalf. The short term goals were to bring to Indians health and medical services of a standard equivalent to that of the population of New York State, as a whole."[26] This assimilationist tone reflected much of the tenor of Indian policy of the period. Even so, the goal of upgrading Indian health care remained an elusive one even well after the state legislature amended it in March 1962. This act mandated the Department of Health ". . . to administer to the medical and health needs of the ambulant, sick and needy Indians residing on reservations."[27] It is important to note that the Department of Health has never focused its attention on Indians off reservations, a fact noted as far back as 1975 by the first deputy commissioner.[28]

The impetus for improvement of these conditions was led by the Seneca Nation Health Action Group, not the Department of Health, and it served as the major advocate group for better health services. Past experiences suggested the limitations of appealing directly for funds from the State Department of Health, so the Senecas worked informally and after work hours with their physicians and nurses, care providers on the reservations, Karen Kalaijian of the Buffalo Office of the New York State Department of Health, and the Harvard School of Public Health. They developed a health care proposal which was submitted to and approved by the United States Indian Health Service. After this and later proposals were funded, federal moneys were allocated for two new modern clinics which were built at the Allegany and Cattaraugus Indian Reservations. These health clinics, developed largely by the initiative of the Seneca people, became the model for the Mohawk Indian health program in New York and have even influenced Indian health services nationwide.[29]

After recounting this Seneca success story, it is little wonder that Iroquois people withhold vital data from the Department of Health and several other agencies. Despite the accomplishments of the Seneca Nation, Indian health care today needs substantial improvement in New York State. Although the Onondagas have recently added a dental clinic, the Tonawanda Band of Senecas are in equally desperate need of a dental clinic, although the internal politics and concepts of sovereignty of their Council of Chiefs prevents them from actively lobbying for it in Albany.[30] Moreover, the Indians of Long Island, especially the Shinnecocks, have health care needs not addressed sufficiently by the Department of Health. In addition, the department, by not having a separate Indian health budgetary category, has placed Indian health services under the administration of the Office of Field Operations Management. This office services migrant laborers, most of whom are aliens, and does not give enough priority to American Indian communities.[31] At a time of federal cutbacks because of the Gramm-Rudman-Hollings amendment, the Indians of the state are again the losers in the bid for needed health services.[32] The state, through its Department of Health, must take up this slack to preserve the gains made by the Senecas and other Indians since the mid-1970s.

The New York State Department of Health also appears to favor one Indian nation over another. It provides a substantially greater amount of per capita funding to the Onondaga Indian health program in comparison to the rest of the state's Indian populations.[33] Even though there are only eight-hundred-fifty Indian residents, mostly Onondaga and some Oneida, living on the Onondaga Indian reservation, they receive nearly 37 percent of the entire state Indian health budget through a combination of direct services and a contract for services with the Onondaga County Health Department. The usual health department explanation for this imbalance is that "the Onondaga Council has refused federal funds and thus the state is making up the difference."[34] The much larger Mohawk and Seneca Nations, both of whom receive substantial federal funding, have far less state health money than the Onondagas.[35] The reason for this discrepancy seems to be the Onondagas' activist reputation, noted as far back as ten years ago by Robert K. Watts, a member of the New York State Health Planning Commission. Writing in 1976, Watts observed in his report: "The Onondagas are a very militant tribe and quite unlike the other Indian tribes I have visited." As savvy Indians "well-wired" to the media, the Onondagas have generated fear in Albany. Ironically, as a traditional Indian council they have succeeded in an untraditional way.[36] Although the Onondagas are deserving of first-rate health care, the Department of Health has not shown similar concern and given equal priority to other Indian communities in the state.

The question of priority affects the responses of other agencies as well. At the Department of Environmental Conservation, Indian matters in the counsel's office are handled on a "floating assignment" basis. As of the summer of 1986, the legal expert on pesticides, with little previous experience in Indian policies, was handling questions involving Indian fishing and hunting rights and overlapping federal and state jurisdiction.[37] Although Indian matters had priority during Commissioner Ogden Reid's tenure at DEC during the Moss Lake controversy, one former special assistant to the commissioner put it bluntly: "Indian concerns seem to matter in State Government only when Indians have rifles pointing at us. When a crisis dissipates, so does State concern for Indian issues."[38] Even the final Moss Lake settlement reflects this axiom. When an agreement was finally about to be reached and the threat of violence ended, the same special assistant for DEC wrote a policy memorandum to Commissioner Peter A. A. Berle placing "Moss Lake Indians" sixth in order of issues that deserved the commissioner's attention. Even at that, the special assistant called the DEC lands to be awarded/leased in the settlement as "of low priority to this Department."[39]

American Indians are designated as "low priority" by other agencies as well. SUNY is a case in point. For the first time in its history, the SUNY Board of Trustees held a public hearing on December 9, 1983 at Nassau Community College "about the lack of an organized curriculum for Native American Studies in the SUNY system." The hearing led to a report in January 1984 by SUNY's Central Office of Academic Programs, Policy and Planning. The 1984 report largely praised SUNY's efforts and did not differentiate between the needs of Native American students and other students taking courses in Native American Studies within SUNY. The mere existence of many excellent and diverse courses in Native American studies scattered throughout the SUNY system pointed out in the report, however, does not mean that the special needs of rural or urban Indian students are being met. The report also was "dead wrong" in explaining why there is a "brain drain" of American Indians from reservation communities. The weak reservation economies in New York cannot support all of the college-educated students trained, not simply as the 1984 report suggests, because "often the graduates choose to remain in the dominant society."[40] It is important to note that only to a limited extent has SUNY committed its great expertise—planning, marketing, economic development—to aid and work with the American Indian communities in necessary efforts at improving reservation economies. When an attempt at overall SUNY institutional outreach was proposed in 1982–1984, with strong Indian support for the idea and a coordinated effort by several SUNY colleges, the plan was killed because of campus rivalries.[41]

SUNY has trailed many other state systems in providing quality higher education in a culturally sensitive way to American Indians.[42] Although the immense university system provides a myriad of course offerings on American Indians, few of its campuses are equipped to handle the special needs of Indian students. Few SUNY catalogs before 1986 contained information about the state's financial aid available to American Indians through the Post-Secondary Aid Program of the New York State Department of Education. Only six colleges in the SUNY system, of sixty-four campuses, have what could be designated "a faculty contact person-advisor" for American Indian students—SUNY/Buffalo, SUNY College of Agriculture and Life Sciences, New Paltz, Oneonta, Oswego, and Potsdam.[43]

Minor programs in American Indian Studies are available at the colleges at New Paltz, Oswego, and Potsdam. Through bureaucratic legerdemain, it is also possible to acquire a contract major at New Paltz in Native American Studies. Because of the loss of two-and-a-third faculty lines since 1978, the minor program at the College at New Paltz centers on three courses in history and a field school in archeology. At SUNY/New Paltz, the two students, one Indian, who have completed a contract major in Native American studies, did it through the advisor's sleight-of-hand and his "going to the wall" with administrators, bureaucrats, and colleagues. The advisor, not a member of the Education Department's faculty, had to set up and personally supervise one student teaching assignment at the St. Regis (Akwesasne) Mohawk Reservation. Because students are bureaucratically discouraged from cross-registering at another SUNY campus and certain courses are not offered on every campus, this same advisor was forced to intercede with the registrar at SUNY/Albany to facilitate acceptance of a New Paltz student in an Iroquoian language class at the Albany campus. At the end of this byzantine process, the student's advisor had to further convince the SUNY/New Paltz registrar to substitute courses in Native American Studies from other campuses since New Paltz no longer offered certain courses because of faculty retrenchment.[44]

The College at New Paltz also sponsored the nationally-acclaimed Eastern Regional Conferences on the Native American from 1972 to 1984. Among other accomplishments, the meetings contributed to the first major analysis of Indian health care in New York by the *New York State Journal of Medicine*. The conferences, three of which were published, brought hundreds of American Indian and non-Indian leaders together and attempted to build bridges and educate non-Indians about native communities and their concerns. This annual effort ended because of budgetary problems, the shifting of the limited internal resources at New Paltz, and the overall lack of institutional priority for the conferences—the director was forced to seek outside funds every year and had no staff to handle the demands of the growing conference. This institutional neglect could also be seen in the SUNY/College of New Paltz gallery's rejection of an exhibition of contemporary Iroquois art in 1982. The college art gallery director at the recommendation of his gallery committee, then composed of faculty and administrators, rejected the exhibition, insisting that it would be more appropriately displayed "at anthropological museums, not college art galleries." Consequently, the exhibit was shifted with success to the famous Mohonk Mountain House five miles away.

In order to comprehend the problems faced by individual American Indian students, the author will focus further on his own campus, the College at New Paltz. In one instance, an American Indian student, from a Longhouse traditionalist background, was falsely accused by her SUNY/New Paltz resident advisor of smoking marijuana after she burnt sage, a common western Indian custom, in her dormitory room. This same student had previously been assigned a non-Indian roommate whose family was being sued for possessing property in the Indian Claims area of the Finger Lakes. When the roommates inevitably came into conflict, the assistant campus housing director could not understand "why there was a problem." Her solution was to shift the American Indian student to a so-called "Third World Dormitory Experience." Within two months of this move, the American Indian student was assaulted in this resident hall and the administrator in charge of the investigation quietly covered up the incident.

Although difficult to believe, the College at New Paltz is actually more progressive with respect to American Indians than most other SUNY campuses. For example, at SUNY/Old Westbury, the vice president for academic affairs was "too busy to come downstairs" to meet with visiting Iroquois chiefs, Algonkian Indian trustees from Long Island, and noted educators attending the first American Indian conference held at a college campus on Long Island.[45] Ironically, the 1982–1984 college catalog at SUNY/Old Westbury reads as follows:

> Old Westbury is distinctive because of its unique commitment to the education of students who, because of age, sex, race, ethnicity, economic conditions, or inadequate secondary school preparation, have been historically bypassed by conventional higher education in the United States. It is the goal of the college to create an educational community in which no one group so predominates that its density becomes the "norm" for the college. The college's philosophy encourages an atmosphere in which each student may truly feel that he or she has as much to offer the educational community at Old Westbury as any other student, while enjoying the rich experience of learning with and from a student body whose diversity is unusual in American higher education.[46]

After suggesting to the author of this report that there was real concern for Indian issues and implying that an American Indian would be hired as adjunct instructor in art to rectify the campus' deficiency in this area, the same SUNY/Old Westbury vice president quickly backed away from this position several weeks later.[47] Instead, in order to counter publicity negative to her campus about the lack of concern for American Indians, this same SUNY/Old Westbury vice president initiated a "token effort" by encouraging her campus to house a small exhibition of contemporary American Indian art. This effort at SUNY/Old Westbury seems quite crass when it is revealed that the same campus offers only two courses in alternate years relative to American Indian cultures.

This lack of sensitivity, interest, and programs for American Indians in the metropolitan region should be understood in larger terms. About fifty percent of the American Indian population in the state lives in the New York City-Long Island area. Yet, neither SUNY or any of the private colleges in this region offers specific programs that can be truly designated "American Indian Studies," except for scattered, uncoordinated coursework at SUNY/Stony Brook.

Other SUNY campuses besides the College at New Paltz offer "programs." At Binghamton, a student can request a major or minor in Native American Studies through the Innovative Projects Board; at Albany, students can request a minor option as well. At the present time, SUNY/Buffalo, which has several Iroquois faculty members (though all but one are on part-time lines), offers five to eight courses a semester and a concentration in American Indian Studies; students receive a B.A. or M.A. degree in American Studies. The program provides special counselling and advisement for Indian students, works with five neighboring reservations in outreach programs, and holds events and an annual conference in the fall. This program has met with resistance in its founding, its development, and its future plans for expansion—both at the campus level and at SUNY Central because of internal campus politics, Indian politics, the smallness of the Indian population, and budgetary restraints.[48]

Because of the successes of two private college programs—St. Lawrence University and Clarkson Institute—in American Indian higher education, the previously documented poor response of SUNY campuses to Indian students, and the lobbying of some Indian and non-Indian educators throughout the state, some changes are now apparent in SUNY. The financial officers of the SUNY colleges have come together and discussed the need to publicize the Post-Secondary State Aid Program available to American Indians.[49] Importantly, the SUNY College of Agriculture and Life Sciences at Cornell was awarded three faculty lines in May 1986, to develop a more formalized program in Native American Studies at Cornell University. This award has been a long time coming since the American Indian Program, an outgrowth of the old Cornell Cooperative Extension Unit to Indian communities, was started in the early 1970s after the college office of minority programs hired an Iroquois Indian in the "sub-professional category." Today forty Indian students participate in the program, half of whom are from New York State. The program's "Extension Associate" provides a counsellor, financial consultant, and recruiter, and cooperates extensively with the native American Advisory Committee of the New York State Department of Education. The program also publishes a journal, *Northeast Indian Studies*, holds an annual conference, and sponsors special events and speakers. The Indian students in the program, it should be pointed out, are not largely in Agricultural and Life Sciences but are scattered in programs throughout the university, including engineering.[50] Hence, the program is potentially ripe for legislative criticism as it uses state funds for students not in the state agricultural college. Moreover, faculty from the SUNY College of Agriculture and Life Sciences have been active in opposing American Indian claims, which undermines the cohesiveness of and support for the American Indian program among the Cornell faculty.

SUNY is not the only state agency which needs to redress past mistakes; however, agencies are often placed or place themselves in difficult positions in attempting to correct commonly recognized poor past performances. At the present time, the State Police has been directed by a court order to actively seek out, train, and hire racial minorities and women as troopers because of past discriminatory practices in recruitment. Despite criticisms by the former director of the Police Academy that the court order should include more active recruitment of Indians as a part of the efforts, the judicial mandate defined racial minorities only in terms of "blacks and Hispanics." Thus, strangely, Indian males are put in the category of "white" by a court order attempting to redress past injustices![51] Moreover, despite growing awareness of Indian concerns in this agency, the Police Academy Training Manual and the four-hundred-hour coursework does little to explain the complexity of the separate Indian legal status from the rest of the New York family.[52]

Since the force's founding in 1917, the relationship of the New York State Police, a division of the executive department, with American Indian populations has been tense at best. The State Police was often the most visible sign of state authority, especially in the rural areas where Indian reservations are generally found.[53] With the congressional transfer of criminal jurisdiction over Indian affairs to law enforcement areas of New York State government in 1948, added tension was brought to Indian-police relations. Added to this uneasy relationship was the fact that few American Indians have been employed at the State Police and that some American Indian nations have their own judicial and legal enforcement systems.

With the Moss Lake crisis, the governor issued to the superintendent of the State Police a specific directive relating to Indian affairs. In order to prevent conflict and bloodshed, the State Police were ordered to enforce criminal jurisdiction only to the limits of reservation lands unless the tribal council formally requested intervention by state troopers.[54] At one reservation, the St. Regis Mohawk (Akwesasne), state troopers in 1979 found themselves face-to-face and armed-to-the-teeth in a tribal dispute in which the elected council appealed for state law enforcement intervention against a rival group; however, state authorities refused to comply. A settlement between the competing Indian political groups was eventually worked out two years later. Because of the persistent tension in Indian-State Police relations, governors Carey and later Cuomo designated Major Leigh Hunt as their trouble-shooter and mediator in these confrontational situations. Hunt, who later became the director of the State Police Academy, has recently been appointed as police commissioner of the city of Syracuse.[55] At the present time, it is unclear who will fill Hunt's important post.

In recent days, the State Police have continued to stay at arm's length in questions related to American Indians.[56] Despite the existence of a federal warrant for the return of the fugitive Dennis Banks, the State Police, because of a directive from Governor Cuomo, refused to enter the Onondaga Reservation and arrest the American Indian Movement activist.[57] Nevertheless, the agency has come into conflict with the Department of Environmental Conservation about DEC's inclusion of Mohawk environmental law enforcement officers in a training program in Albany. When DEC extended an invitation to the Mohawks to take part in law enforcement training procedures, the Indians learned after they reached Albany that they would not be allowed to receive pistol training. The State Police counsel objected to Mohawks carrying weapons since the Indians had no law enforcement authority or right to bear arms without a state permit off of an Indian reservation.[58] Instead of coordination of state Indian policies through a central office, agencies come into conflict which damages overall improvement in State-Indian relations.

Other agencies of New York State government have also not given enough priority to American Indian concerns. In 1971, the Assembly Subcommittee on Indian Affairs recommended that the New York State Department of Commerce "meet with the tribal leaders and members of the reservations in order to explain its function and the services it has available at their request. In order to provide for continual communication, semi-annual meetings should be held on or near the reservation." The report insisted that the department "could appropriately take a more active approach in assisting the Indian with the economic development of the Indian community."[59] Despite these recommendations, this department for a decade ignored the needs of American Indians in the state.

In 1981, the Division of Minority Business Development was created in the New York State Department of Commerce under Governor Carey's Executive Order 117 which mandated "state agencies to promote growth opportunities for minority-owned business." This division, now called the Minority and Women's Business Division after Governor Cuomo's Executive Order 21 in 1983, contains two bureaus: the Business Planning and Development Bureau and the Capital and Economic Development Bureau. The Business Planning and Development Bureau aims to assist firms owned by minorities and women by providing training and technical business skills, helping these firms obtain contracts from state agencies and private corporations, supplying up-to-date industry and market information, and encouraging legislative efforts on their behalf. The Capital and Economic Development Bureau assists these firms in identifying sources of financing and in reviewing loan packages and applications; it also encourages the development of new sources of financing and in reviewing loan packages and applications; it also encourages the development of new sources of financing for these firms and works with other agencies to deposit state funds in financial institutions owned by minorities and women.[60]

At the present time, the MWDB has had limited impact in the American Indian communities of New York State. MWDB does publish a substantial, and frequently updated, minority and women's vendor book containing a sizeable number of entries.[61] American Indian firms are on the list, including several construction companies and a window-cleaning operation in Buffalo; however, these firms were discernible in the listing in the vendor's book because they had designations "American Indian" or "Native American" in their title. Most private firms seeking contracts form the State of New York will go no further than picking the most convenient listing (or those recommended by others) rather than try to determine whether it was hiring American Indians. American Indians, few in number and having limited capital for entrepreneurial activities in New York State, will still be seen as "other" and in most instances will not be selected either by state agencies and/or private firms seeking state contracts.

Although the personnel at MWDB appear to be extremely sensitive to the needs of minority and women entrepreneurs and have held a major state exposition for these firms at Syracuse which included American Indians, they have, like most state officials, limited knowledge of American Indians and their communities. Unlike other branches of the Department of Commerce, they *do* have a special designation for "American Indian."[62]

They have gladly provided technical advice to an American Indian entre-
preneur establishing a cigarette-marketing company but have not built
bridges to the Indian reservation and urban communities. In fact, their
"current" (April 1986) list of Indian contact persons for the purpose of
achieving their stated goals is badly inadequate and outdated, containing
the name of one deceased chief from Onondaga, one retired chief from
Akwesasne, a president of a western New York American Indian historical
society, the misspelled name of one of the Iroquois nations, and no names
of urban Indian community leaders in New York City, Buffalo, Niagara
Falls, Rochester, or Syracuse.[63] Although the president of the Seneca Nation serves as a member of the Western New York Economic Council,[64] a
separate venture from MWBD which was established by the Department
of Commerce, the agency as a whole appears to be responding inade-
quately to the economic crises facing American Indian nations in New
York State.

The New York State Department of State has attempted to fill this
void in the state's economic response to American Indian communities.
The agency is in charge of administering the largest grant assistance program for the poor—the Community Services Block Grant Program—
which it assumed in 1982. This program "provides services aimed at
ameliorating the causes of poverty and has consistently helped to contain
the rate of poverty which now reaches 15 percent of the nation's population." The Department of State program channels its allocations, almost
all federal funds, to well over one hundred "community action agencies,
the Rural New York Farmworkers Organization, limited purpose agencies,
Indian tribes and tribal organization and other community-based organizations across the state providing services to the poor."[65]

Brought in to resolve the Moss Lake crisis, the department's personnel, including the then Secretary of State Cuomo, were exposed to the
grim economic realities that American Indians faced in the state. The
department, working with the Mohawk tribal council, as well as other
agencies, began efforts at economic coordination; however, with the erup-
tion of another tribal political crisis from 1979 to 1981 at the St. Regis
Mohawk (Akwesasne) Reservation, many of these efforts at coordination
were tabled. Nevertheless, certain Department of State efforts in economic planning were well under way by that time—at Akwesasne and
elsewhere.

In 1979, the agency's Division of Economic Opportunity through its
Community and Neighborhood Assistance Program worked with Long
Island Indians to establish the Shinnecock Housing Corporation; two
years later the agency worked with the Iroquois to set up the Mohawk
Housing Corporation. Starting with water and sewage projects, they later
helped secure federal block grants for each nation. One of the ironies

of the Mohawk project was that these Indians, who are a federally-recognized nation, had to file forms with the State of New York showing it had federal tax exempt status. In order to obtain federal funds for housing because of the problem of Indian collateral, the State of New York had to guarantee Mohawk mortgages if there were defaults by individual Indians. One of the weaknesses of these and other important efforts is that ninety-four percent of the agency's Community and Neighborhood Assistance Program is federally financed. In the age of Gramm-Rudman-Hollings, the availability of funding for future program efforts is dubious at best.[66]

The Department of State has also been involved in other efforts in Indian economic development and reservation planning; however, these responses can be considered spotty at best. When the crisis in reservation economies was given more recognition by state officials after Lieutenant Governor Alfred Del Bello's 1983 visit to the Akwesasne Reservation and by the publication of the President's National Commission on Reservation Economies, the Department of State once again focused on providing "community action" economic planning for reservation communities. In a venture presented to one tribal council, the agency attempted to satisfy the needs of the state's kosher meat industry by suggesting that a beef processing plant be initiated at the Akwesasne Indian Reservation. The industry finally settled on a site at the Town of Hancock, half the trucking distance to New York City.[67] In more successful efforts, Department of State personnel in its Coastal Management Program have worked with Brad Smith, a Shinnecock Indian, in the development of the tribe's oyster/aquaculture project, although the state agency funding for the project has come from the Urban Development Corporation.[68] The agency has also helped secure federal moneys for tribal weatherization efforts and other funds from Washington for the maintenance and operations of the Native American Center for the Living Arts (The Turtle) at Niagara Falls, New York.[69]

Unfortunately, much of the limited state effort at American Indian economic development has been focused on propping up The Turtle, rather than community, reservation, or urban Indian development, an area that is largely ignored by state officials. This effort to save The Turtle is the result of state legislative lobbying to redevelop the depressed New York State side of Niagara Falls; apparently, it is also to "assuage" Indian activists in western New York, several of whom are artists and networked to The Turtle. It is clear that the state's delay in imposing financial restrictions on The Turtle's operations was as a result of these two factors.

In May 1970, Duffy Wilson, a prominent Tuscarora sculptor, along with prominent non-Iroquois Indians that included the singer Buffy Sainte-Marie, established the Native American Center for the Living Arts in New York City. The center was devoted to countering racial stereotypes, to promoting the preservation of the visual and performing arts of Native American peoples, and to the development of new forms of creative and cultural expression. In 1975, Wilson moved the center to Niagara Falls, New York.[70] Five years later, as a result of a $4.9 million public works grant from the United States Department of Commerce for a museum building project, The Turtle opened in downtown Niagara Falls; however, this museum and living arts center has been a "money pit" since its opening, obtaining millions of dollars from the New York State legislature and from federal grant programs. Poor initial site selection and poor Indian administration of the facility until 1985 plagued The Turtle from its inception. Despite receiving substantial state moneys, Albany officials, until April 1, 1985, did not provide that The Turtle institute a budgetary system and system of accountability. When The Turtle staff continued to ignore this new arrangement and violate the law, the New York State Comptroller and New York State Attorney General threatened in October 1985 to permanently close down the museum operation. At the present time, the situation appears to have improved somewhat since the National Heritage Trust, which is housed in the New York State Department of Parks, Recreation and Historic Preservation and which helps funnel money to The Turtle, can now make contracts in which the state can specify the type of personnel hired and can oversee bill payments.[71]

Besides limited efforts at promoting true reservation economic development, New York State government has not given priority to a major environmental crisis affecting one of the larger reservations, St. Regis (Akwesasne). Although individual scientists in the departments of Environmental Conservation and Health and at the SUNY College of Veterinary Medicine have worked with the Mohawk community to investigate this crisis and have attempted to get state action to deal with the disturbing conclusions found in their testing, the governor's office and the New York State legislature have not responded. The scientists' agencies until recently have not given this crisis the priority that it deserves.

For years, the St. Lawrence River has been used as a toxic dumping ground by factories along its banks. With the development of the St. Lawrence Seaway project from 1954 to 1959 came an added push for industrialization in the Massena area and the establishment of the General Motors Foundry and the Reynolds Aluminum plant at the Rooseveltown peninsula adjacent to the St. Regis (Akwesasne) reservation. Over the past thirty years, the Mohawk dairy cattle and fishing industries have been virtually eliminated as a result of air and water pollution. The decline of the fishing industry, which had been part of the traditional economy of the community since the seventeenth and eighteenth centuries, has reduced tribal efforts at economic self-sufficiency.[72] This environmental crisis was publicized in 1970 before the Assembly Subcommittee on Indian Affairs by a prominent Mohawk, Dr. Solomon Cook, then a dairy farmer, who blamed the declining prosperity of his herd and the reservation dairy cattle industry on the fluoride pollution from Reynolds and other factories.[73]

Despite continued Mohawk efforts, the agencies of New York State government did little to investigate these Indian concerns until the early 1980s. In the late 1970s and early 1980s, General Motors' plans to expand its operations by developing a DROSS plant (aluminum recovery plant) triggered a huge Mohawk response to stop the expansion. Chief Leonard Garrow along with F. Henry Lickers, a biologist of Seneca heritage who heads the Mohawk environmental monitoring efforts, began new attempts at gaining recognition of these problems from officials in Albany, Washington, and Ottawa.[74] The Mohawk environmental crisis began receiving international media attention only after a major political crisis erupted on the reservation from 1979 to 1981 and only after some Indians and the New York State Police found themselves in a politically explosive stand-off.

The environmental problem still continues and affects the physical and psychological well-being of the Mohawk people who fear for the future of themselves, their children, and their way of life. The Massena Boat Station of the New York State Department of Environmental Conservation, which samples the St. Lawrence River six times per year, in 1982 and 1983 detected mercury mirex pollution; in 1984, chromium pollution; and, in 1985, dicloryl ether, nickel, and zinc pollution, the latter of which was found in each of the annual samples.[75] According to a regional sanitary engineer in the Franklin County Department of Health, "there are 50 parts/billion hot spots of PCBs in the St. Lawrence River."[76]

The General Motors Foundry alone has been cited for dumping 2.7 parts/billion PCBs in the river when the legal limit—no one knows what the health effects are for even the legal limit—is 1 part/billion. Because of this criminal action, the General Motors Central Foundry dump site has been fined and ordered to contain and clean up the site which borders the Racquette Point area of the reservation. This dump site has also been placed on the Toxic Superfund list of the federal Environmental Protection Agency.[77] Significantly, at the present time, the Franklin County Department of Health has found benzene and heavy metals in some non-drinking wells as well as PCB contamination in one well at Racquette Point. According to the county health department, some of the contamination stems directly from arsenic used until twenty years ago by local potato and strawberry farmers and from the high hill deposits of river-bottom clay dredgings from the St. Lawrence Seaway project which scars the landscape today at Racquette Point.[78]

Although no direct link has yet been established (and is extremely difficult to establish) between this pollution and the health of human beings, the DEC wildlife pathology laboratory in Delmar, New York has conclusively shown how frogs, a snapping turtle, a mallard duck, and three shrew species have been seriously affected by this pollution.[79] In another study, conducted by the SUNY College of Veterinary Medicine, the health of cattle was also shown to be affected by this environmental contamination.[80] Since the reservation straddles both sides of the international boundary and pollution from both banks of the St. Lawrence affects the Mohawks, a major health study on the crisis conducted by the Mount Sinai School of Medicine in New York City was submitted to the Minister of Health and Welfare of Canada.[81] In this two-volume report, the investigators studied the potential impact of PCBs, mercury mirex and flouride pollution on reservation residents, with special attention to the Racquette Point area of the reservation. The report concluded that fish consumption per week be reduced for men from 2 lb. to .2 lb., for women from 1.6 lb. to .16 lb., for pregnant women or those planning pregnancy from .16 lb. to 0, and for children from .07 to 0. For an Indian society that has partially subsisted over the years as fishermen, the impact of this crisis is even greater than the health implications caused by a contaminated environment.[82]

Although the environmental crisis is the most serious one affecting the needs of any American Indian population in New York State, state agencies have ignored major concerns of native communities in other areas as well. Today, there is a crisis situation involving the protection and sanctity of Indian burial sites in New York State. Indian burials are being uncovered on private lands on a monthly basis by construction crews, by gravel pit and mining operators, as well as by individuals.[83] Yet, New York State, through its Office of Parks, Recreation and Historic Preservation (OPRHP), has no workable policy mechanism to deal effectively in this culturally and religiously sensitive area. Interagency rivalries and Indian activist politics appear to obscure the real issue here, namely the universal ethical and human concerns involved in resolving this crisis. Both DEC and SED blame OPRHP's inaction.[84] Some OPRHP officials even suggest that the provision in the Indian law awarding the agency supervision in this area was an historical fluke caused during the separation of DEC and OPRHP in the early 1970s and, thus, the issue should not be in OPRHP's jurisdiction.[85] Moreover, other agencies such as the Department of State and the Department of Health, both of which have already-existing legislative mandates dealing with cemeteries, grave-robbing, or body stealing, appear to be abdicating and shifting their administrative and ethical responsibilities in this matter.

In 1971, the New York State legislature passed section 12-a of the Indian Law which was amended to its present form in 1974:

> The office of parks and recreation shall have the power to designate any Indian cemetery or burial ground as a place of historic interest pursuant to subdivision one of section 3.09 of the parks and recreation law provided, however, that such cemetery or burial ground is not located upon any Indian reservation located wholly or partly within the state. No person shall destroy, alter, convert, or in any way impair any such cemetery or burial ground which has been so designated as a place of historic interest or any artifact or other object thereon which is or may be of relevance to the historic interest thereof without the proper express written permission of the office of parks and recreation.
>
> The attorney general, at the request of the office of parks and recreation, is hereby authorized to institute an action in supreme court in the judicial district wherein such cemetery or burial ground is located to enjoin violations or threatened violations of this section.[86]

The act of 1971 occurred after an incident involving burials at the Boughton Hill archeological zone, now known as Ganondagan, which was the major Seneca village during the seventeenth century. In the summer of 1970, while the state was attempting to purchase this property, the site's private owner leased it to persons who proceeded with excavating the land and removing bones and other contents of the graves. Both the Tonawanda Band and Seneca Nation of Indians as well as their friends in western New York protested, but their actions prompted the weak 12-a of the Indian law, only after the site was looted.[87]

Although the so-called "American Indian burial bill" passed with little challenge in 1971 and 1974, there were problems from the beginning with this enactment. The State Office for Local Government as far back as July 1971 expressed a concern that is still seen by some as a major obstacle retarding the resolution of the issue: "The power granted to the historic trust [amended to OPRHP in 1974] by this bill is obviously a restriction or limitation upon the use of private property. It has been held that any limitation on the present use and enjoyment of property constitutes a taking of the property in the sense of this provision (New York State Constitution, Article I, sec. 7)."[88] In sharp contrast to the issue of private property, unmarked skeletal remains uncovered on state and federal projects are already protected by federal environmental and historic preservation laws and procedures exist for their protection. Moreover, section 233 of the New York State Education Law which deals with archaeological permits covers state lands.

The legislation in 1971 and 1974 did not establish regulations to designate and/or place such private sites on the National or State Register, did little to protect *in situ* burials, and did not establish procedures for notifying a property owner of such potential designation and giving him/her an opportunity to be heard with respect to the proposed designation. Nor did the acts of 1971 and 1974 deal procedurally with reburial of Indians disinterred. This last point, reburial, added other headaches to the issue: Are archaeologists forced to rebury, and if so, after how many hours, days, months, or years? Archaeologists have expressed their different opinions on this point, some arguing for total scientific latitude in studying the Indian skeletons as long as is needed; while others recognize and take into account the cultural and religious concerns of the native communities about disinterment and are more willing to work out compromise on the issue.[89]

Ironically, when both American Indians and archaeologists are coming into conflict,[90] more and more sites are being found, not protected from environmental and other factors, and looted by grave robbers. Although state agencies, Indian communities, and archaeologists recognize the problem as expressed in a meeting about the issue called by Secretary of State Gail Shaffer in 1985,[91] the delay in action is causing more losses. Sadly, a repeat situation to the burial crisis of 1970 can happen again today in the State of New York. Although OPRHP has intervened at four discovered burial sites since 1979 to preserve the sites' integrity,[92] one wonders what prehistorical marvels of American Indian history have been lost forever because of state inaction.

Clearly Section 12-a of the Indian law is unworkable. It is also unneeded since the sanctity and the protection of the dead are universal human values not exclusively an "Indian issue," and should not be categorized separately in the New York State law. Indian burials should be protected, as their non-Indian counterparts are, namely by New York State laws that regulate cemeteries and by public health laws and by laws relative to archaeological permits. Sections 4218 to 4221 of New York State's Public Health Law provide sufficiently to deal with this major issue. According to section 4218 of the New York State Public Health Law:

> A person who opens a grave or other place of interment, temporary or otherwise, or a building wherein the dead body of a human being is deposited while awaiting burial, without authority of law, with intent to remove the body, or any part thereof, for the purpose of dissection, or from malice or wantonness or with intent to steal or remove the coffin or any part thereof, or anything attached thereto, or any vestment, or other article interred, or intended to be interred with the dead body, is guilty of misdemeanor.

These laws, along with section 233 of the New York State Education Law dealing with archaeological permits and the removal of human skeletal remains as part of any permitted research project, should be applied by law enforcement officials throughout the state. Thus, what is needed is not new legislation or even new regulations, but interagency cooperation, not agency rivalry. An interagency panel as found in other states should develop an immediate course of action and policy to facilitate and resolve issues relating to unmarked human, Indian and non-Indian, skeletal remains. It should be emphasized that other states, such as North and South Carolina, have made more progress in resolving this issue than New York.[93]

*   *   *   *   *   *   *   *   *   *

The gloomy picture of state operations presented in this chapter cannot be ignored or minimized. Many fine and distinguished civil servants work in New York State government and interact with American Indian communities. They work in the shadows, doing the scientific studies, coordinating agency efforts, overcoming two centuries of distrust, and "putting out the fires" through their diplomacy. They are often not recognized or given credit by a political establishment bent on image-building and winning elections. One such agency has been the New York State Office of the Aging (OA).

OA does not place American Indians into the "other" category and stands in sharp contrast to the non-existent responses of OMH and many other state agencies. OA largely provides services, under the federal Older Americans Act Title III-B Social Support Services Program, to American Indians in New York in three broad categories: (1) Access services (information, referral, transportation, outreach, and other access services); (2) In-home services (homemaker, home health aide, friendly visiting, telephone reassurance, and chore maintenance); (3) Legal services. Title III-C of the Older Americans Act also provides the "Congregate and Home Delivered Meals" Nutrition Program for the Elderly, which includes American Indians.[94]

Although OA's program has severe budgetary limitations and is faced with a 4.3 percent cutback of federal funds as a result of the Gramm-Rudman-Hollings amendment, OA should be lauded for its past efforts. For example, OA has established three state-wide advisory committees that include well-respected American Indian community people from two of the reservations in New York and one urban Indian center: Dr. Solomon Cook from Akwesasne and Jeanne Marie Jemison from Cattaraugus, and Rosemary Richmond, Director of the American Indian Community

House in New York City.[95] Moreover, the agency over the last six years, through a sensitive Aging Services area supervisor who had previously lived in western New York, has made many on-site visits to all the reservations where he has learned firsthand from Indian elders about their needs.[96] OA has worked directly with Randy John and Roxanne Ray of the Seneca Nation of Indians Area Office for the Aging and the St. Regis Mohawk Office for the Aging. Although largely underfunded, OA provides $32,000/year for real costs, not overhead, to each of these two offices. In contrast, OA works with individual county offices of the aging to service the needs of Indian elderly at Tuscaraora, Shinnecock, and Poospatuck. The Tonawanda Band of Senecas, after dissatisfaction with an OA contract to provide services through an off-reservation concern ("Leisure Time"), gets its funding directly from the federal government; while the Onondagas do not participate in any state or federal programs for the aging.[97]

Unlike other agencies, OA administrators are quick to produce Indian needs-assessment studies, Indian annual implementation plans, and candid comment about ways to improve services. If there are two areas of most concern, they are (1) OA's inability to identify and service the urban Indian elderly in New York State; and (2) the intense budget crisis—the program is already substantially underfunded; the Gramm-Rudman-Hollings amendment; and the spiraling costs of providing for an increasingly elderly population.[98]

Two other agencies have redirected their efforts at delivery of services to Native Americans; the Department of Education and the Department of Social Services. Because of these agencies' long historical involvement in Indian communities, they deserve special descriptive analysis and evaluation of their functions and services.

This chapter has concentrated on state services to reservations. If services to reservation communities are poor, then one must characterize services to urban Indian communities as virtually non-existent even though approximately eighty percent of the Native Americans in the state live off-reservation in five cities—Buffalo, New York City, Niagara Falls, Rochester, and Syracuse. Dependent on federal subsidies, American Indian urban centers, such as New York City's American Indian Community House (AICH), face increasing problems finding funds and space for their operations. Except for the moneys that prop up The Turtle, which doubles as an urban Indian center in Niagara Falls, New York State does not contribute to or provide for any of the other Indian centers' operating budgets. Although a few state programs work out of the centers, nearly all the outside funding comes from federal and private sources, and all of the four currently operating centers are close to closing their doors because of federal cutbacks. In New York City, perhaps as much as forty percent of the American Indian community is unemployed. In addition to these real problems, American Indians are the "invisible minority" to state agencies working in an urban setting and are rarely understood except in terms of other minorities' problems. Moreover, tribal division, limited intertribal cooperation, and tribal ethnocentrism stand in the way of unity required to get more equitable distribution of state services.[99]

5

▼▼▼

The Slow Wheels of Progress: The New York State Departments of Social Services and Education and American Indians

> It is therefore suggested that a committee of Indians be appointed on each reservation to meet with the principal and the state supervisor to discuss local school problems and to develop cooperatively a more functional program.
>
> —*Phillip Cowen* Survey of Indian Schools *(a study by the New York State Department of Education), 1940.*

The New York State departments of Social Services and Education are the two state agencies with the longest involvement in administering policies and programs to American Indians. Both agencies are legislatively mandated and have provided Indian services for well over a century. Both agencies also have to bear the burden of past assimilationist policies and paternalistic administration toward Indian communities. Despite a significant turnaround in each agency's Indian administration and programs since 1969, primarily as a result of the appointment of several hardworking personnel of American Indian heritage, the agencies, nevertheless, are extremely slow to respond, in part because they are two of the largest bureaucracies in New York State government. The Native Americans who serve in lower middle-management positions face large-scale ignorance of Indian cultures, history, and legal status even within their agencies. They also have to deal with key administrators who designate Indian social and educational concerns as "low priority."

Department of Social Services

The Department of Social Services (DSS) has a bureau-level administrative structure which provides services to American Indians. This "Bureau of Indian Affairs" provides "consultation information, referral, counselling, advocacy and public relations. In addition, the Bureau coordinates state services to Indian people and serves as liaison between state and federal agencies and Indian Nations/Tribes." Among other responsibilities, the DSS administers Indian home relief, aid to dependent children, child welfare services, old age assistance, and adult institutionalized care to reservation Indians, and employment counselling as well as other forms of counselling assistance. DSS also acts as advocate for court-related actions, gives certification for Social Security, establishes and maintains trust accounts for minors, secures tribal identity upon request, and supports the importance of cultural identity for Native American children both in foster care and adoptive homes.

DSS also is in charge of distributing annuity payments under New York State treaties with various Indian nations—Cayuga, Onondaga, Seneca-Cayuga (Oklahoma), Seneca, St. Regis (Akwesasne) Mohawk, and Tonawanda Band of Senecas—establishing and maintaining trust accounts for Cayuga children, and administering the payment for services of the Onondaga Indian agent, and the attorney for the Tonawanda Band of Senecas. The department also administers, maintains, and supervises the Tonawanda Indian Community House at Akron, New York, which has served the Tonawanda Senecas as a cultural, health, recreational, and social center since the 1930s. In addition, the Indian Affairs Specialist ties in and coordinates other departmental directives, such as the Family and Children Services Division implementation of the federal Indian Child Welfare Act of 1978, which attempted to prevent the breakup of Indian families and which established standards for the placement of Indian children in foster and adoptive homes.[1]

Because of past neglect in providing certain services and overall paternalistic approaches toward Indians, the department has had extreme difficulty in altogether overcoming its historical mistakes in dealing with Indian communities. Moreover, because it is the lead agency in state responses toward Indians under Chapter 39 of the Social Services Law of 1940, the department and its personnel, however hardworking and devoted to improving delivery of services, are blamed by Indians often mercilessly for all the failures of New York State's Indian policies.[2]

The origins of the Department of Social Services can be traced to an 1867 law that established the Board of State Commissioners of Public

Charities. Initially, the board, which had diverse functions, administered poorhouses, institutions for the mentally and physically handicapped, including "lunatic and idiot asylums," and the state school for the blind, the Sailors and Soldiers Home, immigration "clearinghouses," as well as reformatories and orphanages to care for dependent children. It is important to note that the Board of State Commissioners of Public Charities changed its name on several occasions: the State Board of Charities in 1873, the Department of Charities in 1925, the Department of Social Welfare in 1929 and the current Department of Social Services in 1967.[3]

Even before a 1924 state legislative mandate, the department administered to the needs of American Indians. In 1875, the state assumed administrative responsibility for the Thomas Asylum for Orphan and Destitute Children which had been established by Phillip Thomas of the Society of Friends and Asher Wright, a Presbyterian missionary, on the Cattaraugus Indian Reservation in the mid-1850s. By the early years of the twentieth century, the Thomas Asylum was renamed the Thomas Indian School. The State Board of Charities also administered the health clinic at the school, which served as the major state response to Indian health needs until the mid-twentieth century.

Thus, to a significant extent, the State Board of Charities served many of the present functions of the contemporary departments of education, health, housing, and mental hygiene as well as the Division for Youth. Nevertheless, its services were totally inadequate to meet the needs of Indian communities. Outward race discrimination frequently interfered with delivery of relief to poor Indian families. The Board of Charities also classified American Indians in the same categories with youthful offenders and lunatics, a fact not lost on the Indians. Moreover, the Thomas Indian School had, for much of its history, a prison-like institutional quality and an assimilationist focus. Thus, cultural insensitivity, paternalistic charity, and neglect were the early characteristics of the agency's responses to American Indians.[4]

In 1924, the State Board of Charities received a legislative mandate for Indian affairs. The board was to maintain its fiscal responsibility by reimbursing the local Social Services Department for "the full amount expended for administration of Public Assistance and care to eligible, needy Indians and members of their families residing on any Indian reservation in this State."[5] Since 1929, the department has also employed a caseworker or "Indian Affairs Specialist," who has been based in Buffalo. As part of a successful Works Progress Administration project during Herbert Lehman's governorship, the Tonawanda Indian Community House was built through Eleanor Roosevelt's encouragement, federal funding, and Indian labor in the 1930s.[6]

On November 13, 1952, Governor Thomas Dewey created the Inter-departmental Committee on Indian Services which was supposed to eval-uate, integrate, and coordinate services provided by eight state agencies—Commerce, Education, Environmental Conservation, Health, Mental Hygiene, Social Services, State Police, and Transportation—to In-dian reservations, to recommend revisions in the Indian law, and to "for-mulate and put into practice a sound permanent pattern for Indian Administration in this State."[7] Dewey, noting the closing of the BIA's su-perintendency in New York State, insisted that his move was to fill this vacuum and that the state was "now in a position to devote its full efforts to the task of providing the Indians with opportunity to participate in all of the activities of our society." With typical political hyperbole, Dewey maintained that the "State of New York since Colonial times has been vitally interested in the welfare of its Indian citizens. Unlike other States, we have always provided health, education, welfare and other services to the residents of our Indian Reservations rather than looking to the Federal Government to do so."[8] The chairman of this new Interdepartmental Committee had the designation of Director of Indian Services and was assigned to the Albany headquarters of the Department of Social Service. Yet, until the position's demise in 1975, it was held by non-Indian political appointments of the governor, who had little prior knowledge of Ameri-can Indians and their communities, further weakening the Department of Social Services' ability to overcome the legacies of paternalism and ne-glect.

In 1969, the department hired Elma Patterson, an American Indian with an advanced degree in social work from SUNY/Buffalo, as "Indian Affairs Specialist." Having no clearly-defined departmental description of her responsibilities and working in an agency with little knowledge and/or priority to Indian needs,[9] Patterson's impossible task was described by the Assembly Subcommittee Report in 1971: "The full-time social worker, for example, must visit, assist and counsel residents on eight reservations spread from Buffalo to Long Island. It is an overwhelming task." Calling the social services staff "entirely insufficient" to handle and service the needs of the Indian population, the report recommended "added man-power" to provide "a more manageable approach."[10] It is important to emphasize that this situation is as true in 1986 as it was in 1971, despite repeated lobbying by Patterson. Today, Patterson and her secretary, in their Buffalo office, advise and guide Indians, in all the native communi-ties, in educational and vocational planning and in the use of various state, federal, and local resources available to them; encourage commu-nity organizational and self-help efforts; and obtain needed services in connection with problems of health, employment, property rights, recreation, and domestic and social relations. She also serves as one of the state representatives to the Governors' Interstate Council.[11] Despite this all-encompassing role, she is not given the status and recognition she deserves and has been used as a scapegoat by state officials for their own failures in order to quiet the barbs of certain Indian dissidents.[12]

The Moss Lake takeover had a largely negative impact on American Indian social services. John Hathorn, then the director of Indian Social Services and a Republican appointee of Governor Rockefeller, was blamed for the crisis. Because of Democratic political criticism as well as Hathorn's own personal failures to serve as a more fervent advocate for Indian interests in state government, he was fired in 1975 by the newly elected Governor Carey.[13] In fairness to Hathorn, the Assembly Subcommittee Report of 1971 noted "that the interdepartmental committee concept used as an administrative mechanism in the formulation and application of Indian affairs programs, policies and priorities is faulty."[14] It added:

> An interdepartmental committee is one of the least effective means for administering an on-going program; it should be used to solve particular problems and to coordinate policy decisions. It generally lacks strong leadership, has inadequate staffing, and inhibits initiative by any individual department due to the group decision-making process. A stronger organizational concept is needed to administer this state's Indian Affairs program.[15]

The report also pointed out the director's problems with inadequate staffing, as well as the general lack of priority of Indian matters in state government.[16]

When Hathorn was fired in 1975, the position of director of Indian Services was never filled, and, whatever little coordination achieved by the Interdepartmental Committee in the past was lost. For nearly a decade, there has been little overall state coordination of Indian services. During the period, W. Pat Bartlett, the Executive Assistant to the Commissioners of Social Services, served as a contact person for the department's Bureau of Indian Affairs; however, Bartlett, in his words, merely "answered the telephone" rather than coordinated, designed, or initiated policies.[17] Thus, departmental policies from 1975 to 1985 were merely a "holding action" and state government as a whole had a "ten-year hiatus in which Indian affairs were on the back burner."[18]

Despite the solid performance and overwhelming responsibilities of the Indian Affairs Specialist, the department still minimizes here role by not providing her with field workers/case workers—one for the two Long Island reservations and the large Indian population in the New York City metropolitan area and the other for the upstate reservations and urban centers which would allow the Indian Affairs Specialist to plan and coordinate policies. In addition, the Tonawanda Indian Community House, which houses all the reservation social services and community and recreational activities as well as health facilities and library, is also understaffed, having only a superintendent (designated as "custodian" a decade and a half ago) and one maintenance worker. Moreover, although the Tonawanda Indian Community House was designated by state legislation in the mid-1930s as being for the exclusive use of the Indians, DSS and county social services have repeatedly attempted to integrate the facility. Thus, DSS policies appear to be directed at controlling and managing, rather than improving, overall delivery of services to Indian peoples.

Department of Education

The New York State Department of Education has had the longest continuous involvement with American Indian communities in the state. The New York State legislature in 1846 enacted a law providing for school buildings and annual appropriations for the education of American Indians on four of the reservations: Allegany, Cattaraugus, Onondaga, and St. Regis. Later, state-administered schools were specifically established at Shinnecock in 1848, Tonawanda and Tuscarora in 1855, Oneida in 1857, and Poospatuck in 1875. The schools at Oneida were closed in 1889. The rest, except for schools at Onondaga, St. Regis (Akwesasne), and Tuscarora, were closed, starting with Tonawanda in 1931 and ending with the shutting down of the Allegany Reservation School in 1965. In part, these closings were a result of the general movement to centralize rural schools and in part to integrate the races rather than maintain separate Indian educational institutions. Today, only three schools remain, and, except for the Onondaga School, concentrate on early childhood education.[19]

Until 1975 the educational philosophy of these schools was largely to assimilate American Indians into American life. One of the first enactments relating to American Indian education, passed in 1856, was entitled: "An Act to facilitate education and *civilization* [emphasis mine] among the Indians residing within this state."[20] The attitudes of school superintendents and educators of Indian children can clearly be seen in examining any report of the Superintendent of Public Instruction. In 1888, William L. Paxon, the school superintendent at Tonawanda, reflecting total cultural myopia about his Seneca charges, advocated "doing away with the system of reservations, dividing up the lands among them, and making them citizens subject to our laws" in order to make his students better educated and "improve their condition generally."[21] In the same year, W. W. Newman, the superintendent of the Onondaga School, asked: "With so much done for them [Onondagas], why should not the Indians be happy and prosperous?" He then went on to blame failures on the so-called "paganism" of the Indians, the traditional system of Onondaga chiefs as well as the "practical communism" of Indian life that "takes away some of the incentives to personal exertion."[22]

Instead of focusing on the quality of education produced in the schools, these reports largely concentrated on "blaming the victims" or dealt with the improvement of school physical plants and recreational facilities and with school attendance problems. Anna Lewis, an American Indian educator who held the position of associate in the Native American Indian Education Unit, wrote in 1971 that whenever SED saw a problem with and attempted to reform Indian education, it merely built another school facility rather than questioning the philosophy of assimilation.[23]

With the exception of the brief federal New Deal initiatives and experiments in promoting Indian cultures in the 1930s, Indian education changed little until the 1970s. The schools were understaffed, and the quality of the education provided was significantly below average. Until a 1943 state law was enacted, the teachers in the Indian schools were paid at a salary scale far less than their counterparts in non-Indian schools. Indian school drop-out rates were well above the state average.[24] Incredibly, some of the public funds to which Indian nations in New York were entitled were never applied for by state educational administrators until the early 1970s. Moreover, the off-reservation school districts that had large numbers of Indian students, most significantly Lafayette (Onondaga), Niagara-Wheatfield (Tuscarora), Salmon River (St. Regis), and Gowanda (Seneca) took federal moneys for Indian education and rarely gave any of the cultural enrichment courses and/or activities under federal/ state programmatic requirements.[25]

In reaction to this deplorable situation, the St. Regis (Akwesasne) Mohawks, on April 22, 1968, through the efforts of Chief John Cook and Minerva White, organized a boycott of the Salmon River School District. White later described the reason for the boycott:

It is probably hard for whites . . . to understand what it is like knowing who to talk to and not having anyone who will listen when problems arise where your children go to school. We could go to talk to the principal and he would listen to us and agree with us while we were there. But nothing was ever done.[26]

The Mohawks were also infuriated by the refusal of the local school board, their local assemblyman, and Albany SED officials to take their grievances seriously. Their 1968 boycott was spurred on by one teacher's mistreatment of some of his Mohawk students and by the fact that, at that time, Indians could not legally vote in New York State school board elections and were thus excluded from serving on the boards affecting their children's education. The Mohawks were further angered by the Salmon River Central School's receiving of special state legislative funding for improved facilities at a time when their own Mohawk School in the same district was underfunded. Moreover, at the Salmon River Central School District, Title One funding that was earmarked for "Indian education" was used for general education, audio-visual equipment, and the hiring of teachers and nurses.[27]

The Mohawk boycott was followed by one at Onondaga in 1971. This protest centered on the lack of Onondaga community influence and control of their children's education in the off-reservation Lafayette Central Schools, to which Indians were bussed. Led by Lloyd Elm, at that time a science teacher in the school system, and modeled to some degree on the similar Mohawk protest at St. Regis (Akwesasne) in 1968, the Onondagas kept their children out of school in 1971 to call attention to their educational concerns. The Onondagas were reacting to the extremely high drop-out rates among Indian students, the lack of cultural enrichment programs including language instruction, and their limited voice in school district policy. Seeing the decline in knowledge of the Iroquois ways by the younger generation and fearful of the future of their Longhouse religion, they proposed extending their own community school through the twelfth grade. The boycott led New York State Education Department officials to negotiate at the Onondaga Longhouse. Although the boycott did not lead to the creation of an expanded school system on the reservation which the Onondagas wanted, the existing elementary school was expanded to the eighth grade and more awareness of Indian cultural concerns became evident in the Lafayette School District.[28]

The years 1968–1971 also proved a turning point in several other ways. Working with Dean Robert Wells of St. Lawrence University, Chief Cook and Minerva White helped design and introduce the "Upward Bound Program" for St. Regis Mohawk students in grades nine through twelve, and the Institute on the American Indian in Higher Education. White and Cook also helped initiate a Mohawk language class at the Salmon River Central School, and start the Akwesasne Cultural Center (St. Regis Mohawk Library). Working with Anna Lewis of SED, they also helped convince the Teacher Certification Division of SED of the need for special certification requirements for American Indian teachers who taught native languages and cultures and helped initiate the right-to-read program at St. Regis, the first such program operational on an Indian reservation.[29]

Through the efforts of Anna Lewis, educational policymakers became increasingly sensitized to the needs of Indian communities. SED Commissioner Gordon Ambach, then executive deputy commissioner of education, was invited to the St. Regis (Akwesasne) Reservation in the winter of 1971 where he addressed a major convocation on Indian education. There, for the first time, he put forth a major SED policy "redesign" (his words) in a paper entitled "The Education of Indians." He insisted: "We cannot talk about the purposes and programs of Indian education without discussing the goals of Indian society. It follows that we cannot do this without full participation of the Indian community." Ambach outlined the need for (1) sensitivity to Indian differences; (2) the development of programs on Indian culture; and (3) the participation of Indians as teachers, para-professionals, and members of educational advisory committees. He added: "But we can't continue asking them [Indians] to cast off their ties with the past. The past is their prologue just as your past is yours—so help them to build upon it, not apart from it."[30]

Much of what Ambach outlined in his speech had been developed by Lewis, White, and Chief Cook from the time of the Mohawk boycott in 1968. In the late winter of 1971, Lewis, a former teacher at the Onondaga School, and Dale Samuelson wrote a comprehensive five-year plan for improvement of Indian education in New York that specifically built on Ambach's talk. The Lewis-Samuelson plan also called for "Indian Education (advisory or official) Boards made up of tribal leaders (hereditary or elected, and lay), parents and youth for each tribal group in New York. These boards will become the official school boards for that tribe's students, as the tribal group assumes control of the educational program." The plan also called for the establishment of the Onondaga "Demonstration" School, as modeled after the successful Navajo Rough Rock School Project; the creation of an internship-in-leadership program; the expansion of the post-secondary higher educational program; the development of new resource lists and curriculum materials; improved health attention to Indian families; and the establishment of day care centers. Importantly, it pointed out: "Surely, some special consideration must be made eventually for all the problems that encompass the urban Indian."[31]

At the time of the Onondaga protest, the Assembly Subcommittee on Indian Affairs focused much of its investigation on the educational realm, gathering valuable testimony from Minerva White and Onondaga Chief Irving Powless, Jr., about Indian educational needs in New York State.[32]

Besides recommending improved methods of communication among the school districts, the native communities and SED, the assembly subcommittee report urged the establishment of Indian pre-kindergarten (headstart) programs; more focus on drop-out prevention; development of new curriculum materials relating to "New York State Indian culture" increased attention to adult education programs on each reservation; summer faculty training on Indian educational needs; and meetings of school administrators and guidance personnel to explore and implement new programs. It also called for better SED coordination in its bureaus and divisions involved in Indian education and for SED determination of what programs, grants, scholarships, benefits, both public and private, were open to New York State Indian students. SED, according to this report, should inform guidance counsellors in the ten school districts serving Indian communities about these aid programs and train guidance counsellors to be more familiar with the needs of Indian students. Significantly, the report once again repeated the call for the SED's creation of an advisory committee which would include each chief school officer and at least one Indian leader from each of the department's districts and each of the reservations. "This group would meet at least every six months to examine and resolve questions and conflicts arising from the Department's concern for Indian education."[33] This last item, the call for an advisory committee, had been suggested as early as 1940, in one of SED's early studies.[34] It is also important to note that Article 83, Section 4116 of the present New York State Education Law, which was enacted in 1947 but had its origins ninety years earlier, reads:

> In the discharge of the duties imposed by this article, the said commissioner shall endeavor to secure the co-operation of all the several bands of Indians, and for this purpose, shall visit, by himself or his authorized representative, all the reservations where they reside, *lay the matter before them in public assembly, inviting them to assist either by appropriating their public moneys to this object, or by setting apart lands and erecting suitable buildings, or by furnishing labor or materials for such buildings, or in any other way which he or they may suggest as most effectual for the promotion of this object.*[35] [Emphasis mine.]

Despite repeated calls by American Indians for involvement in the education of their children, the first meeting of the commissioner's Native American Education Advisory Committee was convened on January 6, 1986.

In 1973, the SED established the Native American Indian Education Unit under the direction of Lincoln White, a former school superintendent and Mohawk Indian from St. Regis (Akwesasne). From 1973 to 1975, the unit focused its attention on two areas: (1) securing federal moneys into New York for the betterment of Indian education through the Johnson-O'Malley program of 1934 and the Indian Education Act of 1972; and (2) the development of a Board of Regents position paper. Even though SED officials had been informed as early as 1965 that New York State Indian students (and school districts with Indian students) were entitled to federal aid under the Johnson-O'Malley program, SED was slow to respond. Through the efforts of Louis R. Bruce, Jr., the United States Commissioner of Indian Affairs, and close friend of Lincoln White, and intensive lobbying by SED officials including Gordon Ambach, Leo Soucy, and Anna Lewis, Johnson-O'Malley funds were finally secured in 1975; however, for at least seven years, hundreds of thousands of dollars of federal funds were lost, largely because of neglect by some SED administrators. For example, Ronald Daley, the chief of the Bureau of Elementary Schools, never encouraged school districts to go after moneys available for bilingual education nor submitted a formal plan to seek Johnson-O'Malley federal funds before June of 1973.[36]

From 1973 to 1975, the Native American Indian Education Unit worked in the preparation of a Board of Regents policy statement on American Indian education. The Board of Regents first turned their attention to American Indian educational issues in March 1971, at a meeting with representatives of minority groups. As a result of Gordon Ambach's visit to St. Regis in January, American Indians were subsequently invited to this important meeting in Albany. It is important to note that, although the Board of Regents, especially Regents Emlyn Griffith and Laura Chodos and Secretary William Carr, have devoted much attention over the last decade to the improvement of Indian education, the board in March 1971 took up Indian issues as an afterthought, thinking it proper to invite them only after other minority group educators had been invited and only after Commissioner Ambach and Anna Lewis had lobbied for their inclusion. In a letter dated January 28, 1971 to Richard J. Sawyer, the secretary to the Board of Regents, relative to the upcoming Regents meeting with representatives of minority groups, Ambach critically noted:

> No mention of New York State Indians has been made with regard to this meeting. We should definitely have one or two Indians invited and perhaps you would want to have one on the panel. I suggest that you contact Anna Lewis in the School Supervision area. Miss Lewis, who is an Indian, now has responsibility for Indian education programs. I recently joined her and others in a meeting in Massena attended by a number of key Indians interested in education. Miss Lewis would have good suggestions for participants and perhaps for a panel member.[37]

Iroquois representatives were subsequently invited, including Chief John Cook, Lloyd Elm, Janet Jones, Elma Patterson, Maribel Printup, Shirley Snyder, Jacob Thompson, and Minerva White, with Chief Cook serving as a panelist at the March meeting. At the meeting, as a result of the impassioned plea for action made by Minerva White, American Indian educational concerns for the first time were considered important by the Board of Regents. Armed with the Assembly Subcommittee report and the Lewis-Samuelson plan and the convincing arguments made by White, Chief Cook, and Chief Irving Powless, Jr., Assistant Commissioner Leo Soucy, who is of French Canadian and Sioux Indian ancestry, ably cultivated and educated the Regents to Indian concerns.[38] Largely through the initiatives and political power of the Board of Regents, major changes in American Indian education were affected over the next decade and a half.

In 1975, the Board of Regents announced a position paper, "Native American Education," which significantly altered SED's past educational policies with respect to American Indians in New York State. This position paper, number twenty-two in the Board of Regents series, explained the reasons for this major policy shift in the following manner:

> The formal educational programs provided for native Americans in New York State assumed that they desired to become assimilated into the dominant society, while forsaking their tribal heritages. The Regents now recognize that these people prefer to retain their specific tribal cultural identities and life styles and that they wish to exercise the prerogatives of adopting only those components of the dominant American culture that meet their needs. In American history, the State and Federal attempts to terminate tribes, to dissolve their reservation status, and to relocate their people into urban settings have been unsuccessful.[39]

The Board of Regents emphasized the need to create educational programs which "should accommodate specific tribal cultural differences by attempting to provide bilingual and bicultural learning environments to be offered to students at their choice and which enable the Native American to function more effectively in a pluralistic society." Their report recommended (1) the creation of a "Statewide Native American Education Advisory Committee" "to advise and consult with the Commissioner of Education and his staff on educational policies and practices regarding the education of Native Americans in New York State"; (2) "New and improved procedures be established whereby representatives of tribal communities and reservations can have greater involvement in decisions in the education of their children"; (3) the encouragement of school employment policies to enable more Native Americans to be employed as certified instructional and non-instructional personnel; (4) the development of a plan to enable teacher training institutions to provide courses and teacher-training experiences that relate to the cultures and heritages of Native Americans and to establish preservice and inservice teacher-training programs to assist those who teach Indian children; and (5) the revision of the elementary and secondary school curriculum to "assure maximum educational opportunities for Native American children," including the development of special bilingual and bicultural instructional programs and materials in order to increase student ability to learn.[40]

Although much of the Regents Position Paper No. 22 was either needlessly delayed or never implemented, there have, nevertheless, been substantial changes in Indian education since 1975. In a move promoted by the Board of Regents, the New York State legislature passed a bill in 1977 creating and appropriating $175,000 for an Indian public library system, the first of its kind in the United States:[41]

> By a majority vote of the tribal government of an Indian reservation, or upon the request of the tribal government of an Indian reservation, an Indian library may be established, with or without branches, and may make application to the state or other sources for money to equip and maintain such library or libraries or to provide a building or room for its uses. Notwithstanding the provisions of section seven of the Indian law, the board of trustees of such library, on behalf of the tribal government, may acquire real or personal property for use by an Indian library by gift, grant, devise, bequest and may take, buy, sell, hold and transfer either real or personal property for the purposes of such library. No more than one Indian library may be established on a reservation and such library shall serve all inhabitants of that reservation. No such library shall be established on any reservation that has fewer than three hundred permanent residents and one thousand acres of land.[42]

The act also provided for specific means of acquiring and acceptance of surplus library books, a specific formula of apportionment of state aid to Indian libraries and a mechanism for distribution of state aid to either the Indian library board of trustees or directly to the tribal government for a contract for library service. Prior to this act, only one underfunded, underequipped library—the Akwesasne Cultural Center—was operating on the reservations in New York. Although the bill had been in existence for three years and had the support of statewide library associations and three Iroquois councils,[43] it was originally opposed by the Division of the Budget as special interest legislation which did "not provide any special or unique types of library services which are not already provided for." At a time of a major state fiscal crisis, only through Regents lobbying pressure did this revolutionary piece of legislation pass.[44]

Working through the Board of Regents, the Native American Indian Education Unit achieved other goals. Significantly, the state support for

Indian schools has risen from $3,581,107 to $8,000,000 in the last decade, nearly doubling since 1979–1980.[45] In 1977, the state's Postsecondary Aid Program for Indian college students was changed to include off-reservation students; the program was later extended to include enrolled members of New York State tribes or the child of an enrolled member of a New York State tribe.[46] The unit, through Regents pressure, supported the Indian School Board Act and Indian Library Act of 1984, which allowed reservation Indians to serve as members of boards of education and as trustees of public libraries established by school districts.[47] Through its accreditation function the Regents and the Native American Indian Education Unit also supported the creation, incorporation, and chartering of the Seneca-Iroquois National Museum.[48] Moreover, the unit lobbied for improved school facilities, encouraged the development of new curricula, raised standards for teachers and students, and initiated computer-based instruction in 1982 in the Indian schools. The unit has also worked with Clarkson College's "SCOPES" program in developing a model plan to educate American Indians in the engineering sciences. Despite failing to achieve an independent K–12 school district, which was supported by the Native American Indian Education Unit, the Onondagas did establish a K–8 school.[49]

Although there have been significant changes in American Indian education since 1975, SED has delayed, not implemented, or ignored Indian concerns in other areas. The agency was slow to support the so-called "Oath Bill," which would exempt Native American Indian teachers, instructors, and professors from taking the oath of allegiance to the state and its constitution. Because of sovereignty-related concerns, the Iroquois favor this action and had expressed their support for exemption as far back as the 1930s.[50] SED's slowness to act reflects the low priority given Indian education in the agency. Anna Lewis in 1977, in a policy memorandum, "Status of the Native American Education Unit," outlined the weakness of her unit:

Low priority within S.E.D.
Limited staffing.
Limited responsibility for decision making.
Organizationally placed within S.E.D. with units that have no relevance to responsibilities.
Lack of clearly defined policies relating to
Native American education.
Position Paper recommendations not implemented.[51]

Many of Lewis' concerns continued to be ignored until her retirement in 1984.

The low priority assigned to Indian education can be also illustrated by focusing on the Native American Education Advisory Committee's creation, 1984–1986. The committee was finally established after a ten-year delay *only after* Commissioner Ambach feared that one of the planned Board of Regents Bicentennial meetings would be disrupted. According to a memorandum of March 21, 1984, Ambach wrote his deputy commissioner:

> I would like to know the answer to the issue especially in advance of April 6th when you go to the St. Regis Mohawk Reservation for that recognition [Board of Regents meeting]. It is likely that the point would come up there, and I would certainly want to be ready to respond as to what the history has been and, perhaps, some indication for next steps.[52]

Although Ambach, as we have seen, was an early advocate of Indian educational improvement, the letter of March 21 reveals that policy implementation of Regents Position Paper No. 22 had little priority in SED and Indian criticisms were virtually ignored until action was mandatory to prevent a "bad scene" at a scheduled Regents meeting. It should be noted that SED's slowness in creating the Native American Education Advisory Committee and failure to establish the teacher-training and continuing education components of Regents Position Paper No. 22 saved the state nearly $1 million from 1975 to 1985.[53]

As of early 1987, the Native American Indian Education Unit has only two full-time employees, yet has the following responsibilities: counselling American Indians about educational matters on all the Indian reservation communities and five major urban areas; educating their financial aid officers about the state's program for American Indians; processing applications for the state's Postsecondary Aid Program of financial assistance for higher education; working with teachers and administrators in administering and improving educational programs at the state's three Indian schools; supervising school district-Indian nation contracts under state and federal educational programs; bringing an American Indian perspective to state agencies dealing with native peoples; working closely with the newly appointed Native American Education Advisory Committee; and serving the American Indians of the state as unofficial diplomats to Albany by reporting back on legislative and gubernatorial intentions. The associate and bilingual specialist in the unit are also expected to make on-site visits to the three Indian schools. Moreover, the unit, with its one secretary, is also expected to provide all the secretarial and administrative functions needed by the Native American Education Advisory Committee. Despite Associate Dr. Hazel V. Dean-John's linguistic expertise—she holds a PH.D. degree in linguistics from the University of Arizona—she has little time to devote to the much-needed areas of applied linguistics and curriculum reform. Since there are fewer speakers of the Iroquoian languages each year and the languages are being lost, ignoring planning and failing to develop new methods of retention will have grave consequences for the Iroquois people in the future.[54] Moreover, because of the incredible workload on the Native American Indian Education Unit, it cannot focus on other major concerns: (1) new agency regulations to amend its current and Byzantine internship program; (2) a detailed study with recommendations to explore ways of preventing the incredibly high college drop-out of Indian students at New York State colleges; and (3) an analysis of why, despite the expansion of the eligibility of the state's Postsecondary Education Program for Indians, there are fewer Indian students taking advantage of this program than a decade ago.

The Native American Indian Education Unit is also beset by major problems other than overwork. Until recently, the unit was not consulted by other branches within SED in the preparation of Indian-related curriculum materials. In 1986, SED funded and published a dance curriculum for the social studies. Prepared by Artsconnection, it contained inaccurate and culturally insensitive materials about Native Americans and virtually nothing about American Indians in New York State. In the same year, the Bureau of Curriculum Development distributed a field test edition of its new social studies curriculum for the seventh and eighth grades which also contained historical inaccuracies about the Iroquois Confederacy, de-emphasized the role of the Indian in state history, and made no mention that Native Americans are still vibrant cultures in New York state. Only after more than fifty letters of protest were sent to SED by Indian and non-Indian educators about these two faulty curriculum initiatives did SED officials, Indian representatives, and the Board of Regents meet. As a result of a January 8, 1987 meeting, the SED's Division of Program Planning agreed to make revisions in the syllabus and to develop more supplementary educational materials.[55]

Other educational problems affect the Native American Indian Unit and limit its effectiveness. Allowing American Indians the right to serve on school boards throughout the state was an important but mostly symbolic step since the limited size of Indian populations makes the likelihood of their election to school boards slim indeed. Although a few American Indians have won election, their voices will still be limited under this arrangement because of state demographics. Thus, the Native American Indian Education Unit has little political support at the school district level for its initiatives.

As the state's largest bureaucracy, SED has also come into conflict with American Indian communities in one other major area: the New York State Museum's custody of twenty-five wampum belts. In 1968, Chief George A. Thomas, the Iroquois Tadodaho or spiritual leader, initiated the call to return the belts and admitted that "it was was wrong for our grandfathers to give away the wampum. The wampum tells of old, old agreements and passes on the thoughts of our grandfathers. We would like to see them. Our people want to touch them." The "great wampum war," as it has been dubbed by one prominent anthropologist, still rages and has drastically affected the relationship of the Iroquois with the academic community and the New York State Museum.[56]

Wampum is a species of white and purple beads, from the plentiful whelk and the somewhat rarer quahog clam, drilled through from opposite ends with steel awls and strung into strings or woven into belts in geometric designs. Today, twenty-five of these belts are housed in the New York State Museum. The Iroquois did not invent wampum, since its source was outside of their territory; its greatest historic supply was concentrated around Gardiner's Island and Oyster Bay, Long Island, and at Narragansett Bay in New England. Iroquois use of wampum appears to date from the late 1620s; nevertheless, the Iroquois helped endow the belts with meaning and employed "them in all ritually sanctioned transactions for which wampum belts were affidavits. It was they who taught the colonial governors the protocol of treaty making, and as these activities increased so did the demand for wampum." The ritual symbolism and protocol employed by the Iroquois in using the belts was much older than the belts themselves, and largely "derived from the Iroquois paradigm of condolence, a system that every colonial officer" doing business with them had to learn, especially by the middle decades of the eighteenth century, the apogee of British-Iroquois treatymaking.[57]

The Onondagas have argued their case for the repatriation of wampum in legislative hearings, in the media, and in numerous protest demonstrations. Stressing their traditional role as Iroquois wampum keepers, although other Iroquois nations such as the Senecas claim as well as hold their own wampum, the Onondagas insisted upon the religious necessity of restoring the belts. The academic and museum community, although hardly united on the issue of return, insisted that there were few, if any, Iroquois who could read the wampum; focused on the special needs for preservation that only the museum could provide; pointed out that the Onondaga Council of Chiefs itself had agreed in 1898 at a meeting in Albany to allow the University of the State of New York, namely the State Museum, to hold the wampum for safekeeping; and stressed the legality of the contractual transfers of the belts to the museum as well as the New

York State law of 1909 that validated the institution's role as custodians of the wampum. They also maintained that the wampum was not just a part of the Indians' cultural and religious life but part of the history of New York as a whole, and that returning the belts would establish a dangerous precedent for other groups trying to reclaim cultural and religious treasures.[58]

In the Onondagas' eyes, undergoing as they were a new activist and religious awakening, the belts were seen as a way to reconsecrate and restore their ancient role in the League of the Iroquois as keepers of the wampum and capital of the confederacy.[59] Vine Deloria, Jr. has pointed out that the wampum controversy was part of a larger struggle involving not just the return of belts, but questions of treaty rights and sovereignty and even the return of part of the Iroquois homeland. After all, as one Onondaga chief observed: "How could New York State pass a law making itself wampum keepers when it did not have jurisdiction to do so." Thus, the belts' return is seen by Indians today as part of the larger issues involving jurisdiction, tribal sovereignty, and the nature of the federal-Indian relationship. Deloria, for one, has concluded that the Onondagas, in effect, were fighting, as he claimed, to "complete the reintegration of their League on its traditional basis."[60] For the Onondagas, the final insult was a bill, passed in 1971, which allowed the Indians to have possession of five of the belts only after a suitable museum for storage and security of the wampum was built at Onondaga. Because no museum was forthcoming, the Onondagas' disagreement with this caveat, and Seneca claims to the belts, the wampum war still rages.[61]

The State Museum's defensive response to the wampum crisis in the early 1970s was to create a token position for an Indian, namely the full-time position of "Specialist in Indian Culture." The duties of the post included serving as liaison with the Indian communities and assisting with the development of museum-related programs dealing with Indian cultures; aiding in curating the museum's Indian collections and helping arrange for appropriate loans and exhibits of museum materials to Indian communities; preparing and scheduling talks on contemporary Indian culture; advising museum officials on present-day Indian affairs; and arranging seminars and workshops on Indian arts and crafts.[62] SED hired a young Mohawk educator who had little previous experience in the areas necessary to carry out the duties of the post. By being designated as the museum's "Specialist in Indian Culture," he also had the impossible task of working with chiefs and other tribal elders who were his senior in knowledge of traditional ways. Although lasting over ten years in the position, the specialist's effectiveness was dubious from the beginning because of his own limited background, the political climate of Iroquoia in the

1970s, and the museum administrators' lack of commitment at that time to the post.[63]

Today, the New York State Museum, through its Office of Exhibit Planning, is also developing the "Upstate Wing" which will have a significant Iroquoian cultural component when it is completed in 1988–1989. This planned permanent exhibit has an Iroquois advisory committee as well as acknowledged scholarly experts providing valuable input.[64] One of the advisors is an accomplished Onondaga artist, who worked on a provisional basis under a grant, for the museum's Office of State Archeology and has recently been appointed the new "Specialist in Indian Culture."

In sum, although SED and DSS have made substantial progress in overcoming mistakes made in the past, both agencies have still not given enough priority to Indian concerns. According to the most recently available official state statistics, only nine of 4,841 DSS employees are of American Indian or Alaskan Native ancestry while the figure for SED is only six of 4,025.[65] According to a recent letter by former commissioner Ambach to the author:

> We are very aware and sympathetic to the many diverse educational needs of the New York State's Native American students. Despite severe budgetary limitations, several steps have been taken that reflect the Department's commitment to that Unit [Native American Education Unit], including establishing the Commissioner's Native American Advisory Council; assigning Adrian Cook as Dr. Dean-John's assistant; moving the Office of Native American Education Services from the Cultural Education Center to the Education Building Annex where Assistant Commissioner Arnold, to whom the Unit reports, is located; and providing additional stenographic support.[66]

Despite these contentions, SED has not created the necessary administrative structure in the unit to service the educational needs of the state's Indian populations. A similar criticism can be cast at DSS for understaffing its Indian social services programs. Perhaps now, with SED's creation of the Native American Education Advisory Committee after forty-six years of broken promises and needless delay, there is some hope that the voices of American Indians will finally be heard loud and clear in the "Chancellor's Hall" of the massive State Education Department building in Albany.

6

▼▼▼

The Bitter Living Legacy of Robert Moses: New York State Agencies and American Indian Lands

> For almost 200 years the state of New York has, in most cases, dealt with New York indian [sic] tribes in connection with the exercise of the power of eminent domain thereover without approval of federal officials.
>
> —*Louis J. Lefkowitz,*
> *New York State Attorney General,*
> *June 8, 1973*

New York State agencies, most notably the Office of Parks, Recreation, and Historic Preservation (OPRHP), the departments of Law and Transportation, and the Power Authority of the State of New York (PASNY), have a bitter legacy to live down when it comes to improving relations with American Indian communities. No single individual in this century has more personified to the Iroquois the worst in New York State Indian policies than Robert Moses. Although difficult to believe, Tuscarora elders, remembering their battle with Moses and PASNY's plans to take one-eighth of their reservation land base, still play their radios in their homes while talking to outsiders in order to "drown out" what they claim was "state political surveillance" initiated by Robert Moses a quarter-century ago.[1] The passage of time has not overcome the remembrances of and hatred of the "master builder" since Indians are in daily contact with two state parks bearing Moses' name, which were developed directly adjacent to two of their reservations.[2]

Policymakers are affected by the "legacy" in two specific ways. Some, emulating Moses, associate "Indians" only with their "nuisance" value, namely as potential litigants or protesters. These same administrators often have generalized and stereotypical images of Indians as conspiring, combative "hostiles," threatening New York State's growth and future progress. In a letter to Governor Hugh Carey in September 1978, Albert B. Lewis, the former New York State superintendent of insurance, clearly reflected this viewpoint. He recounted to Carey the status of Indian claims which he learned from attending a seminar conducted by attorney Allan Van Gestel of "a firm defending many of the Indian claims in the Northeast area." Lewis insisted that Indian land claims litigation would create catastrophic consequences for New York State. These suits would lead to the suspension of bank mortgage activities and numerous bankruptcies because of questions of clouded title to lands claimed by the Indians. Lewis praised Secretary of State Cuomo's office for attempting to bring federal intervention, suggested the development of a state bail-out plan similar to the Municipal Assistance Corporation receivership during New York City's financial crisis, and urged Governor Carey to obtain maximum federal financial assistance and to call for an emergency session of the Northeast Governors' Conference to deal with the threat of Indian land claims. Lewis warned that many new cases were being contemplated as Indians become "more militant" and "Indian Right [sic] Groups" study federal decisions. To add to the letter's urgency, Lewis reported that the Long Island Shinnecocks were "working with the Native American Rights Fund and will be making claim to areas in Suffolk and Nassau County [sic]." Playing up what he perceived as an Indian conspiracy, he urged the governor to assist the "citizens of western New York, the Mid-Hudson area, Suffolk and Nassau County" as he had done in the 1975–1978 financial crises of New York City, Buffalo, and Yonkers![3]

Other policymakers attempt to quickly redress past mistakes; however, they often make further mistakes which contribute to future problems. In order to prevent conflict with certain more vocal Indian groups, agency policymakers, as the OPRHP case study in this chapter shows, assuage elements in the Indian communities who appear to be threatening and who have the potential of generating unfavorable media attention.

Despite never holding an elected office, Robert Moses, the legendary master builder, wielded unrestrained power for well over forty years. Although associated in the main with transforming the face of New York City and Long Island, its beaches, parkways, and skyline, his influence extended far beyond—to Massena and Niagara Falls, as well as to the backroom political clubhouses of Albany. His critical biographer Robert Caro has observed: "In the shaping of New York, Robert Moses was comparable only to some elemental force of nature."[4] An arrogant, power-hungry individual, he intimidated governors as well as lesser politicians until his political demise under Governor Nelson Rockefeller.

In 1924, Robert Moses wrote *A State Park Plan for New York*, a report that helped shape the direction of park development nationally by shifting the philosophy of parks away from merely conservation; he combined it with the recreational needs of the masses and the means to get to the parks, namely parkway development. He added that the state should develop a park system divided into eleven regional administrations or commissions whose presidents would sit as a "state council of parks," and coordinate, unify, and develop state parks, largely non-existent at the time. The New York State Council of Parks soon became Moses' power base and network to local and regional politicians throughout the state.[5]

From Moses' first involvement with the Iroquois land base in the 1940s, it is clear that he defined reservations as "sacrifice areas" for his idea of progress. In 1945, as head of the New York State Council of Parks, Moses commissioned a study to evaluate the potential impact of the then-proposed Kinzua Dam project on Allegany State Park. When the report was released and announced by Moses the following year, it supported a federal plan to buy the entire Allegany Indian Reservation and remove all the Indians in order to promote flood control and develop the valley for recreational purposes.[6] In the 1950s, Moses turned his attention to the St. Lawrence and Niagara frontier regions, namely the St. Lawrence Seaway and Niagara power development. As chairman of PASNY from 1952 onward, he combined his earlier park interests with new concerns for power development, seaway transport, and heavy industry. By constructing a series of parks and parkways for tourist and recreational purposes, while providing special low rates for St. Lawrence-Niagara frontier residents, he would counter any local opposition to the project. By improving the state's total economic picture, he would satisfy the public utilities' quest for increased profit margins. By sacrificing Indian lands—Tuscarora (560 acres), Akwesasne Mohawk (130 acres), and Caughnawaga Mohawk (1,260 acres)—or those that were claimed by Indians, a small powerless racial minority largely outside of the American electoral process, he would not alienate white voters and their political representatives, especially in the economically depressed North Country of New York State. Moreover, Moses' efforts at industrial development contributed to the wooing of General Motors and Reynolds to the Rooseveltown peninsula, which have had disastrous environmental results to Mohawk life at St. Regis (Akwesasne).[7]

Moses' disdainful attitude towards Indians is best summarized in quoting from a passage he wrote in his book, *Working for the People*, published in 1956:

> This job has its humor. In addition to those who supervise the supervisors, execute the executives and watch the watchmen, we have to contend with St. Regis Indians, who ask the tidy little sum of $34 million for their pre-Revolutionary interest in Barnhart Island, and assorted characters who are

steaming up distant owners on the Great Lakes shorefront to sue us for the rise and fall of the tides.

Moses insisted that these "are merely little incidents that brighten our days."[8] Yet, to all Mohawks, Barnhart Island is still considered their traditional territory despite a state park with a major beach, power houses, high voltage power lines, and two St. Lawrence Seaway ship locks on the island.[9]

Office of Parks, Recreation and Historic Preservation

The bitter legacy created by Robert Moses still seriously affects and undermines the policies of such agencies as OPRHR. Hard-nosed leadership, especially at the regional level, that defines "Indian" as a threat to agency plans for development and expansion co-exists with personnel that are attempting to rectify the insensitivity and mistakes of the Moses era. OPRHP, like its predecessor the State Council of Parks, created by Moses, has had an often stormy relationship with American Indians.

In 1970 two separate agencies were created from the old Conservation Department—the Department of Environmental Conservation (DEC) and the Office of Parks and Recreation (OPR). The latter was "placed in the Executive Department and was assigned the responsibility of maintaining the state's parks and historic sites, as well as providing recreational opportunities for the people of the entire state." Eleven state park regions, largely formed by Robert Moses in the 1920s, were assigned to OPR while the Adirondack and Catskill Parks were put under DEC jurisdiction. Importantly, in 1972 OPR became responsible for the maintenance and operation of thirty-four historic sites as well as the development of the statewide system for historic management from its headquarters at Peebles Island State Park in the environs of Albany.[10]

OPRHP's operations and their relationship to American Indians can be seen by examining three specific areas: (1) Allegany State Park; (2) Sampson State Park; and (3) Ganondagan State Historic Site. Allegany State park, OPRHP's largest facility, spans over 61,000 acres and is noted for its fine hunting, camping, and winter sports, as well as its abundance of native wildlife such as deer, bear, turkey, and raccoon. The Seneca Nation of Indians has tapped into the park's tourist industry through the establishment of their Highbanks Campgrounds and by the building of the Seneca-Iroquois National Museum; however, the two worlds, the Seneca and the park, it is clear, merely peacefully co-exist. Senecas question the legalities of how the park was established in the 1920s, remember past park commissioners' insensitivities to their concerns, and suggest that the park boundaries are incorrect and impinge on tribal lands.[11] It is important to note that three major Salamanca community leaders—Charles Congdon, Thomas Dowd and Albert Fancher—involved in the development of the state park, were also the same non-Indians involved in fighting the Senecas over equitable Salamanca lease payments and were among the strongest advocates of the transfer of federal criminal and civil jurisdiction to New York State in 1948 and 1950.[12]

OPRHP has also resisted having its lands traded off in various Indian land settlements. The 1976 "Lieu Lands Treaty," which will be discussed later, was held up by opposition from administrators of the Allegany State Park Commission.[13] During an attempt to settle the Cayuga land claims with congressional legislation in 1980, George Souhan, a commissioner of the Finger Lakes State Park and Recreation Commission, testified at a Capitol Hill hearing against the "surrendering" of the 1,852-acre Sampson State Park "in a deal cut with the Cayuga Indian Nation." Souhan suggested that the arrangement was "contrary to the best interest of the people of New York State." In revealing testimony, he criticized the Cayugas for "threatening lengthy and costly legal suits" and for "engaging in a warfare of intimidation, tantamount to blackmail." He also criticized what he claimed was the secret decision made by the governor's office in surrendering the park, insisting that state public lands "cannot be thrown into the negotiating table like so many chips at a poker game."[14] Perhaps because of this criticism, OPRHP today has put only 500–550 unused acres of Sampson State Park into a final Cayuga settlement "package," a far cry from H.R. 6631, opposed by Commissioner Souhan, that would have ceded the entire state park to the Cayugas.[15] The effect of Indian claims litigation on the policies of OPRHP is also clearly seen in other ways. Worried about the potential cut-off of federal funds for land and water conservation projects located in various claim areas, John M. Prenderville, then OPRHP's deputy commissioner for Regional Administration, wrote to the governor's director of State Operations in the fall of 1978, pointing out the danger of pending Indian land claims. He concluded that it "is not my intent to be an alarmist, but I thought you should know what is currently happening."[16]

To counter its past conflicts with American Indian communities, the OPRHP, with the support of the governor's office, has finally begun to implement plans for the development of Ganondagan State Historic Site. Ganondagan, formerly called Gannagaro and often referred to by archaeologists as the Boughton Hill site, is the only site within the Bureau of Historic Sites devoted solely to the history and culture of American Indians. It contains the archaeological remains of the major seventeenth-century Seneca village. Ganondagan's village and burial grounds were designated a National Historic Landmark in 1964. Another part of the site, the Fort Hill portion, associated with the massive French Denonville military expedition from Canada in 1687, was listed on the National Register of Historic Places in 1966.[17]

From 1970, the date in which the state first acquired part of the site, until January 1980, little was done to develop, plan, or protect the site.[18] OPRHP, at the regional or statewide level, gave no priority to the site and was even faced with a race discrimination suit by the custodian of the site who was an enrolled Tonawanda Seneca.[19] Since the early 1980s, the Bureau of Historic Sites of OPRHP has received several major federal grants for a site-planning master plan and has hired consultants as well as a site manager, an enrolled Seneca; recently, it has received a state legislative line item appropriation for $147,000.[20] In order to overcome distrust and head off potential problems, it has worked with a committee of Iroquois consultants, not all Senecas.[21]

Unfortunately, OPRHP in attempting to finally redress its poor relationship with the Iroquois—land claims, land exchange, park development and burial issues—has made several blunders which could prove destructive to its efforts in the future. Before 1986, in not fully understanding the Iroquois polity, the agency and its Bureau of Historic Sites personnel had not been balanced and even-handed in their dealings with Indian communities. They have favored the Six Nations' Council of the Iroquois Confederacy by the inclusion of certain native artists and writers, some of whom are political activists, at the expense of the wants and needs of the Seneca Nation of Indians. Although two political leaders of the Six Nations Council were represented from the beginning (1980) of the project, not one Seneca Nation political leader serves as a consultant, even though the site is a Seneca site. Although one well-respected political-religious leader of the separate Tonawanda Band of Senecas is included in the planning, other Seneca leaders from Allegany and Cattaraugus are ignored, leading several former Seneca Nation consultants to resign or purposely boycott the meetings.[22]

Though the site was given special attention in Governor Cuomo's State-of-the-State message in January 1986, the site manager had no staff for the park's operations or clerical assistance to facilitate reports and grant writing as of late May 1986. The site had not been provided with park security to prevent grave robbing or other pilfering. Until mid-May 1986, there was not even a provision for contracting lawn mowing at Ganondagan.[23] Meanwhile, the governor's office "cannot understand why the Governor is discouraged from visiting the site for a campaign whistle-stop and picture-taking session."[24] To further complicate the development of the park, the Bureau of Historic Sites has sunk too much of its funding in saving and restoring a nineteenth-century farmhouse and moving it across the road to Ganondagan to serve as a site visitor center. This farmhouse salvage project, along with the bureau's insistence on saving a small barn, are not related in any way to the American Indian history of Ganondagan.[25]

The Bureau of Historic Sites is also strongly divided about policies relative to Ganondagan. The bureau's foremost archaeologist insists, correctly in my opinion, upon the limited unearthing of the site in order to protect it, respect its religious significance, and insure the possibilities of future study of the site when new technologies allow for it. This preservationist thinking conflicts with others in the bureau who want to dig and unearth the site to find out as much as possible about Seneca history. Although the Bureau of Historic Sites has a ten-year master plan for the development of the site drawn up in response to Division of the Budget concerns about continued high-level funding, one wonders whether the Ganondagan project, the first "State Indian Park," will receive the same political attention and level of funding after the site's official opening in July 1987.[26]

Department of Transportation

The New York State Department of Transportation is one of the oldest agencies in the state involved with providing services to American Indian reservations. The agency has a legislative mandate to maintain roads on American Indian reservations in the state.[27] The agency does not maintain a separate funding category for Indian reservation roads but takes moneys when needed out of general operating funds. The DOT also operates several substations on several Indian reservations, such as the Cattaraugus Indian Reservation where it houses and repairs its equipment.[28] The DOT employs the second largest number of Indians in the state, eighty-seven; this figure is only 0.69 percent of the total DOT work force, but nearly three-and-a-half times the Indian employment average for other state agencies.[29] The DOT has also been involved in positive initiatives in regional transportation planning discussions with the Indian leadership about future commercial development and expansion of economic opportunities for American Indian nations; has put up road signs for tribal museums to encourage tourist development; and has responded to a call by one Indian nation faced with a major oil spill emergency.[30]

Despite these significant overtures, the agency has found itself in the middle of two major controversies with two separate Indian communities since 1970. Each time, the issue was expansion of the existing state highway system. Each time, the DOT came face-to-face with an Indian world which it did not fully comprehend and an issue, land, which had a far different meaning in the two worlds. Each time, state officials ignored, minimized, or were not fully cognizant of the special legalities between federally-recognized Indian populations and Washington, which requires formal federal presence in any and all land dealings. Much like the Oneida case, state officials presumed primacy of jurisdiction over Indians and ran rough-shod over federal Indian law.

In the 1950s, state planners laid out their blueprints for highways which coincided with the push for federal interstate highways during the Eisenhower administration. Included in these plans were Routes 81 and 90, both of which traverse Indian lands today.[31] As part of Cold War defense initiatives, these roads were largely financed by the federal government. In contrast, by the early 1960s, the Department of Transportation planners, unable to justify the development of the new Route 17, the Southern Tier Expressway, on the basis of automobile/truck use or because of the route's strategic importance for the national defense, began fostering and promoting the route as a means of regional economic development for a depressed region from Binghamton to the Ohio border.[32]

In the mid-1950s, the New York State Thruway Authority also negotiated a right-of-way across the lands of the Seneca Nation. In desperate need of money to fight the Kinzua Dam project, the Senecas granted an easement, a 500-foot path for 3.6 miles of the New York State Thruway totaling 300 acres of the Cattaraugus Indian Reservation, for a relatively low compensation of $75,000 to the Seneca Nation and $100,000 to forty individual Indian landholders.[33] One of the principal negotiators for state land acquisitions for the thruway was William C. Hennessy, later commissioner of transportation, chairman of the New York State Democratic Party, and prime negotiator with the Seneca Indians for the Southern Tier Expressway.[34]

In 1971, the DOT faced its first modern crisis with the Iroquois over Onondaga Indian lands. This major struggle was caused by a less-than-sensitive and hard-nosed attitude about highway development expressed by the old-line leadership at the head of the agency who had been initiated in the "Robert Moses school of public works," namely the right of the state to use its alleged powers of eminent domain at will over Indian lands.[35] At the time, the Iroquois, and especially the Onondagas, were undergoing a political resurgence with a young aggressive leadership of new chiefs who had been influenced by growing Indian activist trends across the United States.[36]

In 1971, the DOT implemented a plan to widen Interstate 81 south of Onondaga Reservation lands near Nedrow in order to provide an acceleration lane and improve highway safety. In 1952, the Onondagas had granted the state an easement of over eighty-nine acres of their land for $31,500. The Onondagas argued that the easement agreement specified only repairs and improvements, not additions, and that in any case the 1952 agreement with the state was illegal since it was not approved in advance by the federal government. Thus, in August 1971, about 100 Indians, mostly Onondagas but including Oneidas, Mohawks, and Tuscaroras, went to the road site and sat down to protest the construction project. From mid-August through the end of October, tension built. By early September over 200 Indians were on the highway to make sure the construction was not resumed, and the situation appeared to be a stalemate.

Governor Nelson Rockefeller met with the Council of Chiefs in late October to resolve differences, and a week later, a six-point agreement was reached. The state agreed to abandon plans for the construction of an acceleration lane on Indian lands, to drop charges against Indians arrested, and to consult with the Council of Chiefs at all stages of the highway improvement project. In return, the Onondagas consented to allow the resumption of construction in order to provide a six-and-one-half foot wide highway shoulder, not a lane, with a three-foot wide gravel slope. Once again, the negotiations took place in the Onondaga Longhouse with an agreement signed by the Tadodaho, Chief Leon Shenandoah, and state officials on October 30, 1971.[37]

A second confrontational situation occurred between American Indians and DOT personnel in February 1985, over the expansion of Route 17/Southern Tier Expressway which has been completed through the lands of the Seneca Nation of Indians. Although some Albany political leaders suggest that much of the blame for "DOT's problem with the Indians" in 1985 was caused by so-called "Indian renegades" (their language) intent on destroying the Seneca Nation,[38] state officials' own strategy of negotiating contributed significantly to the crisis. Fearing that an open admission of the need for a federal supervisory role of a state agreement with the Senecas would weaken the state and counties' arguments in the Oneida land claims case, New York officials purposely ignored the requirement of federal presence in Indian land negotiations in acquiring land for the Southern Tier Expressway.[39]

In 1973, the New York State legislature enacted Chapter 31 of the New York State Highway Law authorizing an easement from the Seneca Nation of Indians for the building of the Southern Tier Expressway; in exchange the Senecas were to receive state park lands in compensation for their land loss:

> 1. Notwithstanding any other provision of law, the Seneca Nation of Indians which owns and occupies reservation lands or any real property interest therein as the common property of the Seneca Nation may, by the act of the Seneca Council *and, if required by federal statute or treaty, with the approval of appropriate federal officials,* grant and convey any such lands or real property interest therein to the state for the construction of Route 17 (Southern Tier Expressway) upon such terms and conditions as the Seneca Council shall deem to be just and reasonable. The terms, lands, and real property interest therein as used in this section shall include lands, waters, rights in lands or waters, structures, franchises and interests in land, including lands under water and riparian rights, and any and all other things and rights usually included within the said terms and includes also any and all interests in such land and property less than full title, such as permanent or temporary easements, right-of-way uses, leases, licenses and other incorporeal hereditaments, and every estate, interest or right, legal or equitable.
>
> 2. Notwithstanding the provisions of any other law, the commissioner of transportation is hereby authorized, where such property is identified and requested by the Seneca Nation, to acquire property outside the Seneca reservations, in the same manner as other property is acquired for state highway purposes pursuant to this chapter or to use property under the jurisdiction of the department of transportation, to be exchanged in whole or in part on terms beneficial to the state for Seneca reservation lands or real property interests therein acquired or to be acquired from the Seneca Nation for the construction of Route 17 (Southern Tier Expressway). In order to effect any such exchange the commissioner of transportation is hereby authorized to execute and deliver, in the same of the people of the state, a quitclaim of, or a grant in and to, such property, to the Seneca Nation involved to hold for the benefit of the Nation. Each such instrument of conveyance shall be prepared by the attorney general and, before delivery thereof, shall be approved by him as to form and manner of execution.
>
> 3. Any property granted and conveyed to the Seneca Nation of Indians in exchange for reservation lands or interests in real property pursuant to the provisions of this section shall thereafter be Indian reservation lands, enjoying all the rights and privileges and subject to all the limitations which now or hereafter shall inhere in Indian reservation lands under law.[40] [Emphasis mine.]

Despite the bill's passage, Attorney General Louis J. Lefkowitz objected strongly to the legislation, fearing its implications on the Oneida Indian land claims case and in other New York State-Indian controversies. According to Lefkowitz, New York State's alleged power of eminent domain was employed in Indian matters for almost two hundred years without approval by federal officials. To now include the formal provision in state legislation that federal permission was necessary before Indian land transactions with the state could be accomplished was, to Lefkowitz, a "serious admission" of state culpability in the past. According to Lefkowitz:

> This bill, which in effect would authorize federal approval of such transactions, might be construed as a serious admission against interest [sic] by the state of New York. It might be stated that its failure to secure such approval in previous transactions would cause a failure of title as to such lands.[41]

Lefkowitz went on to criticize other aspects of the bill:

> A further statement in the bill that the grant be made "upon such terms and conditions as the Seneca Council shall deem to be just and reasonable" constitutes a surrender of the inherent sovereign powers of the State of New York. Existing laws of the State of New York provide whatever authority is needed to acquire Seneca Indian reservation land for highway purposes. Until all present litigation on this subject has been finally judicially determined it would be legally hazardous for this bill to be approved. It would recognize the necessity for federal approval of the exercise of the power of eminent domain over Seneca Indian reservation lands.[42]

The attorney general then concluded by maintaining that it "would be preferable that all the lands required for [the] Southern Tier Expressway be acquired by appropriation pursuant to the provisions of Section 30 of the Highway Law," namely through the state's alleged power of eminent domain. Gratuitously, Lefkowitz suggested that an "Agreement of Adjustment" with the Senecas could be prepared for the settlement of the claim arising by reason of such appropriation.[43] Despite Lefkowitz's objections, Governor Rockefeller signed the bill into law as a result of pressures from DOT officials who had been lobbying for the route since the early 1960s—and who were less concerned about future legal fall-out than was the Department of Law.

Figuring that the Route 17 land negotiations were a good avenue to bring other outstanding issues to the attention of officials of the New York State government, the Seneca Nation of Indians Council was willing to sit down with regional and state administrators of the DOT. Both sides understood full well that the Kinzua Dam project (1956–1966) cast a heavy shadow on Seneca-DOT relations since the loss of Indian lands to the federal Army Corps of Engineers in the 1960s was still fresh in the Senecas' minds. The painful loss of over 9,000 acres of prime farm land for the building of the Kinzua Dam was remembered by all the tribal leadership. Moreover, the removal of the 130 Indian families from the "take area" had undermined traditional life, had taken the Indians away from the Allegheny River and the source of their medicinal plants and spirituality, and caused psychological trauma for those Indians relocated from the isolated rural existence to ranch-style housing clusters at Jimersontown (Salamanca) and at Steamburg. Because of this history, several council members feared, and expressed in council, that the DOT was intent on "acquiring title" to Indian lands.[44]

Realizing the Senecas' sensitivity over loss of lands in the Kinzua Dam project and fearing an Onondaga-style confrontation, DOT officials, in a highly irregular fashion, agreed to negotiate on a wider range of issues, much more than the expansion of Route 17, the Southern Tier Expressway. In the process, Commissioner Raymond Schuler and his assistant William Hennessy also went beyond the legal limits of state authority and jurisdiction. Even after the Lefkowitz letter, Hennessy negotiated an easement land settlement with the Senecas without formal federal supervision under the provisos of the Trade and Intercourse Acts. Attempting to prevent a repetition of the Route 81 crisis, Hennessy negotiated with the Senecas for four years. State officials and the Senecas reached an accord only after Hennessy convinced the governor to pay the Senecas double compensation—money and land exchange—for the easement and only after Seneca President Robert Hoag was allowed to address the New York State legislature. The Senecas, desperate for funding for economic development because of over fifty percent unemployment, desirous of tax relief, and pushing for the improvement of abysmal health facilities and conditions, approved both the agreement and the memorandum of understanding in July 1976, with a vote 12–0, with four abstentions.[45]

Under this agreement, sometimes referred to as the "Lieu Lands" Treaty, the Seneca Nation of Indians received $494,386 under the provisions of the agreement with interest at the rate of six percent from April 1, 1972. The Senecas also received 795 acres of lieu lands (out of Allegany State Park) from New York State. In return, the Senecas granted to the state's DOT an easement for highway purposes only and agreed to the application of Section 30 of the New York State Highway Law for purposes of the agreement. In effect, the "Lieu Lands Treaty" facilitated the completion of the final uncompleted thirteen-mile segment of the Southern Tier Expressway, in the environs of Salamanca. The agreement exclusively dealt with "the claim of the Seneca Nation of Indians for its tribal interest in the appropriated property" and was exclusive of any and "all claims of lessees and allottees." Although there was an original provision, later crossed out, listing secretary of the interior approval of the agreement, the only signatories to the "Lieu Lands Treaty" were Senecas Robert C. Hoag, Genevieve R. Plummer, and Calvin E. Lay, Commissioner Raymond T. Schuler of the DOT and Gerald G. Hall of the New York State Department of Audit and Control.[46] It should also be noted that, separate from this "Lieu Lands Treaty," the DOT eventually allocated $1.3 million to be paid in the future to individual tribal members whose land was affected by the Route 17 construction and to non-Indian lessees whose rental lands were also affected. As previously mentioned, the Allegany State Park Commission delayed the negotiations with its initial refusal to accede to the DOT's trade-off of park lands for Seneca tribal lands as compensation to the Indians.[47]

On the same day, the DOT and the Senecas signed a "Memorandum of Understanding." It called for the DOT to construct and maintain two access roads of one-half mile each within the lieu lands, to maintain certain roads within the Cattaraugus Reservation, and to continue to maintain existing roads within the boundaries of the nation's reservation "in as good or better condition than other comparable roads in the state system of highways." The Memorandum of Understanding also conveyed a small triangular parcel in the Crick's Run area of Allegany State Park to the Seneca Nation, gave the Indians of the Allegany Reservation preference in gravel contracts, and prevented building on a "buffer zone" area between Red House Road and the replacement acreage.[48]

The Memorandum of Understanding also dealt with a variety of issues that the Senecas believed had not been addressed in the past by New York State government:

To the maximum extent feasible, and consistent with the authorities conferred upon the Department by the New York Transportation Law, the New York Highway Law, and any and all other related statutes, the Department shall:

(a) encourage and support legislation or administrative action which exempts the Nation and its members from state laws regulating hunting, fishing, and trapping activities, and which authorizes the transportation of game by members of the Nation on all state roads located outside the boundaries of the Nation's reservations.

(b) encourage and support federal and state proposals the purpose of which is to facilitate improved medical services, medical facilities, and health care for members of the Nation;

(c) encourage and support legislation or administrative action which authorizes special licensing privileges, including the waiver of licensing fees, for motor vehicles owned by members of the Nation;

(d) support, upon being requested to do so by the Nation, the efforts of the Nation to obtain from the New York Bureau of Recreation funds with which to promote tourism on the Nation's reservations;

(e) recommend to appropriate authorities the utilization of state and federal funds to establish a mini-bus transportation system on the Nation's reservations; and

(f) encourage and support legislation which, for the purpose of promoting and facilitating industrial development on the Nation's reservations, provides relief from state taxes, including corporation and excise taxes, for corporations and enterprises which commence commercial activities on the Nation's reservations.[49]

Because the negotiations occurred after the 1971 Onondaga battle along Route 81 and during the Moss Lake tensions of 1974–1977, long neglected Indian issues were addressed by state officials in the "Memorandum of Understanding." Once the Route 17 land issue was "settled" in a signed agreement with the Senecas in the summer of 1976, Indian issues once again faded into the shadows and much of the memorandum was never implemented. Ironically, both state officials and the leadership of the Seneca Nation saw the land issue as bargaining points during the negotiations. When the Seneca lands were transferred and a potential Route 81 or Moss Lake situation did not materialize right away, the important issues discussed by state officials and the Senecas in council in 1975–1976 were once again given limited priority by New York State government. As former Commissioner Raymond Schuler succinctly put it: "State officials only seem to take Indians seriously when the Indians have rifles in their hands."[50]

The drafting of the "Lieu Lands Treaty" led to problems nearly a decade later. As early as 1977, both the responsible opposition to tribal leadership and fringe elements within the Seneca Nation began questioning the actions of the council in signing the agreement, especially what they perceived as the limited or non-existent federal role in the negotiations to watch over and protect the Indians' interest.[51] Soon Senecas began to recall the traumatic days of Kinzua when they were forced into bad leasing or easement agreements on the white man's terms. In 1977, one year after the agreement, Lou Grumet, the special assistant to Secretary of State Mario M. Cuomo, expressed concern about this agreement:

> Emily Young sent me the attached letter from the Department of the Interior concerning the Seneca Treaty Ray Schuler executed last year. According to this letter the treaty was not executed correctly. This could be the beginning of yet another problem with the Indians and constitutes another reason for the Division of Native Americans.[52]

To complicate and intensify the growing crisis, the DOT began monetarily compensating non-Indian leaseholders for lands condemned for Route 17, and many Senecas questioned and objected to this move.[53] By late 1984, when the construction "cats" finally started to move on Indian land, the crisis boiled over. Soon after, in February 1985, Senecas began to block Route 17 highway construction and one small but extremely vocal element began to use the agreement of 1976 to attempt to overthrow the

existing tribal political structure. Although eventually the protest dissi-
pated and the highway spur south of Salamanca was completed, the Seneca political consciousness was raised and more Seneca involvement and
attendance at council meetings has resulted.[54]

Today, fully aware of their past mistakes and of Indian views and
concepts of land and sovereignty and fearful of "bad press," most DOT
officials readily admit that they cannot arbitrarily dictate acquisition of
Indian and/or non-Indian lands as in the days of Robert Moses. Unfortunately, because of fears of future "Indian uprisings," they suggest that they
service state roads traversing Indian reservations only when and if they are
asked to do so by Indian tribal councils.[55] Because of the near-total but
conscious separation of certain Indian governments from the political process in the state, certain needed state operations including road repairs
remain neglected because of the unwillingness of tribal councils to seek
out the aid of state agencies, including DOT officials. Consequently, the
roads, especially at the Tonawanda Indian Reservation, appear to be in
desperate need of overhaul and repair.[56]

Power Authority of the State of New York

The Power Authority of the State of New York (PASNY) is another
agency that has been directly involved in Indian land issues since its
founding in 1931. Under the aggressive leadership of Robert Moses,
PASNY's chairman from 1952 to 1968, the authority came into conflict
with Indian land rights at the Tuscarora and Akwesasne Reservations,
when it led the fight for the Niagara Power project and the St. Lawrence
Seaway project. Besides expropriating a substantial amount of land at
Tuscarora and callously running rough-shod in its dealings with these Indians in the 1950s, Moses also ignored Mohawk land claims. PASNY was
also largely responsible for encouraging heavy industry, General Motors
and Reynolds Aluminum, to relocate to the Rooseveltown peninsula adjacent to the St. Regis (Akwesasne) Mohawk Reservation. The resulting air
and water industrial pollution from these two added factories as well as
callous hazardous waste disposal policies contributed to the health crisis at
the Akwesasne Reservation previously discussed in Chapter 4.[57]

In more recent years, PASNY, because of the success of the Oneidas in
the United States Supreme Court in 1974 and increased attention to eastern Indian land issues, has begun to take Indian claims seriously and has
developed strategies to deal with them. In March 1978, worried about the
"St. Regis Mohawk" claim to Barnhart Island "where the Power Authority's St. Lawrence Power Project is located," Frederick R. Clark, then

chairman of PASNY, wrote to the governor's chief-of-staff, Robert Morgado. In his letter, Clark made it clear that PASNY's trustees felt insulted that their representative had been excluded from a meeting on this subject in the governor's office. Clark not so subtly threatened that any monetary claims settlement awarded the Indians from PASNY's coffers would "be passed through to the Power Authority customers." He added that PASNY had decided to hire "the services of a professional person or organization" to educate the public about the significant dollars in claims.[58] The same day, Clark expressed similar concerns about PASNY's $1 billion power plant on Barnhart Island threatened by the Mohawk land claim in a letter to Governor Hugh Carey. Clark criticized the Interior and Justice departments for their roles in promoting the suit and chastized Thomas Frey, Carey's director of State Operations, for excluding PASNY from land settlement discussions because of the "immense value of the St. Lawrence power plant and the effect that a large dollar settlement may have on power users."[59]

Morgado politely replied four days later. In his letter Morgado claimed that Secretary of State Cuomo would "make every effort to familiarize his staff with your concerns" since he was the key figure for the state in the specific Indian negotiations. In order to emphasize Cuomo's role, Morgado reiterated: "Since the Power Authority has not been at the negotiating table up to this point, I feel it would be better for all parties concerned if we worked through the Secretary of State." Once again, it is clear from the documents that Mario Cuomo had a central role, this time smoothing the ruffled feathers of a powerful agency head annoyed about the lack of consultation in state-Indian land negotiations. Importantly, today (January 14, 1987) PASNY is represented at the land claims negotiations table and has observer status at a recently-convened land claims meeting held at the United States Capitol.[60]

The Department of Law

The Department of Law has been the chief legal adversary of American Indians in New York State government. Working with the governor's counsel, attorneys in the Department of Law represent the state and its interests countering litigation brought by American Indian nations. Since these same Indian nations are largely outside of the political participatory-lobbying process, many of the complex issues affecting their status and/or communities end up being determined in courts of law. Thus, New York State officials insist that they are merely protecting the state's sovereignty in opposing American Indian nations' attempts to extend their sovereignty by intervening against the Indians in court tests.[61] Yet, Indian elders remember that the department has had a long history as an adversary, was a major advocate of congressional transfer of Indian criminal and civil jurisdiction to the state, intervened on behalf of the City of Salamanca in early legal disputes over the Seneca leases, opposed Indian land claims from World War I to the present, and helped expropriate Tuscarora Indian lands in the Niagara Power project only a quarter-century ago.[62]

Through the Department of Law's legal efforts, the agency helps promote state jurisdiction over these same nations. They intervene on behalf of state as well as county interests in Indian land claims suits and supply the legal expertise and law enforcement for agencies, including the Department of Taxation and Finance's efforts attempting to impose the state sales tax on Indian reservations.[63] In addition, the New York State attorney general's formal and informal published opinions have on many occasions dealt with Indian issues. Over the past decade and a half, the attorney general and his staff, in cooperation with the counsels and commissioners of other agencies have interpreted the applicability of the New York State Public Health Law to the state's Indian communities, have expressed two opinions on the power of the state to apply its personal income tax to Indians, have dealt with a question of Indian police forces' legal authority off of reservations, determined the legal authority of the state to license Indian-run bingo games, and have evaluated the constitutionality of one of the major provisions of the education law that affects post-secondary Indian students.[64]

Since 1974, the Department of Law has spearheaded the legal battle against the Oneida, Cayuga, and Mohawk land claims, but with little success. They have been beseiged by landholders and their legislators affected by these claims, have attempted to clarify the status of the litigation, and have warned, especially after 1977, about the seriousness of these suits in messages to the governor's office. It should be noted that the attorneys in the Department of Law do not make the final decisions affecting state-Indian policies and frequently ask the governor's office for advice as to the course of action the agency should pursue relative to Indians.[65] They also cooperate with other agencies' counsels, such as OPRHP, State, DEC, PASNY, and federal agencies and work out memoranda of understanding in quasi-legal attempts to resolve strategies in dealing with Indian issues.[66]

Before the 1970s, the Department of Law treated Indian land issues too casually and gave them little priority. In their suits in defense of other agencies, they even made open admissions of illegality in state land transactions with the Indians. In the late 1950s, PASNY attorney Thomas F.

Moore, Jr., then working with the legal staff of the Department of Law against the Tuscaroras, admitted this fact:

> Except for the period 1790 to 1793, New York made a practice of purchasing Indian rights of aboriginal occupancy without the intervention of the Federal Government. . . . While as our memorandum shows . . . , New York purchased some Indian land rights at Federal treaties subsequent to 1793, in most instances when it purchased such rights it did so without Federal intervention. A vast part of the territory within the State was purchased by the State without such intervention. *The present day title to this area depends upon the validity of these purchases.* Invariably when such purchases were challenged the courts have sustained them.[67]

New York State Attorney General Lefkowitz made similar comments during the late 1950s, minimizing the state liability.[68] Moreover, one of his assistant attorneys general, Julius Sackman, dismissed Indian contentions, arguing that the Trade and Intercourse Acts did not apply to the State of New York. Sackman insisted that the proper legal remedy was the federal Indian Claims Commission or the New York State legislature which could pass enabling legislation allowing an Indian land suit in state courts.[69]

As late as September 27, 1977, in a letter to the law firm of Gajarsa, Liss and Sterenbech, representing the Mohawks in their land claim, the New York State Attorney General Lefkowitz and the Assistant Attorney General Jeremiah Jochnowitz minimized the 1974 Oneida (and Passamaquoddy) decision. He insisted the case was on appeal and "we are optimistic that will be reversed. The facts in this case [Mohawk] and in the Passamaquoddy and the Oneida cases differ, moreover we have additional defenses to any litigation which might be brought by the St. Regis Mohawk Tribe of New York State which we deem to be meritorious." While dismissing the legal merits, the attorney general and assistant attorney general stated that they would be "prepared to discuss the matter whenever and wherever you suggest."[70]

The Department of Law, however, by the late 1970s, responded to the seriousness of the various Indian land claims. In a meeting with Gerald C. Crotty, then assistant counsel in the governor's office, Jochnowitz and Solicitor General Shirley Siegel "advised that the Cayuga land claim was not frivolous and that it would take years to litigate to a final solution." Jochnowitz and Siegel advised the governor "that during such litigation real estate titles in this claims area would be almost completely disrupted thus causing economic losses to landowners in the claims area." The department then helped work out a provision in a memorandum of understanding, at the urging of the attorney general, "whereby the Federal Government will hold New York State and its political subdivisions harmless against any and all Indian claims in the claims area."[71]

Today, neither the Department of Law, the Governor's office, nor the other agencies of New York State government take Indian land claims issues for granted or minimize the Indian legal efforts in bringing successful suit. To a larger degree, the agency's past attitudes in this regard was partly conditioned by the previously-mentioned "Robert Moses mind-set." Progress was not defined in terms of protecting and preserving rooted Indian communities or the restoration of their former land base. Indian lands were agency, state, regional, national and international "sacrifice areas" to be expropriated when needed.

PART III

Conclusion

7
▼▼▼

Summary and Recommendations

Introduction

New York State-American Indian relations today are in crisis, the depth of which is not fully understood by Albany policymakers. Consequently, state Indian policies made in the governor's office, legislature, and agencies are in drastic need of restructuring. The state government's inability to serve its American Indian populace, as this study documents, is not a new development created over the past two decades. At the heart of this crisis are unresolved Indian land issues dating from the late eighteenth and nineteenth centuries that continue to fester and result in continuing distrust. Although these land issues are found to some degree elsewhere, New York officials have trailed their counterparts in other states such as Connecticut, Maine, Massachusetts, and Rhode Island in reaching land settlements with the Indians. Moreover, the delay has had an adverse impact on other areas of New York government's relationship to native peoples.

Past and more contemporary efforts directed at improving the state's relationship to Indian communities have only contributed to this crisis. From 1888 to 1950, state officials periodically reassessed Indian affairs; however, nearly all of these efforts to solve the so-called "Indian problem" ended by "blaming the victims," rather than making noticeable improvements and building trust. In 1952, Governor Dewey's attempts at agency coordination resulted in the creation of the Interdepartmental Committee on Indian Affairs. Unfortunately, this effort was weakened by colonial-like administration and paternalistic approaches. Until the early 1970s, the state made little or no attempt to consult with Indian leaders about anything. Furthermore, from the early 1950s to the 1970s, state-Indian relations actually worsened as a result of the high-handed land acquisitions policies of Robert Moses and his subordinates in the state highway, power, and transportation bureaucracies.

Since 1970, New York officials have frequently spoken about the need to restructure Indian policy in the state and have often proclaimed a "new day" in the state's relations with American Indian nations. In 1970–1971, the Assembly Subcommittee on Indian Affairs held extensive hearings to reassess past policies and to provide necessary reforms. In 1976, Governor Carey and the DOT heralded a "new day" when New York signed an accord with the Seneca Nation over state acquisition of Indian lands for the completion of the Southern Tier Expressway (Route 17). In 1977, Secretary of State Cuomo proclaimed a "new day" when state officials resolved the Moss Lake crisis. In 1981, Governor Carey revealed his plans for a "new day" by the establishment of a state Indian office. In 1984 and again in 1986, Governor Cuomo reiterated Carey's call for an office, but this time within the framework of the Department of State; however, as we have seen, nowhere in the governor's *Three-Year Report* of January 1986, which extensively documented Cuomo's accomplishments in office, were American Indians even mentioned. Thus, the promises of improved performance by a variety of state policymakers have never been carried out, adding to the Indians' cynicism and further suspicion of Albany officials.

The Governor's Office

Because of the power of his office, the governor must lead the way in building bridges to the state's Indian populations. He should immediately create a "Governor's Advisory Commission on Indian Affairs" composed of representative leaders form reservation and urban communities. In order to alleviate the distrust that American Indians have about New York State government, the governor and his staff could, with all deliberate speed, seriously push for the equitable settlements *now* of the major outstanding Indian land disputes currently existing in New York State. Realizing that federal involvement is essential to the settlement process, the governor could focus his staff's efforts at drafting federal legislation and making an unprecedented lobbying effort on behalf of congressional and the public-at-large's acceptance of a settlement. To facilitate settlement, the governor's office would also be wise to negotiate *only* with the formally recognized leadership of the Indian nations bringing suit.

The governor's office could help set a favorable climate for these Indian land claims settlements by developing and participating in a massive public education campaign through thirty- to sixty-second "spots" on radio and television in order to educate New Yorkers about the history, contributions, and separate legal status of American Indians. Unlike western states such as New Mexico, citizens in New York (and their representatives) and other eastern states are largely ignorant about American Indians and their special relationship to the United States and the State of New York. This ignorance retards progress in every area since constitutionally, legislatively, and historically American Indians are set apart from other Americans.

Settlements of Indian land claims could also be coordinated with other state initiatives designed to overcome the present poor economic climate in American Indian communities. It should be noted that after land claims settlements in Connecticut and Maine, American Indians in these states, most notably the Mashantucket Pequot and Passamaquoddy Indians, have made tremendous economic progress.[1] In order to plan for land claims settlements and the resolution of the Salamanca lease impasse, the governor's office could push legislation creating a Native American Research Institute within the State University of New York to develop master plans. This institute could be composed of experts in agriculture, applied anthropology, business, economics, geography, history, and sociology. The institute could also focus, after completion of these initial tasks, on problems affecting urban Indian communities, the most neglected native population in New York State.

Because of the pressing economic problems facing American Indians in New York State and because of the poor record of achievement of the Department of Commerce in this area, the governor's office should develop initiatives, but all must be done with the cooperation and support of tribal and urban Indian leaders. For example, the governor could appoint American Indians, nominated by tribal and urban Indian communities, to work with a member of his staff to help coordinate or develop multi-agency initiatives (Commerce, Labor, State, Agriculture, Finance and Taxation, Urban Development Corporation). These appointees would also be in charge of grant development, needs assessment studies, manpower development, and workshop skills training as well as cooperating with American Indian communities to develop trust which would lead to better data retrieval. Secondly, the governor's office could work with Indian communities in lobbying Congress to designate New York's Iroquois reservations as federal economic opportunity zones, in order to foster entrepreneurial activity; at the same time, state officials could award state economic opportunity zone status to the two Indian communities on Long Island which are not federally recognized. These zones on reservation land mainly use tax breaks to woo industries to communities, thereby creating jobs.

The governor's office could direct its attention to improvement in other major areas. The governor could designate the St. Regis (Akwesasne) Reservation and environs a "state health emergency" and appoint a trouble-shooter to coordinate the Department of Environmental Conservation, Health, State and Parks, the New York Power Authority, Commerce, and St. Lawrence Development Authority responses with respect to this major environmental crisis. The resolution of this crisis could receive top priority by New York State officials at all levels.

In order to facilitate improvement of state services to American Indians and build trust, the governor could create a "Governor's Advisory Commission on Native American Concerns." This body would serve as the advocate and ombudsman for American Indians in state government. Since a formalized Native American Advisory Committee has been established by the State Department of Education and is already meeting, the governor could add weight to this effort by naming these same Indians to his new commission.

To further efforts at coordination of state agency policies, the governor's director of State Operations should commission the preparation of a Manual of Indian Affairs and Procedures—the last one in existence is dated December 1, 1954—in order to provide background information to state agencies about the history and unique legal status of American Indian nations and their lands in New York State.[2] The governor should also reconstitute the Interdepartmental Committee on Indian Affairs composed of representatives of all agencies providing services to Indian communities. This committee could be coordinated on a rotating basis by the Indian Affairs specialist in the Department of Social Services and the associate of Native American Education. The director of State Operations could serve as an ex-officio member of this committee and should report to the governor about Indian as well as agency needs. The committee would also work with the previously mentioned Governor's Advisory Commission to educate agency policymakers about Indians and their needs.

The New York State Legislature

The New York State legislature has in the past largely abdicated its legal responsibilities to American Indian communities. In order to overcome this neglect, the legislature could help transform Indian policy in New York by establishing permanent standing committees on Indian Affairs in the state senate and state assembly. These newly-constituted legislative subcommittees, among other things, would direct their attention to the environmental crisis at the St. Regis Mohawk (Akwesasne) Reservation, the human skeletal remains issue, and to the higher education needs of American Indians. The subcommittees could also hold hearings in the major urban centers of Buffalo, Niagara Falls, Rochester, Syracuse, and

New York City in order to formulate a legislative program for urban Indians.

As part of a new legislative program, the New York State legislature could start by abolishing section 12-a of the New York State Indian Law. In its place, the New York State Health Law, section 4218 could be implemented and enforced in order to prevent the desecration of Indian grave sites. In addition, the State Education Department's draft proposal of procedures, which includes the creation of an interagency panel, could be adopted.[3] The interagency panel would, as indicated in the New York State Department of Education proposal, consult with those individuals with special concerns about human burials, including American Indian leaders, and be sensitive to the ethical and cultural responsibilities of its task.

The New York State legislature could also create a new Regents district to geographically encompass all the reservation communities in New York State, and, with it, the appointment of a Regent to serve this newly established district. Allowing American Indians the right to serve on school boards throughout the state was an important but mostly symbolic step since the limited size of Indian populations makes the likelihood of their election to school boards slim indeed. Although a few American Indians have won election, their voices are too limited under this arrangement. In order to overcome this problem and give recognition to the special and unique needs of educating American Indians, the state legislature could establish a "Native American Indian District," since the Board of Regents has been since 1971 the Albany arena most responsive to the improvement of Indian educational needs.

To recognize Indian cultural and political sensibilities, the New York State legislature could also pass the American Indian Oath Bill, which has been bottled up in committee for several years. This bill would eliminate the requirement that all teachers of American Indian descent swear allegiance to the state and its constitution. The requirement offends Indian political, cultural, and religious sensibilities and may even prove to be a violation of the federal American Indian Religious Freedom Act of 1978, although it has never been tested. Moreover, New York State, either through executive or legislative action, should follow New Jersey's example by finally granting state recognition to the Ramapo Indians.

State Agencies

New York State agency officials could work with the suggested Governor's Advisory Commission on Native American Concerns and the reconstituted Interdepartmental Committee on Indian Affairs to improve state services. This effort could be furthered by actively recruiting American Indians for employment in state government, especially in the departments of Commerce, State, and the Division of Human Rights. The following state agencies with historic tensions with Indian communities, after consultation with the tribal councils in the state, could immediately create Native American advisory boards composed of their own employees of American Indian descent as well as recognized American Indian leaders: the Department of Transportation, the Office of Mental Health, the Department of Environmental Conservation, the New York Power Authority, and the New York State Police. The Bureau of Historic Sites' Native American Advisory Committee for the Ganondagan State Park could be broadened to include more representation from the Tonawanda Band of Senecas, and the Seneca Nation, including member(s) from these two Seneca governments.

Importantly for the improvement of the criminal justice process, the New York State attorney general's office, in conjunction with the Indian tribes and the New York State Police and the governor's special assistant for criminal justice matters, could hold a series of symposia for state and local peace officers and jurists spelling out the unique legal status of American Indians in New York State. These symposia could include legal experts who would provide reliable information about treaty rights, civil and criminal jurisdiction, customary law, tribal courts, hunting and fishing exemptions, etc. Through education, state and local peace officers and jurists would become more aware of Indian rights and concerns.

The New York State Department of Education could expand the Native American Education Unit by hiring two additional full-time personnel. These two employees would serve, mostly in the field, as State Education Department liaisons with the three Indian schools and numerous school districts and public and private colleges in the state with large Indian student populations in order to facilitate communication, educate guidance counsellors and financial aid officers, coordinate policies, investigate problems, and improve overall educational delivery. The present supervisor and bilingual specialist could serve primarily as educational planners, curriculum and linguistic specialists, legislative initiators, and the State Education Department liaisons to the Native American Education Advisory Committee. Because of the workload of the office, a support staff is required, including a secretarial line. By freeing up the two existing positions for educational policy analysis purposes, the unit could focus on other major concerns: (1) new agency regulations to amend its current and Byzantine internship program; (2) a detailed study with recommendations to explain ways of preventing the incredibly high college drop-out rate of Indian students at New York State colleges; and (3) and analysis of why, despite the expansion of the eligibility of the state's Postsecondary Education Program for Indians, there are fewer Indian students taking advantage of this program than a decade ago. SED's New York State Museum could also return wampum belts sought by the Iroquois community(ies) only after it is carefully determined which Iroquois community(ies) are today properly entitled to the wampum and only after some general arrangements for the preservation and security of said belts are established as specified in earlier New York State legislative enactments.

The New York State Department of Social Services could expand its Indian Services by hiring two caseworkers—one for the two Long Island reservations and the large Indian population in the New York City metropolitan area and the other for the upstate reservations and Indian urban centers. This action would free the Indian Affairs Specialist and allow her to plan and coordinate policies. The department could add two new posts to the Tonawanda Indian Community House: (1) assistant superintendent, and (2) community worker, a position designed to work specifically with reservation Indian youth as guidance counsellor for employment and school, alcohol and drug education, and in recreational activities. In addition, the department and county social services should not attempt to integrate the Tonawanda Indian Community House by allowing non-Indians to use this facility since the state legislative enactment creating the facility in the mid-1930s specifically designated the center as being for the exclusive use of the Indian population.

Conclusion

In sum, New York State officials have the great opportunity to make a dramatic shift in the implementation of American Indian policies to overcome historic neglect in this area. Leadership begins at the top with the implementation of real changes—settlement of existing Indian land claims; the hiring of additional culturally sensitive and informed personnel; and the improvement of state services to Indian communities through administrative reorganization. James MacGregor Burns, the noted political scientist and former advisor to President John F. Kennedy, has written that political "leadership, however, can be defined only in terms of, and to the extent of the realization of, purposeful, substantive change in the conditions of people's lives." Burns concluded, emphasizing: *"The ultimate test of practical leadership is the realization of intended, real change that meets people's enduring needs."*[4]

8
▼▼▼

Afterword

Since this study was completed at the end of 1986, little has changed in New York State American Indian policies to warrant major revisions of this book's conclusions. Then as now state-Indian land disputes are festering and retarding overall improvement. Nevertheless, state-Indian land negotiations have resumed with New York officials' main efforts focused on the resolution of the Mohawk Indian land claim. Although it appears that the Power Authority of New York has shown more willingness to cede some of its excess lands in the St. Lawrence River Valley to the Mohawks, no land settlement is in sight at the present time. Perhaps more disappointing is the near-total impasse on the other three Indian land claims, those of the Cayuga, the Oneida, and the Stockbridge-Munsee. Moreover, the Seneca-Salamanca lease controversy remains unresolved, although negotiations between the Indians and city officials appear likely to resume again, in the fall of 1987, after a five-year hiatus.[1] While these stalemates continue, state officials as well as those connected to Indian policy matters in New York continue to insist that the governor's office has plans for a new Indian office for the coordination and improvement of services. Yet, as of the late summer of 1987, these statements appear to be hollow promises.[2]

Other issues also remain unresolved, including controversies about the application of the state's sales tax, the custody of wampum, and the protection and sanctity of human skeletal remains. Some reservation gas dealers have been selling gasoline to Indians and non-Indian customers at a low rate because of what they claim as exemption from state fuel taxes. Previously, the United States Supreme Court has decided that states can tax reservation sales to non-Indians and require Indian entrepreneurs to keep records to differentiate between sales to Indians and non-Indians. Yet, in May 1987, the New York State Court of Appeals unanimously decided that Indian nations are not required to prepay state fuel taxes set by the New York State Tax Commission. The Court of Appeals ruled "that Congress has pre-empted the field of regulating trade with Indians on reservations and has left 'no room' for the application of supplementary state tax laws, such as the one here at issue, that impose 'additional burdens' on Indian traders." This continuing controversy may soon end up being resolved by the nation's highest court in Washington, D.C.[3]

Despite the Museum of the American Indian's recent decision to return several wampum belts to the Iroquois Indians of the Six Nations Reserve at Ohsweken, Ontario, no similar resolution of the wampum controversy has been reached by the New York State Museum and Iroquois leaders.[4] Moreover, New York State also continues to have no policy relative to the protection of human skeletal remains. A recent case in Louisiana, *Charrier v. Bell*, the so-called "Tunica Treasure Case," may have a bearing on what happens in New York State. Between 1968 and 1971, Leonard Charrier, a prison guard and self-proclaimed "amateur archaeologist," removed materials from 150 burial sites on the Trudeau Plantation, private lands owned by non-Indians. He later attempted to sell the cultural artifacts to Harvard University's Peabody Museum. The district court, in a decision affirmed by the Louisiana Court of Appeals, insisted that the Tunica-Biloxi Tribe of Louisiana was the lawful owner of the artifacts since the common law doctrine of abandonment did not apply to burial materials. Although the case did not pertain to human skeletal remains, the major archaeological controversy in New York, the Louisiana court did set a major precedent by reasoning that a contemporary Indian nation's burial site and its contents remain as tribal interest even after alienation of land to private owners.[5]

The responses of state officials to the problems of urban Indians has also continued to be dismal. For example, the space needs required for counselling, education, health and social services of American Indians in New York City, nearly half of the state's Indian population, have taken a "back seat" to Albany and Manhattan officials jockeying to keep the Museum of the American Indian from moving to Texas or Washington, D.C. Personnel in the governor's office in particular have also conveniently "passed the buck" and shifted blame for the state's neglect of urban Indians to Reaganomics. According to a recent letter written by Governor Cuomo's chief-of-staff to the director of the American Indian Community House of New York City:

> Our strong support for the latest plan to keep the Museum in New York should not, however, be misconstrued as acquiescence of the other Federal actions that have cut back assistance to Native American-run organizations on reservations and in cities such as the American Indian Community House, Inc. Given the unique Federal role vis-a-vis Native Americans, such cutbacks represent an abdication of an important national responsibility.

> In addition to supporting the Museum's efforts to secure a viable future, we will continue to support efforts to ensure that the needs of all New Yorkers, including Native Americans, are met.[6]

In other areas, state officials have made somewhat more headway. In 1987, New York State's Post-Secondary Aid to American Indian students was increased from $1000 to $1350. The Division of Alcoholism has initiated plans for a Native American advisory council and is preparing a needs assessment study on American Indians.[7] At a symposium held in June 1987 at the Cattaraugus Indian Reservation, knowledgeable state personnel from the Western New York Development Corporation addressed forty Seneca participants about state opportunities for Indian people, job training, and job development assistance, as well as regional economic development programs. This was a hopeful beginning to a long-neglected state concern, namely reservation economic development. This effort appears to complement the Senecas' own efforts at diversifying their economy away from an over-reliance on bingo, tax-free gasoline, and cigarettes. They have sought Japanese foreign investment, have worked with the United States Small Business Administration, and have attempted with Interior Department personnel to secure a "Federal Tribal Enterprise Zone."[8] The Indians' goal is not massive industrialization but the creation of more cottage industries "that are not threatening to the lifestyle of native peoples."[9]

After years of needless delay and waste, Ganondagan State Park was finally dedicated in July of 1987. As a result of the fine efforts of site manager G. Pete Jemison, many Senecas from all their communities in western New York were participants in the dedication of this site, the major Seneca village of the late-seventeenth century. Importantly, Lieutenant Governor Stanley Lundine, long considered even-handed in his relations with the Indians, was sent as the official representative of the governor. Although other states such as Ohio, Wisconsin, and New Mexico have had a long tradition of state involvement of this kind, Ganondagan is the first state-managed Indian heritage site in New York. Thus, if properly managed, Ganondagan has the opportunity to help New Yorkers better understand the rich Native American history of their state.[10]

New York State Indian policy appears to be at a crossroads. Governor Cuomo, in his January 6, 1988 Message to the Legislature, has publically promised that the state "must do more to resolve Indian land claims, provide better services to Indian communities and improve overall state—Indian relations." Only time will tell if state officials will continue to make false promises and confront Indian communities in the courtroom or work with the recognized leadership of these same communities to achieve permanent settlements and overcome two hundred years of distrust.

Stan Fox, Larry Pierce, and Raymond Jimerson of Iroquois American Post No. 1587 at the Fall Festival on the Cattaraugus Indian Reservation south of Buffalo. September 1985.
Credit Line: *Rochester Times-Union.*

Many Indians in New York, such as Clete Laffin of Rochester, specialize in working on high steel. October, 1985.
Credit Line: *Rochester Times-Union.*

Arlinda Locklear, attorney for the Native American Rights Funds and a Lumbee
Indian, arguing the Oneida land claims case before the United States Supreme
Court. March, 1985.
Credit Line: Courtesy of Arlinda Locklear and the Native American Rights Fund.

Governor Thomas Dewey at groundbreaking ceremony for St. Lawrence Seaway Project (1954). Robert Moses seated on the right.
Credit Line: Thomas E. Dewey Papers, Department of Rare Books and Special Collections, Rush Rhees Library, University of Rochester.

Moses-Saunders Power House. Barnhart Island near St. Regis (Akwesasne) Reservation. July 4, 1975.
Credit Line: PA7–11892G Courtesy of the New York Power Authority.

Troubled Water: Mohawk Indian John Sawatus fishes in the polluted St. Lawrence River with the Reynolds Aluminum Plant looming in the background. October 1985.
Credit Line: *Rochester Times-Union.*

Robert Moses in front of Robert Moses Niagara Power Plant near Tuscarora Reservation. July 19, 1963.
Credit Line: PA7–25726 Courtesy of the New York Power Authority.

Robert Moses Niagara Power Plant and Reservoir built on condemned Tuscarora land. June 8, 1983.
Credit Line: PA7–46358 Courtesy of the New York Power Authority.

Edison Mt. Pleasant, a Tuscarora chief, and his wife, Ruth, visiting the site of her childhood home, a portion of Tuscarora land beside the Niagara River north of Niagara Falls which was taken by the state following a dispute with the Tuscaroras and flooded more than 20 years ago for use as a PASNY reservoir. October, 1985. Credit Line: *Rochester Times-Union.*

NOTES

▼▼▼▼▼▼▼

PREFACE

1. See for example Rennard Strickland, *The Indians in Oklahoma* (Norman, Okla.: University of Oklahoma Press, 1980); Gretchen M. Bataille, et al., eds., *The Worlds Between Two Rivers: Perspectives on American Indians in Iowa* (Ames, Iowa: Iowa State University Press, 1978); J. Donald Hughes, *American Indians in Iowa* (Boulder, Colo.: Pruett Publishing Co., 1977); Paul A. W. Wallace, *Indians in Pennsylvania* (Harrisburg, Pa.: Pennsylvania Historical and Museum Commission, 1961, reprinted 1975); Ronald N. Satz, *Tennessee's Indian Peoples: From White Contact to Removal, 1540–1840* (Knoxville, Tenn.: University of Tennessee Press, 1979). For a survey of state-Indian relationships by a former BIA official, see Theodore W. Taylor, *The States and Their Indian Citizens* (Washington, D.C.: U.S. Dept. of the Interior, Bureau of Indian Affairs, 1972). For an official study of federal, state, and tribal jurisdiction, see *American Indian Policy Review Commission, Final Report: Task Force Four: Federal, State, and Tribal Jurisdiction* (Washington, D.C.: U.S.G.P.O., 1976). One exception to the dearth of state studies is Elizabeth Ebbot and Judith Rosenblatt, eds., *Indians in Minnesota*, 4th ed. (Minneapolis, Minn.: University of Minnesota Press, 1985).

2. Laurence M. Hauptman, *The Iroquois and the New Deal* (Syracuse, N.Y.: Syracuse University Press, 1981); and *The Iroquois Struggle for Survival: World War II to Red Power* (Syracuse, N.Y.: Syracuse University Press, 1986).

3. Laurence M. Hauptman, *Formulating American Indian Policies in New York State, 1970 to 1986: A Public Policy Study*. A report submitted to the governor of New York and American Indian Nations, Sept. 1, 1986 (unpublished).

4. Sally M. Weaver, *Making Canadian Indian Policy: The Hidden Agenda, 1968–1970* (Toronto: University of Toronto Press, 1981).

5. Stephen L. Pevar, *The Rights of Indians and Tribes* (New York: Bantam, 1983), p. 99.

6. 25 U.S.C.A. 232 and 233. See Appendix I for the text of the jurisdiction bills.

7. See Appendices II and III for census figures.

8. See chapters 2 and 5 for New York State land policies. For the policy of mediation, see Luther Bliven, "Cuomo on Banks," *Syracuse Post-Standard*, March 8, 1983; Steve Carlic, "The Negotiator: Howard Rowley Brings Casual Approach to Some Critical Talks," *Syracuse Post-Standard*, Feb. 24, 1986. See also Richard Kwartler, " 'This Is Our Land': The Mohawk Indians v. the State of New York," in: *Roundtable Justice: Case Studies in Conflict Resolution: Reports to the Ford Foundation* (Boulder, Colorado: Westview Press, Inc., 1980), pp. 7–18. For the policy of jurisdiction, see Hauptman, *The Iroquois Struggle for Survival*, chapters 2–4. This jurisdictional issue has been especially played down in dealing with the Mohawk and Onondaga Indians since 1974. It is important to note that, on occasions, some Indian leaders

themselves have requested the state's enforcement of criminal jurisdiction. This request occurred during the Moss Lake occupation (1974–1977) and at the "Akwesasne siege" (1979–1981) and was turned down by state officials fearing the intensification of the conflict and bloodshed between Indian and Indian and Indians and non-Indians. Interviews of Ward DeWitt (assistant commissioner of Corrections), April 7, 1986 and Major Leigh Hunt (director of the State Police Academy), May 7, 1986. Major Hunt was named the police commissioner of the City of Syracuse in 1986.

9. New York State Assembly Subcommittee on Indian Affairs of the Standing Committee on Governmental Operations, *Final Report* (Albany, 1971).

10. *Ibid.*, p. 7.

11. Hauptman, *The Iroquois Struggle for Survival*, pp. 179–203. For the New England Indian land settlements, see Jack Campisi, "The Trade and Intercourse Acts: Land Claims on the Eastern Seaboard," in: *Irredeemable America: The Indians' Estate and Land Claims*, Imre Sutton, ed. (Albuquerque, N.M.: University of New Mexico Press, 1985), pp. 337–362. For one successful Indian land claim (Maine) and one Indian land claim loss (Massachusetts), see Paul Brodeur, *Restitution: The Land Claims of the Mashpee, Passamaquoddy and Penobscot Indians of New England* (Boston: Northeastern University Press, 1985).

12. Subcommittee on Indian Affairs, *Final Report* (1971), pp. 29–33.

13. *Ibid.*, p. 53.

14. Laurence M. Hauptman, Iroquois Field Notes, 1971–1986. I have previously discussed the origins of this phenomenon in *The Iroquois Struggle for Survival*, pp. 177–214 in references to the late Wallace Mad Bear Anderson.

CHAPTER 1

1. Cuthbert W. Pound, "Nationals Without a Nation: New York State Tribal Indians," *Columbia Law Review* 22 (February 1922), p. 99.

2. Gerald Gunther, "Governmental Power and New York Indian Lands—A Reassessment of a Persistent Problem of Federal-State Relations," *Buffalo Law Review* 8 (Fall 1958), pp. 1–26.

3. Marcus H. Johnson to George W. Manypenny, Nov. 25, 1856 with attached notice of sale of lands for taxes dated Oct. 10, 1856, Records of the New York Agency, 1829–1880, Office of Indian Affairs, 1824–1881, Microfilm Reel 588, RG75, National Archives, Washington, D.C.

4. Joint Resolution of New York State Assembly and Senate, Jan. 18, 1871 with attached letter of transmittal by John Hoffman, Jan. 30, 1871, Records of the New York Agency, 1829–1880, Office of Indians Affairs, 1824–1881, Microfilm Reel 591, RG 75, National Archives, Washington, D.C.

5. See Chapter 2.

6. This fact can be ascertained from even a casual reading of New York State legislative investigations of Indian affairs from 1882 to 1945.

7. Henry S. Manley, "Buying Buffalo from the Indians," *New York History* 28 (July 1947), pp. 313–329; Norman B. Wilkinson, "Robert Morris and the Treaty of Big Tree," *Mississippi Valley Historical Society* 60 (Sept. 1953), pp.

257–278; Barbara A. Chernow, "Robert Morris: Genesee Land Speculator," *New York History* 58 (April 1977), pp. 195–220; Anthony F. C. Wallace, *The Death and Rebirth of the Seneca* (New York: Random House, 1970).

8. Jack Campisi, "New York-Oneida Treaty of 1795: A Finding of Fact," *American Indian Law Review* 4 (Summer 1976), pp. 71–82; and his "The Trade and Intercourse Acts," pp. 337–362. See *Oneida Indian Nation of New York, et al. v. County of Oneida, New York, et al.*, 94 S.Ct. 772.

9. See Barbara Graymont, *The Iroquois in the American Revolution* (Syracuse, N.Y.: Syracuse University Press, 1972).

10. Reginald Horsman, *The Frontier in the Formative Years, 1783–1815* (New York: Holt, Rinehart and Winston, 1970), pp. 30–31.

11. For Duane's views, see *Public Papers of George Clinton*, VIII, pp. 328–332.

12. Barbara Graymont, "New York State Indian Policy After the Revolution," *New York History* 57 (Oct. 1976), p. 440.

13. *Ibid.*, p. 443.

14. Richard Morris, ed., *John Jay: The Making of a Revolutionary: Unpublished Papers, 1745–1780* (New York, Harper and Row, 1975), II, pp. 659–660.

15. Graymont, "New York State Indian Policy . . . ," pp. 442–443.

16. *Ibid.*, pp. 444–445.

17. *Ibid.*, pp. 449–451.

18. Quoted in *Ibid.*, p. 451.

19. *Ibid.*, p. 453.

20. *Public Papers of George Clinton*, VIII, p. 354.

21. *Ibid.*, p. 355.

22. Jack Campisi, "Ethnic Identity and Boundary Maintenance in Three Oneida Communities." (Unpublished Ph.D. dissertation, Albany: State University of New York at Albany, 1974), pp. 93–94.

23. *Ibid.*, pp. 94–102.

24. See note 7; see also Hauptman, *The Iroquois and the New Deal*, pp. 70–71, 88–90.

25. Gunther, "Governmental Power and New York Indian Land . . . ," pp. 7–9.

26. Quoted in *Ibid.*, pp. 9–10.

27. Helen Upton, *The Everett Report in Historical Perspective: The Indians of New York* (Albany, N.Y.: New York State American Revolution Bicentennial Commission, 1980), pp. 73–74; George Abrams, *The Seneca People* (Phoenix, Ariz.: Indian Tribal Series, 1976), p. 72; William N. Fenton, "Toward the Gradual Civilization of the Indian Natives: The Missionary and Linguistic Work of Asher Wright (1803–1875) Among the Senecas of Western New York"; *Proceedings* of the American Philosophical Society 100 (1956), pp. 567–581. See Chapter 5.

28. Laurence M. Hauptman, "Senecas and Subdividers: The Resistance to Allotment of Indian Lands in New York, 1875–1906," *Prologue: The Journal of the National Archives* 8 (Summer 1977), pp. 105–116; and Laurence M. Hauptman, "Governor Theodore Roosevelt and the Indians of New York State," *Proceedings* of the American Philosophical Society 119 (February 1975), pp. 1–7.

29. Quoted in Upton, *The Everett Report*, p. 52.

30. Quoted in *Ibid.*, p. 55.
31. Laurence M. Hauptman, Iroquois Field Notes, 1971–1987. This report has been frequently brought to my attention by Indians as proof of New York State's "real" intentions in dealing with Indians.
32. New York State legislature, Assembly Special Committee to Investigate the Indian Problem Appointed by the Assembly of 1888. *Report* (Assembly Document No. 51) (Albany, N.Y., 1889), pp. 41–45, 68, 73–74, 78–79, 405–506. For Sims, see pp. 406–417. For Cusick, see pp. 456–483, 506.
33. Theodore Roosevelt to Oscar Straus, William Walker, Darwin James, Albert K. Smiley and Philip C. Garrett, Dec. 4, 1900, Theodore Roosevelt MSS., Microfilm Reel 319, XII, 34–42, Library of Congress.
34. The report can be found in United States Board of Indian Commissioners, *32nd Annual Report, 1900* (Washington, D.C., 1901), pp. 20–22; a rough draft can be found in the Smiley Family MSS, Box 87, Haverford College, Haverford, Pa.
35. See, for example, New York State legislature, Assembly Special Committee to Investigate and Ascertain the Extent of the Powers Possessed by the State to Regulate and Control the Affairs and Property Rights of the Indians, *Report* (Legislative Document No. 40) (Albany, N.Y., 1906).
36. Quoted in Gunther, "Governmental Power and New York Indian Lands . . . ," pp. 12–13.
37. See Chapters 2 and 6.
38. Hauptman, *The Iroquois Struggle for Survival*, pp. 21–22.
39. *Ibid.*, pp. 22, 250 n 22.
40. Barbara Graymont, ed., *Fighting Tuscarora: The Autobiography of Chief Clinton Rickard* (Syracuse, N.Y.: Syracuse University Press, 1973), p. 95.
41. *United States v. Boylan*, 265 F. 165 (1920).
42. New York State legislature [Everett Report] Assembly. *Report of the Indian Commission to Investigate the Status of the American Indian Residing in the State of New York . . . March 17, 1922* (unpublished). For more on the Everett Report, see Hauptman, *The Iroquois Struggle for Survival*, pp. 179–203.
43. *Deere, et al. v. St. Lawrence River Power Co., et al.*, 22 F.2d 851 (1927).
44. *United States v. Forness*, 125 Fed. Rep. 2d Series 928 (1942); 37 F.Supp. (1941). For the Salamanca lease controversy, see Chapter 2.
45. New York State, *Legislative Document No. 52* (Albany, N.Y., 1944), p. 32.
46. See Hauptman, *The Iroquois Struggle for Survival*, Chapter 3.
47. New York State legislature, Joint Legislative Committee. *Report*, Feb. 25, 1944 (Albany, N.Y., 1944); "Forness Case Decision Termed Reproach to State and Nation," *Salamanca Republican-Press*, Aug. 5, 1944.
48. Quoted in Arch Merrill, "Salamanca Lease Settlement," *American Indian* 1 (Spring 1944), p. 7.
49. Graymont, ed., *Fighting Tuscarora*, p. 95; "Salamanca Seeks to Enjoin Indians from Taking Lands," *Buffalo Evening News*, Aug. 28, 1942; "Defendants File Answers in Indian Lease Cases," *Salamanca Republican-Press*, Nov. 25, 1942.
50. New York State legislature. *Report* of Joint Legislative Committee on Indian

Affairs, March 15, 1945, found in *New York State Legislative Document No. 51* (Albany, N.Y., 1945), pp. 3–5.

51. Hauptman, *The Iroquois Struggle for Survival*, Chapter 3. See Appendix I for the text of the two bills.

52. Albert Abrams and Everett Parker, Memorandum of Chief's Council of the Tonawanda Band of Seneca Indians, July 6, J. R. McGrath MSS., Box 28, "Indian Legislation—Proposed Legislation, Senatorial, 1947–1949," Truman Library, Independence, Mo.

CHAPTER 2

1. Hauptman, *The Iroquois and the New Deal*, Chapter 1.

2. For a full discussion of the origins of jurisdictional transfer, see Hauptman, *The Iroquois Struggle for Survival*, pp. 31–64.

3. See Hauptman, *The Iroquois and the New Deal*, pp. 6–7; and Hauptman, *The Iroquois Struggle for Survival*, pp. 45–64.

4. Interviews of Assemblymen Maurice Hinchey, Feb. 25, 1986; Melvin Zimmer, March 11, 1986; and Daniel Walsh, March 13, 1986; and State Senators Jess Present, March 12, 1986; and James Donovan, April 17, 1986; Executive Deputy Commissioner (Labor) John Hudacs, March 10, 1986; Regent Laura Chodos, Feb. 24, 1986; Leo Soucy (former assistant commissioner of Education), March 4, 1986; Adrian Cook, Feb. 24, 1986; Dr. Hazel V. Dean-John, March 19, 1986; and Fernando DiMaggio (former legislative staffer for the Assembly Subcommittee on Indian Affairs), April 17, 1986.

5. For the history of contemporary Iroquois land loss, see Hauptman, *The Iroquois Struggle for Survival*, pp. 85–178. See also Graymont, ed., *Fighting Tuscarora*, pp. 138–152.

6. William A. Starna, "Indian Land Claims in New York State: A Policy Analysis." (Report submitted to the Governor's office, August 1987, published by the Nelson A. Rockefeller Institute of Government, Fall, 1987), p. 5. For further evidence, see Hauptman, *The Iroquois Struggle for Survival*, Chapter 10.

7. Campisi, "Trade and Intercourse Acts . . . ," pp. 337–362.

8. New York State Legislature, Assembly Subcommittee on Indian Affairs of the Standing Committee on Governmental Operations, *Public Hearings*, Nov. 18, 1970 (Albany, 1970), p. 41.

9. *Ibid.*, pp. 41–42.

10. See Hauptman, *The Iroquois Struggle for Survival*, Chapter 10.

11. *Ibid.*

12. *Ibid.*

13. 94 S. Ct. 772.

14. Laurence M. Hauptman, Oneida Indian Field Notes, 1977–1986.

15. U.S. Sup. Ct. 83–1065; 83–1240–opinion.

16. New York State, *Legislative Document No. 15: Report of the Joint Legislative Committee on Indian Affairs, 1959* (Albany, 1959), p. 4; Exhibit III: Memo-

randum of Law and Fact, pp. 16–17, undated, contained in petition of Feb. 9, 1968, attached to letter of Joseph Califano to Jacob Thompson, Feb. 28, 1968, Lyndon Johnson MSS., White House Central Files, Box 3, IN/A-Z, LBJ Library, Austin, Texas.

17. The anti-settlement correspondence is immense. See, for example, Frederick R. Clark (chairman of PASNY) to Robert J. Morgado, March 6, 1978; Hugh Carey to Louis Lefkowitz, Feb. 4, 1978; Albert B. Lewis (superintendent of Insurance) to Hugh Carey, Sept. 18, 1978, Hugh Carey Records, Subject Files, Reel 104, New York State Archives, Albany. Peter Borzilleri (New York State Wine Grape Growers, Inc.) to Hugh Carey, May 15, 1979; Michael DelGuidice to Peter Borzilleri, May 29, 1979; Richard McGuire (New York Farm Bureau) to Hugh Carey, May 27, 1980; Gary Lee to Hugh Carey, Feb. 21, 1979, Nov. 20, 1980; Marilyn Schiff to Ward DeWitt; Madison County legislature Resolution Requesting Ratification of the "Allegedly Invalid Treaties and the September 8, 1981 Extinguishment of the Aboriginal Titles to the Land Being Claimed by Native Americans," Sept. 8, 1981; Sean Walsh to Governor Hugh Carey, June 17, 1980; Governor Hugh Carey Records, Subject Files, Reel 65, New York State Archives, Albany.

18. United States Congress, House of Representatives, Committee on Interior and Insular Affairs, *Hearings on H.R. 6631: Settlement of the Cayuga Indian Nation Land Claims in the State of New York*, March 3, 1980, 96th Cong., 2nd sess. (Washington, D.C., 1980); United States Congress, Senate, Select Committee on Indian Affairs, *Hearings on S. 2084: Ancient Indian Land Claims*, 97th Cong., 2nd sess. (Washington, D.C. 1982). For the Iroquois protest against the Ancient Indian Land Claims Settlement Act, see Barry Snyder (president of the Seneca Nation of Indians) to Governor Hugh L. Carey, March 8, 1982; Chief Corbett Sundown (chairman, Council of Chiefs, Tonawanda Band of Senecas), Feb. 23, 1982; Grand Council of the Houdenosaunee The Six Nations Iroquois Confederacy Onondaga Nation to President Ronald Reagan, Feb. 14, 1982, Governor Hugh Carey Records, Subject Files, Microfilm Reel 65, New York State Archives, Albany.

19. For a full discussion of the history of the issue, see Laurence M. Hauptman, "The Historical Background to the Present Day Seneca Nation-Salamanca Lease Controversy: The First Hundred Years, 1851–1951," Rockefeller Institute of Government, *Working Paper No. 20* (Fall, 1985).

20. Interview of Assemblyman Daniel Walsh. Lou Grumet to Mario Cuomo, Sept. 15, 1976, Moss Lake Indian Negotiations, New York State Department of State Records, Series 726, New York State Archives, Albany; Robert C. Batson to Ward DeWitt, July 28, 1981, Governor Hugh Carey Records, 2nd term, Subject Files, Microfilm Reel 65, New York State Archives, Albany.

21. United States Congress, House, *Congressional Record*, 57th Congress, 2nd sess. 1902, 36, pt. 1, p. 337.

22. Salamanca City Attorney David Franz Testimony, House of Representatives, Committee on Interior and Insular Affairs, Hearings on the Salamanca leases, No. 7, 1985, Washington, D.C.

23. Prepared statement of Robert Batson, Associate Counsel, New York State Department of State, House of Representatives, Committee on Interior and Insular Affairs, Hearings on the Salamanca leases, Nov. 7, 1985, Washington, D.C.

24. Mayor Ronald Yehl (Salamanca) to Governor Hugh Carey, Oct. 13, 1981, Governor Hugh Carey Records, Subject Files, Microfilm Reel 65, New York State Archives, Albany. The Seneca Nation also has a small land claim pending (50 acres) centering on the area around Cuba Lake. Interviews of Assemblyman Daniel Walsh and State Senator Jess Present.

25. Interview of Robert Batson, Jan. 16, 1986, Albany.

26. Interviews of Assemblyman Daniel Walsh and State Senator Jess Present.

27. Robert P. Whelan (NYS Commissioner of Health) to Louis J. Lefkowitz (NYS Attorney General), March 18, 1977; Subject Files of the 1st Deputy Commissioner, New York State Department of Health Records, Box 16, acc. #13, 307–82A, New York State Archives, Albany. Formal Opinions of the Attorney General, 1976 (Albany, 1976), pp. 54–55. Lou Grumet to Mario Cuomo, Sept. 15 and 24, 1976, Moss Lake Indian Negotiations, New York State Department of State Records, Series 726, New York State Archives, Albany. Anna Lewis to Mr. Caruso, et. al., Oct. 1, 1970, records of the Native American Indian Education Unit, New York State Department of Education Records, "Regents Research Files," Box 1, Series 729, New York State Archives, Albany. Interview of Dr. Hazel V. Dean-John (Native American Indian Education Unit), April 8, 1986, Albany.

28. New York State Comptroller, Department of Audit and control, "New Issue, Official Statement, $3,500,000,000 State of New York 1986 Tax and Revenue anticipation Notes," April 11, 1986, pp. 48–49.

29. Laurence M. Hauptman, Iroquois Field Notes, 1976–1986.

30. Interviews of Assemblymen Melvin Zimmer and Maurice Hinchey; State Senator Jess Present; Dr. Henrik Dullea; Jeff Cohen; and Dr. Hazel V. Dean-John.

31. Interviews of Robert Batson, Jan. 16 and March 6, 1986, Albany. Robert Batson to Lou Grumet, July 22, Aug. 10, 1977; Batson to Mario Cuomo, Aug. 14, Oct. 23, Dec. 4, Dec. 11, 1978, Moss Lake Indian Negotiations, New York State Department of State Records, Series 726, New York State Archives, Albany. Robert J. Morgado to Caroline Drake, Sept. 19, 1980; Michael Finnerty to Joe Quetone, Aug. 19, 1982. Robert Batson to Files, Feb. 13, 1979; Batson to Thomas Frey, Jan. 11, 1979; Batson to Nikolaus Satelmajer, May 20, 1980; Batson to Ward DeWitt, July 28, 1981; Batson to Evan L. Webster, Jan. 20, 1981, Governor Hugh Carey Records, Subject Files, Microfilm Reel 65, New York State Archives, Albany. Statement of Robert Batson, Associate Counsel, New York State Department of State, Seneca Nation-Salamanca lease hearings, United States House of Representatives, Committee on Interior and Insular Affairs, Nov. 7, 1985. Interview of Howard Rowley, March 17, 1986, Rochester. Steve Carlic, "The Negotiator." Howard Rowley has purported to be part Mohawk to add to his credentials about being a competent mediator of Indian disputes. He has also insisted that he is "on loan" from Rochester Gas and Electric (RGE) Company to serve the New York congressional delegation. RGE has a stake in land claimed by the Cayuga Indians. Moreover, several members of the New York congressional delegation have been critical of Rowley for not reporting to them. Lou Grumet to Mario Cuomo, Sept. 9, 1976, Moss Lake Indian Negotiations, New York State Department of State Records, Series 726, New York State Archives, Albany. Congressman Matt McHugh, p.c., Oct. 28, 1986, New Paltz, N.Y.; Laurence M.

Hauptman, Seneca Field Notes, 1985–1986. For more on Howard Rowley, see Laurence M. Hauptman, "Hauptman Answers Rowley," *Akwesasne Notes* (Late Spring, 1987), p. 29.

32. Marc Humbert, "Governor's New Chief of Staff Set to Take Charge of Nuts and Bolts," *Albany Times-Union*, Sept. 18, 1985. *New York Red Book, 1984–1985* (Albany, 1985), p. 434.

33. *Ibid.*

34. Mario Cuomo, *Forest Hills Diary: The Crisis of Low Income Housing* (New York: Random House, 1974); Kwartler, "This Is Our Land . . . ," pp. 7–17.

35. Interviews of Louis Grumet, March 24, 1986, Albany; Howard Rowley, March 17, 1986, Rochester; and Martin Wasser, April 11, 1986, New York City. Grumet was the special assistant to Secretary of State Cuomo and is now executive director of New York State School Boards Association. Martin Wasser was the senior counsel for the New York State Department of Environmental Conservation from 1975 to 1977. Both Grumet and Wasser were directly involved in the Moss Lake negotiations.

36. For the earlier occupation, see Hauptman, *The Iroquois Struggle for Survival*, pp. 148–150. Although the Moss Lake occupation (1974–1977) has been written about previously, no one has taken advantage of the extensive (three boxes) correspondence in Moss Lake Indian Negotiations, New York State Department of State Records, Series #726, New York State Archives, Albany; or the Governor Hugh Carey Records, Subject Files, Reel 104, New York State Archives, Albany. For a synoptic analysis which failed to take full advantage of these materials, see Gail H. Landsman, "Ganienkeh: Symbol and Politics in an Indian-White land dispute" (Ph.D. dissertation, Catholic University of America, Washington, D.C., 1982); see also Landsman's "Ganienkeh: Symbol and Politics in an Indian/White Conflict," *American Anthropologist* 87 (Dec. 1985), pp. 826–839.

37. Mario Cuomo to "The File," Nov. 4, 1976; Robert Batson to Secretary Cuomo, Aug. 14, 1978, Moss Lake Indian Negotiations, Series #726, New York State Archives, Albany.

38. Mohawk (Akwesasne) Tribal Council to Governor Malcolm Wilson, Nov. 25, 1974; Mario Cuomo to Mohawk Chiefs Rudolph Hart, Charles Terrance, and Leonard Garrow, Feb. 7, 1977, Moss Lake Indian Negotiations, New York State Department Records, Series #726, New York State Archives, Albany; Mohawk (Akwesasne) Tribal Council to Governor Carey, March 14, 1977; Carey to Mohawk (Akwesasne) Tribal Council, April 14, 1977, Governor Hugh Carey Records, Subject Files, Microfilm Reel 104, New York State Archives, Albany.

39. Robert Batson to Mario Cuomo, Aug. 14, 1978. In order to attempt to defuse the political damage for not consulting beforehand with county legislators about the Moss Lake settlement, Cuomo later addressed the Clinton County legislature. Importantly, today county legislators are consulted about the status of the Cayuga land claims and are brought into the process. This change was a direct result of the political *faux pas* at Moss Lake. Interview of Howard Rowley.

40. Interviews of Louis Grumet, Martin Wasser, and Howard Rowley. Rowley, for one, kept bringing other issues besides land into the discussions while Cuomo,

almost immediately, realized that "the land idea is basic." Louis Grumet to Mario Cuomo, Oct. 22, 1976. For Rowley's role, see Grumet to Cuomo, Sept. 9, 24, 1976 and Sept. 6, 1977, Moss Lake Indian Negotiations, New York State Department of State Records, Series 726, New York State Archives, Albany. For divisions in the Indian world intensified by Moss Lake, see Lincoln White to Dr. Thomas Sheldon, Jan. 27, 1975, Records of the Native American Indian Unit, Box 1, New York State Department of Education. State Senator James Donovan was a leading critic of Governor Carey's and Secretary Cuomo's handling of Moss Lake. Interview of James Donovan. James Donovan to Governor Hugh Carey, April 17, 1975, Governor Hugh Carey Records, Subject Files, Microfilm Reel 104, New York State Archives, Albany. Donovan to Attorney General Louis Lefkowitz, July 6, 1977; Secretary of State Cuomo to Senator Donovan, July 25, 1977, Moss Lake Indian Negotiations, New York State Department of State Records, Series #726, New York State Archives, Albany. Interview of Fred DiMaggio; Elma Patterson, p.c., May 28, 1986.

41. Cuomo postscript to Memorandum from Lou Grumet to Secretary Cuomo, Nov. 15, 1976.

42. Mario Cuomo to Louis Grumet, Oct. 11, 1976; Cuomo to "The File," Nov. 4, 1976, Moss Lake Indian Negotiations, New York State Department of State Records, Series #726, New York State Archives, Albany.

43. Chiefs Ellsworth George and Clarence Blueye (Tonawanda Council of Chiefs) to Fred DiMaggio, Feb. 6, 1975, Moss Lake Indian Negotiations, New York State Department of State Records, Series #726, New York State Archives, Albany.

44. Lou Grumet to Secretary Cuomo, Dec. 8, 1976; Grumet to Cuomo, Dec. 8, 1976; interviews of Louis Grumet and Martin Wasser. Secretary of State to Lou Grumet, Jan. 17, 1977, Moss Lake Indian Negotiations, New York State Department of State Records, Series #726, New York State Archives, Albany.

45. Mario Cuomo to the chiefs of the Mohawk Nation and to the chiefs of the Grand Council of the Six Nations of the Iroquois Confederacy, July 27, 1977, Moss Lake Indian Negotiations, New York State Department of State Records, Series #726, New York State Archives, Albany.

46. Kwartler, "This Is Our Land . . . ," p. 11.

47. See Starna, "Indian Land Claims . . . ," pp. 30, 32, 38.

48. Laurence M. Hauptman, Mohawk Field Notes, 1975–1986. For Cuomo's exaggerated goals for Ganienkeh, see Mario Cuomo to James Donovan, July 25, 1977.

CHAPTER 3

1. Ray D. Apodaca (executive director, Texas Indian Commission and national president of Governors' Interstate Council on Indian Affairs), p.c., June 2, 1986; Bruce Jones (executive director, North Carolina Commission on Indian Affairs), p.c., April 7, 1986.

2. Elma Patterson (supervisor of Indian Social Services, New York State Department of Social Services), p.c., May 28, 1986. Interviews of Hazel V. Dean-

John (supervisor of Native American Indian Education Unit, New York State Department of Education), March 19, 1986, Albany; John Adrian Cook (bilingual specialist, Native American Indian Education Unit, New York State Department of Education), Feb. 24, 1986, Albany; Ramona Charles (superintendent, Tonawanda Indian Community House), May 14, 1986, Tonawanda Indian Reservation; and Robert Batson (associate counsel, New York State Department of State), Jan. 16 and March 6, 1986, Albany. Robert Batson, p.c., March 25, 1986.

3. Subcommittee on Indian Affairs, *Final Report*, pp. 10–14.

4. *Ibid.*, p. 7.

5. John Hudacs et al. to the Governor, Re: Suggestions for Improving New York State Indian Affairs, Sept. 10, 1975; New York State Assembly, Subcommittee on Indian Affairs, "A Reorganization Proposal for New York State's Administration of Indian Services," New York State Department of State Records, Moss Lake Indian Negotiations, Series #726, New York State Archives, Albany.

6. Joseph Lisa to Governor Hugh Carey, June 5, 1975, Governor Hugh Carey Records, Subject Files, Microfilm Reel 104, New York State Archives, Albany. For Lisa's mediating role, see Lisa to Chief Leon Shenandoah, Feb. 4, 1975; Lisa to Michael Del Guidice, Feb. 10, 1975; Lisa to Peter A. A. Berle, June 16, 1975; Lou Grumet to Mario Cuomo, Sept. 8, 10 and 13, 1976, New York State Department of State Records, Series #726, Moss Lake Indian Negotiations, New York State Archives, Albany.

7. New York State legislature, Assembly, Subcommittee on Indian Affairs, "A Reorganization Proposal for New York State's Administration of Indian Services," New York State Department of State Records, Series #726, Moss Lake Indian Negotiations, New York State Archives, Albany.

8. John Hudacs, et al. to the Governor, Memorandum: Suggestions for Improving New York State Indian Affairs, Sept. 10, 1975.

9. *Ibid.* For reaction to the Hudacs proposal, see the Division of the Budget's analysis of the reorganization; John Corrigan to Ray Harding and John Hudacs, March 22, 1976; Robert Kerker to John Corrigan, Jan. 19, 1976, New York State Department of State Records, Series #726, Moss Lake Indian Negotiations, New York State Archives, Albany.

10. Mario Cuomo to Governor Hugh Carey, Memorandum: 1980 Legislative Agenda—Indian Affairs, Nov. 5, 1979, Governor Hugh Carey Records, Subject Files, Microfilm Reel 65, New York State Archives, Albany.

11. Interviews of Gerald Crotty, Henrik Dullea, and Jeff Cohen.

12. Marilyn Schiff to Cheryl Parsons Reul, Memorandum: Office of Indian Affairs, Nov. 27, 1979; and Schiff to Michael Del Guidice, Memorandum: Office of Indian Affairs/Interdepartmental Committee on Indian Affairs, undated, Governor Hugh Carey Records, Subject Files, Microfilm Reel 65, New York State Archives, Albany.

13. "Governor Carey Proposes Creation of a State Division of Native American Services," Press Release, April 2, 1981.

14. Interviews of Gerald Crotty and Henrik Dullea.

15. Laurence M. Hauptman, Iroquois Field Notes, 1975–1986.

16. Governor Mario Cuomo, *Message to the Legislature, Jan. 4, 1984* (Albany, 1984), p. 6.

17. Governor Mario Cuomo, *Message to the Legislature, Jan. 8, 1986* (Albany, 1986), p. 91–92.

18. *Ibid.*, p. 130.

19. *Ibid.*; Governor Mario M. Cuomo, *Messages to the Legislature*, Jan. 5, 1983; Jan. 4, 1984; Jan. 9, 1985.

20. Draft of "Executive Order to Provide Coordination of State Services to Native Americans," undated. Interviews of Henrik Dullea (director of State Operations, governor's office), April 18, 1986 and Jeff Cohen (policy analyst, governor's office), April 11, 1986, Albany; Jeff Cohen, p.c., May 7, 1986.

21. Hauptman, *The Iroquois Struggle for Survival*, chapters 2–4.

22. *Ibid.*, p. 184.

23. Interview of Fernando DiMaggio.

24. Interviews of James Donovan, Jess Present, Maurice Hinchey, and Melvin Zimmer.

25. Interview of James Donovan.

26. *Ibid.*; James Donovan to Governor Hugh Carey, April 17, 1975, June 27, 1975, Governor Hugh Carey Records, Subject Files, Microfilm Reel 104, New York State Archives, Albany. Donovan to Attorney General Louis J. Lefkowitz, July 6, 1977; Mario Cuomo to Donovan, July 25, 1977; and Donovan to Carey, Aug. 2, 1978, New York State Department of State Records, Series # 726, Moss Lake Indian Negotiations, New York State Archives, Albany.

27. New York State Executive Budget, 1986–1987. "An Act to Amend the State Law in Relation to the Cost of Certain Indian Land Claims."

28. New York State legislature, Assembly Standing Committee on Governmental Operations, *Annual Report, 1980* (Albany, 1980), p. 11.

29. Governor Mario M. Cuomo, *Three-Year Report* (Albany, 1986).

30. Laurence M. Hauptman, "Circle the Wagons," *Capital Region* 2 (Feb. 1986), pp. 29–31, 52–53.

31. Paul Moore, p.c., April 30, 1986.

CHAPTER 4

1. It is impossible to ascertain all the areas of New York State government that touch on life in American Indian communities because of the multitude of agencies and because these same agencies do not list American Indians separately from "other New Yorkers." Interview of Robert Kerker (Division of the Budget), May 20, 1986, Albany.

2. Interview of Michael Davis (New York State Department of Civil Service), June 9, 1986; Michael Davis, p.c., Feb. 9, 1987. For the last published state employee figures relating to American Indians, see New York State Department of Civil Service, *Ethnic Survey of New York State Agency Work Force, 1982* (Albany, 1985), p. 13. Nelson A. Rockefeller Institute of Government, *1984–1985 New York State Statistical Yearbook*, 11th edition (Albany, 1985),

p. 19. United States Department of Commerce, Bureau of the Census, *Subject Reports: American Indians 1980* (Washington, D.C., 1985).

3. This definition is listed on all ethnic surveys done by the New York State Department of Civil Service.

4. Marilyn G. Schiff to Michael Del Guidice, Feb. 25, 1980, Governor Hugh Carey Records, Subject Files, Microfilm Reel 65, New York State Archives, Albany.

5. Interview of Yvette Jones (affirmative action officer, New York State Department of State), Feb. 25, 1986, Albany.

6. See Chapter 2 for an analysis of Robert Batson's role.

7. James Edwards (chairperson of the Native American Affirmative Action Committee of the New York State Division of Human Rights), p.c., May 1, 1986. It should be noted that Governor Cuomo in his State-of-the-State address placed Indian concerns *after* his statement criticizing the South African government's policy of apartheid.

8. *Ethnic Survey . . . , 1982*, pp. 66–74.

9. John W. Kalas (SUNY/Research Foundation), p.c., June 3, 1986. Interview of Chief Oren Lyons, May 6, 1985, Old Westbury, New York. Chief Lyons is associate professor of art at SUNY/Buffalo, the only full-time Iroquois faculty member in SUNY! Nancy Johnson (SUNY/Buffalo American Studies Program), p.c., May 20, 1986.

10. *Ethnic Survey . . . , 1982*, pp. 66–74. Michael Davis, p.c., Feb. 9, 1987.

11. Interviews of Ward DeWitt (assistant commissioner of Corrections), April 7, 1986, Albany, and Roy Black, April 7, 1986, Esopus, New York. Mr. Black, an Iroquois Indian, was a deputy regional administrator at the Department of Corrections.

12. Interview of John Hudacs (executive deputy commissioner of Labor), March 10, 1986, Albany; Leonard Gaines (New York State Department of Commerce, Data Center), p.c., April 7, 1986.

13. Paul Moore, p.c., April 29, 1986.

14. Interview of Julia Wilson (New York State Department of Social Services, Bureau of Policy Research), May 19, 1986, Albany.

15. Dr. Morris Cohen (Office of Mental Health), p.c., May 22, 1986; Dr. Carole Firman (assistant commissioner of Mental Health), p.c., April 30, 1986.

16. New York State Office of Mental Health, *Five Year Comprehensive Plan for Mental Health Services, 1985–1990* (Albany, 1986), pp. 35–36.

17. New York State Division of Alcoholism and Alcohol Abuse. *Five-Year Comprehensive Plan for Alcoholism Services in New York State, 1984–1989: Focus on Research, Planning and Professional Development, Final 1987 Update.* Albany: DAAA, 1986. Interviews of William Barnette, June 10, 1986; and Kallen Martin, Feb. 20, 1986, Albany, N.Y. See also "Alcohol and Drug Abuse Conference a Success," *Indian Time* Aug. 21, 1986, p. 1.

18. Robert Batson, p.c., March 16, 1986; and Joseph Brett (regional director, New York State Department of Commerce), Ogdensburg, New York, April 7, 1986. Mr. Brett was totally uninformed about Indians in the North Country and their entrepreneurial needs.

19. Michael Ellrott (New York State Department of Health, Bureau of Biostatistics), memo to Laurence M. Hauptman, April 8, 1986. Kathryn B. Surles, *Update on the Health Status of American Indians in North Carolina: A Special Report Prepared for North Carolina Commission of Indian Affairs, June, 1985* (Raleigh, N.C.: North Carolina State Center for Health Statistics, 1985).

20. Karen Kalaijian to Donna Glebatis-Feck, June 7, 1983; Elma Patterson to Karen Kalaijian, May 19, 1983. (Both copies of these two letters were provided to me by Michael Ellrott.) Interview of Karen Kalaijian, May 7, 1986, Albany.

21. Interviews of James Feck (Office of Field Operations Management, New York State Department of Health), March 25, 1986; Karen Kalaijian; Drs. Elmer Green and Jayantha Kumar (Bureau of Dental Health, New York State Department of Health), May 7, 1986, Albany. Theodore Rebich, Jr., Jayanth Kumar et al., "The St. Regis Environmental Health Issue: Assessment of Dental Defects," *Journal of the American Dental Association,* CVI (May 1983), pp. 630–633; and the same authors' "Dental Caries and Tetracycline-stained Dentition in an American Indian Population," *Journal of Dental Research,* LXIV (March 1985), pp. 462–464.

22. Cuomo, *Message to the Legislature, Jan. 8, 1986,* pp. 91–92.

23. Commissioner Robert P. Whalen (Health Department) to Everett Rhoades (American Indian Policy Review Committee), Jan. 5, 1976, New York State Department of Health Records, Subject Files of the Commissioner, acc. #13, 307–82, Box 36, New York State Archives, Albany.

24. William Leavy to Mr. Coffey, Sept. 20, 1977, New York State Department of Health Records, Subject Files of the 1st Deputy Commissioner, Box 16, acc. # 13, 307–82A, New York State Archives, Albany; Assembly Subcommittee on Indian Affairs, *Report, 1971,* pp. 41–43.

25. Interview of Dr. Henry P. Staub, May 4, 1977, New Paltz, New York. Henry P. Staub, et al., "Health Supervision of Infants on the Cattaraugus Indian Reservation, New York: The Record Is No Better than in Big City Slum Areas," *Clinical Pediatrics,* XV (Jan. 1976), pp. 44–52. D. W. Kaplan in cooperation with the Seneca Nation of Indians, *Seneca Nation of Indians: Indian Health Proposal, March 1, 1975* (Boston, 1975). See also Laurence M. Hauptman, ed., "Symposium: American Indian Medicine and Problems," *New York State Journal of Medicine,* LXXVIII (April-July 1978).

26. Quoted in Karen Kalaijian, *Indian Health Services in Western New York State: Past, Present and Future,* p. 5, found in New York State Department of Health Records, Subject Files of the 1st Deputy Commissioner, Box 16, acc. # 13, 307–82A, New York State Archives, Albany.

27. New York State Public Health Law, amendment to Chapter 22, section 201 (March 1962).

28. Dr. A. G. Baker to Dr. Campbell, June 24, 1975, New York State Department of Health Records, Subject Files of the 1st Deputy Commissioner, Box 16, acc. #13, 307–82A, New York State Archives, Albany; Dr. David Axelrod to P. Millrock, Sept. 30, 1981, New York State Department of Health Records, Subject Files of the Executive Deputy Commissioner, Box 7, acc. #13–307–83A, New York State Archives, Albany.

29. Interviews of Wini Kettle, July 27, 1977, Cattaraugus Indian Reservation, Marilyn Anderson and Norma Kennedy, Henry Staub, May 4, 1977, New Paltz, New York; and "Seneca Nation Health Department Celebrates Tenth Anniversary," *O-HI-YOH-NOH: Allegany Indian Reservation Newsletter* April 23, 1986, pp. 1, 4–5.

30. Interview of Ramona Charles, May 14, 1986.

31. Elma Patterson, p.c., May 28, 1986; New York State Department of Health, *Annual Report, 1984* (Albany, 1985), pp. 47–48; interview of James Feck.

32. "St. Regis Mohawk Health Services—Reduction in Funding," *Indian Time* May 30, 1986.

33. See Appendix II.

34. Interview of James Feck; William Leavy, p.c., June 12, 1986.

35. See Appendix IV.

36. Robert K. Watt to Dr. Kevin Cahill, Aug. 16, 1976, New York State Department of Health Records, Subject Files of the Commissioner, acc. #13, 307–82, Box 36, New York State Archives, Albany.

37. Interview of Telisport Putsavage, May 8, 1986, Albany.

38. Interview of Martin Wasser.

39. Martin Wasser to Peter A. A. Berle, March 18, 1977, New York State Department of Environmental Conservation Records, Commissioner Beale Subject Files, Box 17, acc. #13, 063–83, New York State Archives, Albany. Wasser had given Indian affairs top priority in his memo to Commissioner Ogden Reid on March 8, 1976. New York State Department of State Records, Moss Lake Indian Negotiations, series #726, New York State Archives, Albany. For Wasser's views, see Martin B. Wasser and Louis Grumet, "Indian Rights—The Reality of Symbolism," *New York State Bar Journal*, L (Oct. 1978), pp. 482–485, 514–518; and Wasser's "Sovereign New York and Sovereign Mohawks," *North Country Life* (Summer 1977), pp. 4–5, 16; and Wasser, "The Six Nations and the State," *Conservationist*, XXX (Jan.-Feb. 1976), pp. 36–37.

40. Michael Reynolds, SUNY Office of Academic Programs, Policy and Planning, *Report on Native American Studies* (January 1984).

41. This proposal, "The Arthur C. Parker Institute," had the formal support of Seneca, Mohawk, Oneida, Schaghticoke, Pequot, Mashpee and Wampanoag Indians as well as faculty cooperation from SUNY/New Paltz, SUNY/Oneonta, SUNY/Stony Brook, and SUNY/Fredonia.

42. See Charlotte Heth and Suzanne Guyette, *Issues for the Future of American Indian Studies* (Los Angeles: UCLA American Indian Studies Center, 1986).

43. This data is compiled from reading each of the SUNY catalogs over a ten-year period and speaking to colleagues in the history, anthropology, and American Indian studies programs at the colleges and university centers of SUNY.

44. The author is the coordinator of the Native American Studies Program at SUNY/New Paltz. All references made about the New Paltz campus are based upon his own administrative and teaching experiences.

45. Laurence M. Hauptman to Selby Hickey (vice president, SUNY/Old Westbury), April 16, June 4, 1985; Hickey to Hauptman, May 14, 1985; interview of Selby Hickey, May 6, 1985, SUNY/Old Westbury. Sid Cassese, "Indians Call for Degree Programs," *Newsday* May 7, 1985.

46. See the mission statement. SUNY/Old Westbury, *College Bulletin, 1982–1984* (Old Westbury, New York, 1982), p. 3.

47. See note 41.

48. Interviews of Chief Oren Lyons, May 6, 1985, SUNY/Old Westbury and Andrew Jackson, March 21, 1986, Buffalo. Nancy Johnson, p.c., May 27, 1986. The above individuals are all involved in the administration of the SUNY/Buffalo American Indian program. Chief Lyons, an Onondaga chief, is associate professor of art at SUNY/Buffalo and heads the American Indian program.

49. Ed Hauser (SUNY/New Paltz financial aid officer), p.c., Feb. 6, 1986.

50. Dr. David Call (dean of the College of Agriculture and Life Sciences), p.c., May 21, 1986.

51. Interview of Major Leigh Hunt.

52. *Ibid.; New York State Police Manual* (Albany, 1986); New York State Legislative Commission on State-Local Relations, *New York's Police Service: Perspectives on the Issues* (Albany, 1985), pp. 151–168. The latter report contains the course outline for basic training of police officers in New York State as of January 1, 1986. See also "State Legislative Audit Assails Police Training," *New York Times* Sept. 28, 1986, p. 44.

53. *New York's Police Service*, pp. 31–32.

54. Interviews of Ward DeWitt and Major Leigh Hunt. See Donna Snyder, "Two Arrested on Gambling Charges," *Jamestown Post-Journal*, Sept. 3, 1987.

55. Interview of Major Leigh Hunt.

56. See "Indians' Rage at Illegal Bar Fuels Upstate Fire," *New York Times*, May 12, 1986.

57. Bliven, "Cuomo on Banks."

58. Interview of Telisport Putsavage.

59. Assembly Subcommittee Report, p. 45.

60. New York State Department of Commerce, *Annual Report, 1981* (Albany, 1981), pp. 1–3. Interviews of Samuel Johnson and Fran Genovesi (MWBD, New York State Department of Commerce), April 18, 1986; MWBD informational sheet.

61. New York State Department of Commerce, *Directory of Minority and Women-Owned Business Enterprises* (Albany, 1986). Some firms listed include: Native American Construction, Inc., Native American Window Cleaning, and American Indian Builders and Suppliers. For other problems relative to this program, see "More Charges of Cheating in Minority Hiring," *New York Times*, Aug. 3, 1986, p. 6.

62. *New York State Minority and Women-Owned Business Enterprise Certification Program Fact Sheet.*

63. Native American List provided by Fran Genovesi. Interviews of Samuel Johnson and Fran Genovesi.

64. Kevin Hurley (New York State Department of Commerce—Buffalo Regional Office), p.c., April 7, 1986.

65. New York State Department of State, *Annual Report, 1984* (Albany, 1985), p. 6.

66. Interview of Rosa Castillo-Kesper, May 5, 1986, Albany. The Department of State and Department of Housing have made some recent strides in the improvement of Indian housing. See "Mario M. Cuomo Recognizes Iroquois Village," *Indian Time* Sept. 4, 1986, p. 1.

67. Robert Batson talk at SUNY/Oneonta, July 12, 1985. "Lieutenant Governor to Visit Hogansburg," *Syracuse Post-Standard* Aug. 18, 1984.

68. Interview of Neil MacCormick (New York State Department of State Coastal Management Program), May 8, 1986. Sandra Cadwalader, "Facts of (Oyster) Life," *Indian Truth* 255 (February 1984), pp. 5–7.

69. Interview of Rosa Castillo-Kesper.

70. For The Turtle, see Hauptman, *The Iroquois Struggle for Survival*, Chapter 12.

71. Mark Lyon (National Heritage Trust, New York State Department of Parks, Recreation and Historic Preservation), p.c., May 20, 1986; Laurence M. Hauptman, Iroquois Field Notes, April 1985. I attended the Iroquois Communications Conference at The Turtle on April 21–22, 1985, and have discussed The Turtle's operations with many Iroquois people as well as present and former staff members who must remain nameless here.

72. See Hauptman, *The Iroquois Struggle for Survival*, Chapter 8 for added background.

73. Assembly Subcommittee on Indian Affairs, *Hearings*, Massena, New York, Sept. 19, 1970. For Mohawk reactions to this crisis, see virtually any issue of *Indian Time* in 1985 or 1986.

74. Gary Gunther (senior sanitary engineer, Franklin County Department of Health, Saranac Lake), p.c., May 6, 1986; Victor Pisani (St. Lawrence County Health Department), p.c., April 30, 1986; interview of Henry Lickers, July 11, 1985, Oneonta, New York.

75. Ray Gabriel (Division of Water, New York State Department of Environmental Conservation), p.c., May 12, 1986.

76. Gary Gunther, p.c., May 6, 1986.

77. "General Motors to Clean Up Toxic Dump Site," *Indian Time* May 10, 1985.

78. Gary Gunther, p.c., May 6, 1986.

79. Ward Stone, *ENCON Progress Report RAGTW Project No.: W–4*, April 1, 1985–March 31, 1986.

80. Lennart Krook and G. A. Maylin, "Industrial Fluoride Pollution: Chronic Fluoride Poisoning in Cornwall Island Cattle," *Cornell Veterinarian*, 69, Suppl. 8 (1979), pp. 1–70.

81. Irving Selikoff, E. Cuyler Hammond, and Stephen Levin, *Environmental Contaminants and the Health of the People of the St. Regis Reserve*, a report submitted to the Minister of Health and Welfare of Canada (New York: Mount Sinai School of Medicine, 1984–1985), 2 vols.

82. *Ibid.*, II, p. 126.

83. Interviews of Wint Aldrich (special assistant to the commissioner of the New York State Department of Environmental Conservation), May 8, 1986, Albany; George Hamell (Office of Exhibit Planning, New York State Museum), June 9, 1986, Albany; Ben Kroop (New York State Bureau of Historic Sites, Office of Parks, Recreation and Historic Preservation, May 20, 1986, Peebles

Island, New York; Bruce Fullem (archaeologist, Office of Parks, Recreation and Historic Preservation), May 12, 1986, Albany; Paul Huey (archaeologist, Office of Parks, Recreation and Historic Preservation), July 10, 1986, Peebles Island, N.Y.; Robert Funk and Philip Lord (Office of State Archaeology, New York State Department of Education), Feb. 20, 1987, Albany.

84. Interviews of Wint Aldrich and George Hamell.

85. Interview of Bruce Fullem.

86. New York State Indian Law, Legislative Bill Jackets, L 1971, c. 1195 and L 1974, c. 460.

87. Memorandum Re: S. 3284A and A. 3842-A, Legislative Bill Jacket L 1971, c. 1195, New York State Archives, Albany.

88. J. Harry Penrose (counsel to New York State Office for Local Government) to Michael Whiteman (governor's counsel), July 1, 1971, Legislative Bill Jacket, L 1971, c. 1195.

89. See "Issues in Archeology: The Questions of Reburial: Archeologists Debate the Handling of Prehistoric Human Skeletal Remains," *Early Man Magazine* (Autumn 1981), pp. 25–27. For an insightful analysis of this issue, see Lawrence Rosen, "The Excavation of American Indian Burial Sites: A Problem in Law and Professional Responsibility," *American Anthropologist*, LXXXII (1980), pp. 5–23.

90. For the Indians' position, see Chief Irving Powless, Jr. to Governor Hugh Carey, May 20, 1982, Governor Hugh Carey Records, Subject Files, Microfilm Reel 65, New York State Archives, Albany.

91. Interviews of Wint Aldrich and Bruce Fullem. Office of Parks, Recreation and Historic Preservation, Proposed Rule Making Hearings Scheduled: Designation of Indian Burial Grounds, I.D. No. PKR—41-84-00002-P.

92. Interview of Bruce Fullem. The "burial issue" is of national and international dimensions. See Peter H. Lewis, "Indian Bones: Balancing Research Goals and Tribes Rights," *New York Times* May 20, 1986. National Indian organizations have been active on this issue: Suzan Shown Harjo (executive director, National Congress of American Indians) to Lorraine Mintzmeyer (director, Rocky Mountain Region, National Park Service), May 7, 1986; Raymond D. Apodaca (national president of Governors' Interstate Indian Council), May 16, 1986. Letters provided author by Robert Batson.

93. Interviews of Robert Funk and Philip Lord; New York State Museum, "Draft Proposal: Unmarked Human Skeletal Remains," Jan. 5, 1987; New York State Education Law, section 233; New York State Public Health Law, sections 4216–4221; Thomas D. Burke (chief archaeologist, State of North Carolina) to Charles Vandrei, April 18, 1985, letter and packet of materials relative to North Carolina burial legislation; *General Statutes of North Carolina*, chapter 70: Indian Antiquities, Archaeological Resources and Unmarked Human Skeletal Remains Protection (1981). See Appendix VI.

94. Interview of Colwyn Allen (Aging Services area supervisor, New York State Office for the Aging), June 3, 1986. New York State Office for the Aging, *Annual Report, 1983-1984* (Albany, 1985), pp. 7–8, 33–35.

95. OA, *Annual Report, 1983-1984*, pp. 34–35. Interview of Jeanne Marie Jemison, March 21, 1986, Cattaraugus Indian Reservation. For the past half-

dozen years, I have had the privilege of seeing the positive features of this OA Seneca program in my visits to the Cattaraugus Reservation.

96. Interview of Colwyn Allen.

97. *Ibid.* Interview of Ann Cortese (New York State Senate Committee on the Aging), May 27, 1986, Albany. Interview of Ramona Charles, May 14, 1986.

98. Interview of Colwyn Allen. Seneca Nation of Indians Area Office for the Aging, *Four Year Plan for Older Americans Act and New York State Community Services for the Elderly Programs*, April 1, 1984–March 31, 1988; Randy John, *Annual Implementation Plan (Older Americans Act) for the Seneca Nation of Indians Area Office for the Aging*, Oct. 1, 1986-Sept. 30, 1987 (III–B), Jan. 1, 1986 to Dec. 31, 1986 (III–C).

99. American Indian Community House Fact Sheet. Rosemary Richmond to (AICH) to Morris Udall, Jan. 30, 1987. Douglas Martin, "Indians Quarrel Over Customs House," *New York Times* Feb. 5, 1987; and Martin's "Indians in New York City Search for a Better Life," *New York Times* March 22, 1987; "Indians: Past, Present and Future," *New York Times* Feb. 8, 1987, editorial. AICH News Release, "Indians Are Not Quarreling with Museum," Feb. 6, 1987. Interview of Rachel Sequoyah O'Connor (board member, AICH), July 10–13, 1985, Oneonta, N.Y.; Elma Patterson, p.c., Feb. 27, 1986; interview of Keith Reitz, July 21, 1982, June 8, 1984, Rochester, N.Y.

CHAPTER 5

1. New York State Department of Social Services, *Annual Report, 1985* (Albany, 1986), p. 55. This analysis is also based on reading the Annual Reports of the New York State Interdepartmental Committee on Indian Affairs from 1960 to 1975.

2. Chief Irving Powless, Jr. (Onondaga Council of Chiefs) to Governor Hugh Carey, Feb. 3, 1975, New York State Department of Education, Records of the Native American Education Unit, Box 1, New York State Archives, Albany. Please note that DSS records are closed and no records are available from the late 1930s onward except those of the Thomas Indian School which are housed at the New York State Archives.

3. I have learned much about the history of the State Board of Charities from Cornell "Corky" Rinehart, a senior fellow at the Rockefeller Institute, and I acknowledge and thank him for his help.

4. Thomas Indian School (and Orphan Asylum), *Annual Reports*, 1856–1956. See Hauptman, *The Iroquois Struggle for Survival*, pp. 11–14.

5. New York State Interdepartmental Committee on Indian Affairs, *Annual Report, 1973–1974* (Albany, 1974), p. 15.

6. Hauptman, *The Iroquois and the New Deal*, Chapter 7.

7. Quoted in Assembly Subcommittee on Indian Affairs, *Report, 1971*, p. 10.

8. Quoted in New York State Interdepartmental Committee on Indian Affairs, *Annual Report, 1974–1975* (Albany, 1975), p. 3.

9. Elma Patterson, p.c., May 29, 1986.

10. Assembly Subcommittee on Indian Affairs, *Report, 1971*, p. 12.

11. Patterson, p.c., May 28, 1976. Interview of Elma Patterson, April 15, 1972, New Paltz, N.Y. Elma Patterson to Kenneth L. Payto (acting deputy assistant secretary of Indian Affairs, U.S. Department of the Interior), Nov. 6, 1981, Governor Hugh Carey Records, Subject Files, Microfilm Reel 65, New York State Archives, Albany.

12. Martin Wasser to Ray Harding, Jan. 28, 1976; Wasser to Ogden Reid, March 8, 1976; Lou Grumet to Mario Cuomo, Nov. 15, 1976, New York State Department of State Records, Series #726, Moss Lake Indian Negotiations, New York State Archives, Albany.

13. Patterson, p.c., May 28, 1986; W. Pat Bartlett, p.c., April 8, 1986.

14. Assembly Subcommittee on Indian Affairs, *Report, 1971*, p. 11.

15. *Ibid.*

16. *Ibid.*, pp. 10–12.

17. Bartlett, p.c., April 8, 1986.

18. *Ibid.*; Patterson, p.c., May 28, 1986.

19. New York State Department of Education, Native American Indian Education Unit, *Indian Education in New York State* (Albany, undated). Informational hand-out distributed by Native American Indian Education Unit periodically updated since first prepared by Ruth Birdseye in mid-1950s.

20. *Ibid.*

21. New York Department of Public Instruction, *Thirty-Fourth Annual Report, 1888* (Albany, 1888), p. 765.

22. *Ibid.*, p. 763.

23. See the remarkable document, Anna M. Lewis and Lillian T. Samuelson, *"We Shall Live Again": A Positive Approach for Survival of a People, Proposal for Indian Education in New York State, March 1971* (Albany, 1971). This report is available through the Native American Indian Education Unit.

24. *Ibid.*, p. 12.

25. Interview of Leo Soucy (assistant commissioner of Education), March 4, 1986, Albany; H. E. Hyden (associate solicitor, U.S. Department of the Interior) to commissioner of Indian Affairs, Memorandum: Status of New York Indians, May 12, 1965; Ronald P. Daly to Leslie N. Gay, Jr. (Branch of Tribal Operations, BIA), Jan. 31, 1973; Leonard F. Bersani (chairman, Assembly Subcommittee on Indian Affairs), Oct. 3, 1972; George Brun to Barry Knussman, April 7, 1972; John J. Bardin to Thomas D. Sheldon, March 28, 1982; Bardin to Sheldon, March 29, 1972; Gordon M. Ambach to Henry G. Williams (acting director, Office of Planning Services), Jan. 23, 1975; Ambach to Sheldon, Feb. 27, March 13, 1975; Ambach to Harry Rainbolt (area director, Eastern Area, BIA), March 7, 14, 1975; Lincoln White to Leo Soucy, Feb. 6, 1975; White to Soucy, Memo: Status of Johnson-O'Malley State Plan, Feb. 26, 1975; Louis R. Bruce Jr. to chief of Division of Public School Relations, Nov. 13, 1970; Bruce to chief, Division of Employment Assistance, June 29, 1971; Bruce to Maribel Printup, Aug. 18, 1971. New York State Department of Education Records, Native American Indian Education Unit, Johnson-O'Malley Act Project Files, 1971–1977, Series 728, Acc. #80–32, New York State Archives, Albany.

26. Roy H. Sandstrom, ed., *Educating the Educators: A Report of the Institute on "The American Indian Student in Higher Education," St.. Lawrence University, July 12–30, 1971* (Canton, N.Y., 1971), pp. 30–36. Minerva White's article in this pamphlet is entitled "The St. Regis School Boycott."

27. *Ibid.*, pp. 17, 30–36. Chief John Cook and Minerva White to commissioner of Education, April 20, 1968, New York State Department of Education, Records of the Native American Indian Education Unit, Box 2, Series # 13143–85, New York State Archives, Albany.

28. Lloyd Elm, "Educating the Native American: The Lollypop of Self-Deceit," talk at Herkimer Community College, December 1972. Richard Case, "Onondagas Petition State: Unusual School Plan," April 25, 1971 and Case's "Onondagas Concerned About School Hassle," Oct. 15, 1972, both found in *Syracuse Herald-American*.

29. Interviews of Anna Lewis, June 10, 1983, Albany; and Leo Soucy, March 4, 1986, Albany.

30. Gordon M. Ambach, "The Education of Indians," speech before the Third Annual Conference on Indian Education, January 14, 1971, Massena, N.Y.

31. Lewis and Samuelson, "We Shall Live Again."

32. See for example Assembly Subcommittee on Indian Affairs, *Hearings at Massena, New York, Sept. 19, 1970* (Albany, 1970), pp. 2–82.

33. Assembly Subcommittee on Indian Affairs, *Final Report (1971)*, pp. 37–40. For the work of the subcommittee, see also Matthew F. Doherty, "Toward a Better Tomorrow," *New York State Education*, LVIII (April 1971), pp. 16–17 (entire issue devoted to American Indian education). Joseph M. Reilly to Commissioner Ewald Nyquist, Sept. 15, 1971, New York State Department of Education, Records of the Native American Indian Education Unit, Box 2, Series #13143–85, New York State Archives, Albany.

34. Phillip A. Cowen, *Survey of Indian Schools* (Albany, 1940), p. 41.

35. New York State Education Law, c. 820 (1947).

36. Interviews of Anna Lewis and Leo Soucy. Interview of Louis Bruce, Jr. and Lincoln White, June 30–July 1, 1982, Washington, D.C.

37. Gordon M. Ambach to Richard J. Sawyer, Jan. 28, 1971, New York State Department of Education, Records of Commissioner Ewald Nyquist, Box 3, Series #BO 467–80, Regents Folders Meetings (Jan. 1971-Sept. 1971), New York State Archives, Albany.

38. Interview of Leo Soucy. Richard Sawyer to Albert Berrian, et al., March 18, 1971 with attached lists of "Staff invitees to Minority Meeting on March 25" and "Representatives of Minority Groups," Records of the Board of Regents for "Meeting With Minority Groups," March 24–26, 1971, material made available by the Board of Regents.

39. Regents of the University of the State of New York, *Position Paper No. 22: Native American Education* (Albany, 1975).

40. *Ibid.*

41. Interview of Regent Laura Chodos, Feb. 24, 1986, Albany.

42. New York State Education Law, c. 476 (1977).

43. Dadie Perlov (executive director, New York Library Association) to Governor Hugh Carey, July 13, 1977; Margaret Jacobs (Akwesasne Library director) to

Governor Hugh Carey, May 15, 1977; Stanley Ransom (director, Clinton-Essex-Franklin Library System), July 19, 1977, found in (Legislative Bill Jacket) New York State Education Law, c. 476 (1977), New York State Archives, Albany. Ewald Nyquist to Board of Regents, Oct. 15, 1975, Records of Regents Meeting of Oct. 22–24, 1975.

44. New York State Division of the Budget, 10-Day Budget Report on Bills, July 21, 1977, (Legislative Bill Jacket) New York State Education Law, c. 476 (1977).

45. These figures were provided the author by the Native American Indian Education Unit and acquired through the reading of the New York State Legislative Budget since 1970.

46. (Legislative Bill Jacket) New York State Education Law, c. 257 (1978), New York State Archives, Albany; interview of Leo Soucy.

47. (Legislative Bill Jacket) New York State Education Law, c. 1105 (1985), Governor's Office Files (Rosemary Hannan).

48. Regents of the University of the State of New York, *Journal* (June 22–24, 1977), pp. 744–745; *Journal* (July 29, 1982), p. 277.

49. Interviews of Dr. Hazel V. Dean-John, Anna Lewis, Leo Soucy and John Adrian Cook. Anna Lewis to Leo Soucy, Jan. 5, 1979, Oct. 6, Dec. 16, 1980, Jan. 5, 1981; Ben Lindeman to Anna Lewis, March 1, 1983; Soucy to Chief Irving Powless, Jr., Dec. 16, 1980; Olga M. Vaughn to Anna Lewis, March 1, 1983, with attached report on visit to Onondaga school; John T. Bochenek to Soucy, Dec. 23, 1980; Thomas D. Sheldon (deputy commissioner, SED) to Onondaga Council of Chiefs, March 7, 1972; Onondaga Indian Reservation Special School District Staff Report, undated; Anna Lewis, report of meeting with Irving Powless, Jr., Oren Lyons and Lloyd Elm, April 14, 1971; Gordon Ambach to Chief Powless, April 24, 1978, New York State Department of Education, Records of the Native American Indian Education Unit, Series # 13143–85, Boxes 1 and 2, New York State Archives, Albany. Chief Irving Powless, Jr., to Laurence M. Hauptman, March 23, 1987, letter in author's possession.

50. Interview of Dr. Hazel V. Dean-John. The Oath bill is S. 4942 (Jess Present) and A. 2325 (Maurice Hinchey) and has been held up in the New York State Senate.

51. Anna Lewis to Leo Soucy, Memo: Status of the Native American Education Unit, Nov. 17, 1977, New York State Department of Education, Records of the Native American Indian Education Unit, Box 1, New York State Archives, Albany.

52. Commissioner Gordon Ambach to Gerald Freeborne, March 21, 1984, Records of the Board of Regents Meeting (1984). This material was made available to me by the Board of Regents.

53. See the estimates of annual cost of implementing Regents Position Paper No. 22: Stanley Raub to Thomas Sheldon, April 7, 1975, with attached summary entitled "Fiscal Requirements," New York State Department of Education, Records of the Native American Indian Education Unit, Series #729, Research Files for Regents Policy Statement, Box 4, New York State Archives, Albany.

54. Interviews of Leo Soucy, Anna Lewis, Hazel V. Dean-John and John Adrian Cook.

55. John Kahiones Fadden to Laurence M. Hauptman, Feb. 7, 1987, letter in author's possession. Laurence M. Hauptman Field Notes, Sept. 1986-Feb. 1987; "Haudenosaunee Meets New York State Education Department," *Indian Time* Jan. 28, 1987, p. 1. Artsconnection, *Dance: A Social Study* (Part IV: Native Americans) (Albany: New York State Education Department, 1986).*Field Test Edition: Social Studies 7 and 8: United States and New York* (Albany: New York State Department of Education Bureau of Curriculum Development, 1986). There is a desperate need for SED to prepare new Indian-related curriculum materials. The new fourth grade local history unit is a place to start. For the best curriculum-related materials on New York State American Indians, see Hazel W. Hertzberg, *The Great Tree and the Longhouse* (New York: Macmillan Co., 1966). The Native American Indian Education Unit has published a summary guide entitled: *Iroquois and Algonquian Indians: An Historical Perspective and Resource Guide* (Albany: New York State Department of Education, Native American Indian Education Unit, 1984).

56. "Wampum Belts Asked: Chief [Thomas] Demands State Return Them," *Syracuse Herald Journal* March 25, 1967.

57. Interviews of Oren Lyons and Lee Lyons, Sept. 8, 1984, Syracuse, N.Y.; interview of William N. Fenton, May 18, 1983, Slingerlands, N.Y.

58. William N. Fenton, "The New York State Wampum Collection: The Case for the Integrity of Cultural Treasures," *Proceedings of the American Philosophical Society*, 115 (Dec. 1971), pp. 440, 442, 446; Noah T. Clarke, "The Wampum Belt Collection of the New York State Museum," *New York State Museum Bulletin*, 288 (July 1931), pp. 85–124.

59. Fenton, "The New York State Wampum Collection"; and "Albany's Side of the Issue: State Expert on Indian Affairs Says Belts Belong in Albany," *Syracuse Herald American* March 28, 1971; Richard Case, "Indians v. New York State: Wampum Belt Dispute Has Wide Ramifications," *Syracuse Herald American* March 28, 1971; New York State legislature, Subcommittee on Indian Affairs, Hearings at the Onondaga Longhouse, Sept. 1, 1970, pp. 13–66. Arnold Bloom to John G. Broughton, Memo: Preparation for News Conference, April 21, 1970; Broughton to Rev. John E. Hines (bishop, Episcopal Church), April 21, 1970, New York State Department of Education, Records of Commissioner Ewald Nyquist, Series #BO 467–80, Folders for Regents Minutes, Jan.-May, 1970, New York State Archives.

60. Vine Deloria, Jr., *God Is Red* (New York: Dell, 1973), pp. 19–20.

61. Interview of Oren Lyons, Sept. 8, 1984. "Rocky Signs Bill Giving Wampum Belts to Indians," *Syracuse Herald-Journal* July 2, 1971.

62. Assembly Subcommittee on Indian Affairs, *Final Report*, p. 22.

63. Laurence M. Hauptman, Mohawk Field Notes, 1975–1985. Interview of Philip Tarbell, Dec. 7, 1981, New Paltz, N.Y.

64. Interview of George Hamell (Office of Exhibit Planning, New York State Museum), June 3, 1986, Albany.

65. New York State Department of Civil Service, *Ethnic Survey of New York State Agency Work Force, 1982*, pp. 66, 72.

66. Commissioner Gordon Ambach to Laurence M. Hauptman, Jan. 31, 1986, letter in author's possession.

CHAPTER 6

1. Interviews of Chief Edison Mt. Pleasant and Ruth Mt. Pleasant, Nov. 30, 1984, Tuscarora Indian Reservation.

2. There are Robert Moses State Parks, regionally administered by the Niagara Frontier Parks Commission and the Thousand Island Parks Commission, which border the Tuscarora Reservation and St. Regis (Akwesasne) Mohawk Reservation, respectively. A third Robert Moses State Park is regionally administered by the Long Island Parks Commission.

3. Albert B. Lewis to Governor Hugh Carey, Sept. 18, 1978, Governor Hugh Carey Records, Subject Files, Microfilm Reel 104, New York State Archives, Albany.

4. Robert Caro, *The Power Broker: Robert Moses and the Fall of New York* (New York: Random House, 1974), p. 830.

5. *Ibid.*, p. 166. See Hauptman, *The Iroquois Struggle for Survival*, Chapters 8 and 9.

6. "State Council of Parks Backs Federal Plan to Buy Reservation and Remove Indians: Proposal Linked with Kinzua Dam; Would Develop Allegany Valley for Recreation," *Salamanca Republican-Press* Jan. 21, 1946. CEC (Charles E. Congdon) to William N. Fenton, Dec. 4, 1964, William N. Fenton MSS., Box: Kinzua Dam III, American Philosophical Society, Philadelphia.

7. See Hauptman, *The Iroquois Struggle for Survival*, Chapter 8.

8. Robert Moses, *Working for the People: Promise and Performance in Public Service* (New York: Harper, 1956), p. 186.

9. See Hauptman, *The Iroquois Struggle for Survival*, Chapter 8.

10. New York State Office of Parks, Recreation and Historic Preservation, *People, Resources, Recreation, 1983: New York Statewide Comprehensive Recreation Plan, March, 1983* (Albany, 1983).

11. Interviews of Cornelius Abrams, Jr., March 20, 1986; and George Abrams, Aug. 26, 1983, Allegany Indian Reservation. Hauptman, Seneca Nation Field Notes, 1975–1986.

12. For the development of the park, see Charles E. Congdon, *Allegany Oxbow: A History of Allegany State Park and the Allegany Reserve of the Seneca Nation* (Little Valley, N.Y.: Straight Publishing, 1967), pp. 1–10. For Congdon and Dowd, see Hauptman, *The Iroquois Struggle for Survival*, pp. 32–37.

13. Interview of Raymond Schuler (former commissioner of Transportation), June 3, 1986, Albany.

14. United States, Congress, House of Representatives, House Committee on Interior and Insular Affairs, *Hearings on H.R. 6631: Settlement of the Cayuga Indian Nation Land Claims in the State of New York, March 3, 1980* (Washington, D.C., 1980), pp. 394–400.

15. Interview of Bruce Fullem.

16. John M. Prenderville to Thomas Frey, Nov. 29, 1978, with attached letter of John C. Stokes to Commissioner Orin Lehman, Oct. 25, 1978, Governor Hugh Carey Records, Subject Files, Microfilm Reel 104, New York State Archives, Albany.

17. New York State Office of Parks, Recreation, and Historic Preservation, Bureau of Historic Sites (Ben A. Kroup), *Master Plan for Gannagaro State Historic Site* (Albany, 1985), pp. 1, 5.

18. Interviews of G. Pete Jemison (Ganondagan Site Manager), May 15, 1986, Victor, N.Y.; Ben A. Kroup (Gannagaro NEH Grant project director), May 20, 1986, Peebles Island, N.Y.

19. E. Patricia Boland to Kenneth Burroughs (Department of Civil Service), Feb. 24, 1977; "Description of Duties" for Historic Site Assistant (Gannagaro), March 14, 1977; Stanley Winter (OPRHP) to Jack Prenderville and Al Caccese (OPRHP, Finger Lakes Region), June 22, 1978; Rosa Maria Castillo-Kesper to Stanley Winter, June 20, 1978; "Description of Duties" for Historic Site Assistant, May 9, 1979; Stanley Winter to Ed Lynch (OPRHP), May 21, 1979; Dick Haberlen (OPRHP) to Stanley Winter, March 18, 1980; "Indian Says Racism Cost State Post," *Knickerbocker News* June 25, 1981.

20. Interviews of Ben Kroup and G. Pete Jemison; OPRHP, *Master Plan for Gannagaro; New York State Budget, 1986–1987; Capital Projects* (Albany, 1986), p. 429.

21. Interview of Ben Kroup.

22. Hauptman, Seneca Field Notes, 1984–1986.

23. Cuomo, "State-of-the-State," (1986) p. 130.

24. Interviews of Ben Kroup and G. Pete Jemison.

25. Interview of G. Pete Jemison.

26. *Ibid.*; Governor Mario M. Cuomo, *Message to the Legislature*, Jan. 7, 1987 (Albany, 1987), p. 53. For more on Ganondagan, see *Turtle Quarterly*, I (1986), pp. 2–16, 24. See also OPHPR Bureau of Historic Sites three publications: *Art from Ganondagan (Albany, 1986); Ethnological Trail Boughton Hill* (Albany, 1986); and John Mohawk, *War Against the Seneca: The French Expedition Against the Seneca* (Albany, 1986).

27. New York State Highway Law, Section 53. See Appendix V.

28. Interviews of John Mladinov (New York State executive deputy commissioner of Transportation), Feb. 26, 1986, Albany; Donald Ketchum (regional director, Buffalo Office, Department of Transportation), May 15, 1986, Buffalo.

29. New York State Department of Civil Service, *Ethnic Survey*, p. 72. Interview of Michael Davis.

30. Interviews of John Mladinov, Donald Ketchum; Raymond Schuler (former New York State commissioner of Transportation), June 3, 1986, Albany; and John Hennessy (assistant to the regional director, Buffalo Office, Department of Transportation), May 15, 1986.

31. For the 1950s push for highway development, see Mark Rose, *Interstate* (Lawrence, Kan.: University Press of Kansas, 1979). Interviews of Raymond Schuler; and Norman Hurd (former secretary to Governor Rockefeller), Feb. 26, 1986, Albany.

32. Interview of Raymond Schuler. For the further development of the plan, see Joseph M. Tocke (regional planning engineer, Region 5) to G. Tanner, "Memo: Ten-Year Construction Program Update, Region 5, Nov. 2, 1973 (with Oct. 1973 update)," Folder: Region 5 10-Year Plan, 1973–1983, New York State Department of Transportation Records, #BO626, Highway Development Planning and Progress Files, 1921–1975, Office of Planning and Development, New York State Archives, Albany.

33. Interview of Arthur Lazarus, Jr. (Seneca Nation attorney), July 17, 1982, Buffalo. See Hauptman, *The Iroquois Struggle for Survival*, chapters 6–7. "Indians Grant Right of Way to Thruway," *Buffalo Courier-Express* Oct. 6, 1954; "Seneca Nation to Get $75,500 from Thruway," *Salamanca Republican-Press* Sept. 23, 1954; "Seneca Indians State OK Pact on the Thruway," *Fredonia Censor* Sept. 23, 1954. Newsclippings found in New York State Thruway Authority Records, Series BO588-85, Office of Public Information, Box 7, File: "Indians," New York State Archives, Albany.

34. Interview of Jess Present.

35. Interviews of Raymond Schuler and John Mladinov; interview of William Hennessy, July 9, 1986, Albany.

36. See Hauptman, *The Iroquois Struggle for Survival*, pp. 217–222.

37. *Ibid.*, pp. 221–222.

38. Interview of Jess Present.

39. Louis J. Lefkowitz memorandum for Governor, Re: Assembly Bill 4020, Senate Bill 20,005-A, June 8, 1973. (Legislative Bill Jacket), New York State Highway Law, c. 962 (1973), New York State Archives, Albany.

40. New York State Highway Law, Section 31.

41. Lefkowitz to Governor, June 8, 1973.

42. *Ibid.*

43. *Ibid.*

44. For the development of the Southern Tier Expressway on the Allegany Indian Reservation, see Governor Hugh Carey Press Release, Jan. 31, 1975; Carey to the Traditional Seneca Peoples Government, Feb. 4, 1975; Raymond Harding (secretary to Governor Carey) to James Tully (commissioner of Taxation and Finance), April 23, 1975; Harding to Peter C. Goldmark, Jr. (director, Division of the Budget), April 23, 1975; Harding to Vito Castellano (first deputy commissioner of Commerce), April 23, 1975; Harding to President Robert C. Hoag (Seneca Nation of Indians), Aug. 22, 1975; Carey to Hoag, Sept. 4, 1975; Raymond Schuler (commissioner of Transportation) to Governor Carey, July 7, 1976; Carey to Hoag, July 28, 1976; Harding to Carey, Jan. 22, 1975; Carey to Elliott Tallchief (Traditional Seneca Peoples Government), Aug. 5, 1975; Traditional Seneka (sic) Peoples Government, May 30, 1975, Governor Hugh Carey Records, Subject Files, Microfilm Reel 104, New York State Archives, Albany. For the history of the Kinzua Dam, see Hauptman, *Iroquois Struggle for Survival*, chapters 6–7. I have learned much from the following American Indians about this tragedy: Cornelius Abrams, Jr., George Abrams, the late Merrill Bowen, George Heron, Jeanne Marie Jemison, Dr. Hazel V. Dean-John, and Wini Kettle; as well as from the late Pauline Seneca (Cayuga), who was the widow of President Cornelius Seneca.

45. Seneca Nation of Indians, minutes of a special council meeting, June 28, 1976, in author's possession; interview of Raymond Schuler.

46. Agreement (Robert C. Hoag and Raymond T. Schuler, Signatories) Between the Seneca Nation of Indians and the People of the State of New York for the Southern Tier Expressway, Cattaraugus County, June 28, 1976; Memorandum of Understanding Between New York State Department of Transportation and Seneca Nation of Indians, July 28, 1976; Seneca Nation of Indians Special Session, Council Minutes, June 28, 1976.

47. Agreement Between the Seneca Nation and the People of the State of New York, July 28, 1976.

48. Interview of Raymond Schuler.

49. Memorandum of Understanding, July 28, 1976.

50. Interview of Raymond Schuler. See Chapter 3 for Martin Wasser's similar comments.

51. Emery H. Williams to Stanley D. Doremus, July 9, 1977, New York State Department of State Records, Moss Lake Indian Negotiations, Series #726, New York State Archives, Albany. Traditional Seneka (sic) Peoples Government to President of the United States, May 30, 1975, Governor Hugh Carey Records, Subject Files, Microfilm Reel 104, New York State Archives, Albany.

52. Lou Grumet to Secretary of State Mario Cuomo, July 19, 1977, New York State Department of State Records, Moss Lake Indian Negotiations, Series # 726, New York State Archives, Albany.

53. Interviews of George Abrams and John Mladinov.

54. Hauptman, Seneca Nation of Indians Field Notes, 1985–1986; Emily Campbell and Donna Snyder, "Expressway Work Stalled," *Salamanca Press* Feb. 22, 1985; "Dissident Senecas Hold March," *Olean Times Herald* Feb. 25, 1985; "Protesting Senecas March on Highway," *Buffalo News* Feb. 24, 1985; Eric Paddock, "Senecas Bar Construction on Expressway," *Bradford [Pa.] Era* Feb. 21, 1985; and Paddock's "Standoff: DOT Hopes Seneca Nation Can Intercede," *Bradford Era* Feb. 23, 1985; Rosemary Daley, "Hennessy Seeks Facts from Senecas," *Olean Times Herald* May 31, 1985. List of Demands (handout), Feb. 23, 1985, copy in author's possession. The list included demands to abolish eminent domain and Route 17 and 219 as well as the recognition and protection of Iroquois villages, burial sites, and artifacts. The list also charged the Seneca Nation Council, the BIA and New York State with "fraudulent conspiracy and collusion in dealing with Seneca lands," and accused the Interior Department of ignoring its "trust responsibilities to the Seneca People."

55. Interview of John Mladinov.

56. This conclusion is based on the author's visit to the Tonawanda Indian Reservation, May 14, 1986, and his interview of Ramona Charles, superintendent of the Tonawanda Indian Community House.

57. See Hauptman, *The Iroquois Struggle for Survival*, chapters 8–9.

58. Frederick R. Clark to Robert J. Morgado, March 6, 1978, Governor Hugh Carey Records, Subject Files, Microfilm Reel 104, New York State Archives, Albany.

59. Frederick R. Clark to Governor Hugh Carey, March 6, 1978, Governor Hugh Carey Records, Subject Files, Microfilm Reel 104, New York State Archives,

Albany. "Land Claims Meeting Held in Washington," *Indian Time* Jan. 16, 1987, p. 1.

60. Robert J. Morgado to Frederick R. Clark, March 10, 1978, Governor Hugh Carey Records, Subject Files, Microfilm Reel 104, New York State Archives, Albany.

61. Interview of Dr. Henrik Dullea.

62. See Hauptman, *The Iroquois Struggle for Survival*, chapters 2, 3, 9; also see Graymont, *Fighting Tuscarora*, p. 95. The major Department of Law "opponent" of the Iroquois from the 1920s to the 1950s was Henry Manley, an attorney and historian.

63. Jean Coon (assistant solicitor general) to Governor Hugh Carey, Aug. 22, 1975, Carey to Attorney General Louis Lefkowitz, Feb. 4, 1976; Lefkowitz and Jeremiah Jochnowitz, Sept. 27, 1977 to Gajarsa, Liss and Sterenbech, Esq., Governor Hugh Carey Records, Subject Files, Microfilm Reel 104, New York State Archives, Albany. Louis Lefkowitz to Commissioner Robert Whalen (Health), Oct. 18, 1976, Records of the New York State Board of Health, Subject Files of the Commissioner, Box 36, acc. #13, 307–82, New York State Archives. *Herzog Brothers Trucking, Inc. v. The State Tax Commission of the State of New York*, Supreme Court, Albany County, Special Term, Dec. 6, 1985, Calendar No. 38.

64. New York State Department of Law, *Formal Opinions of the Attorney General*, 1973 (Albany, 1973), pp. 16–18; *Formal Opinions of the Attorney General*, 1976, (Albany, 1976), pp. 54–55; *Formal Opinions of the Attorney General*, 1977 (Albany, 1977), p. 76; *Informal Opinions of the Attorney General*, 1977 (Albany, 1977) (contained in *Formal Opinions of the Attorney General*, p. 254); *Formal Opinions of the Attorney General, 1978* (Albany, 1978), pp. 7–9, 79–80; *Formal Opinions of the Attorney General, 1975* (Albany, 1975), pp. 83–84.

65. Coon to Carey, Aug. 22, 1975.

66. Interview of Telisport Putsavage (DEC).

67. Quoted in Exhibit III: Memorandum of Law and Fact contained in petition of Feb. 9, 1968, attached to letter of Joseph Califano to Jacob Thompson, Feb. 28, 1968, Lyndon Johnson MSS., White House Central Files, Box 3, IN/A-Z, LBJ Library, Austin, Tex.

68. *Ibid.*

69. Exhibit II: Julius L. Sackman memorandum for Louis Lefkowitz, Aug. 3, 1967, attached to Califano letter to Thompson, Feb. 28, 1968. See note 65.

70. Louis Lefkowitz and Jeremiah Jochnowitz to Gajarsa, Liss and Sterenbech, Esq., Sept. 27, 1977.

71. Gerald C. Crotty, Memo to the Files, Aug. 22, 1979, Governor Hugh Carey Records, Subject Files, Microfilm Reel 65, New York State Archives, Albany.

CHAPTER 7

1. "A New Band of Tribal Tycoons," *Time* March 16, 1987, pp. 56–57.

2. New York State Department of Social Welfare, *Manual of Indian Affairs and Procedures (Including Historical Data)* (Albany, 1954).

3. See Appendix VI for excerpts from SED's draft proposal.

4. James MacGregor Burns, *Leadership* (New York: Harper & Row, 1978), p. 461.

CHAPTER 8

1. "PASNY Lands Up For Sale," *Indian Time* Feb. 11, 1987; "The New York Power Authority," *Indian Time* June 10, 1987. "Hoag: Seneca-Salamanca Lease Talks Could Resume in the Fall," *Olean Times-Herald* July 23, 1987. For the progress of the Mohawk land claims negotiations, see for example, "Land Claims Meeting Held in Washington," *Indian Time* Jan. 16, 1987; and "Land Claims Held in Nikentsiake," *Indian Time* March 11, 1987.

2. Lieutenant Governor Stanley Lundine, in addressing the audience at the dedication of Ganondagan State Park on July 18, 1987, repeated what New York State officials have said about the imminent establishment of an Indian office. See also Howard Rowley, "Response to Laurence Hauptman Article," *Akwesasne Notes*, Late Spring 1987 as well as the author's response to it in the same issue. Also see Laurence M. Hauptman, "Circle the Wagons: N.Y. State vs. the Indians," *Capital Region* 2 (Feb. 1987), pp. 29–31, 52–53, which prompted Rowley's reaction.

3. Bob Maas, "Gas Distributors' Sales Tax Collection Eliminated," *Olean Times-Herald* May 8, 1987; David Ernst, "Prepaid Taxes on Reservation Ruled Unlawful," *Buffalo News* May 8, 1987; "State Loses in Indian Tax Case," *Salamanca Press* May 8, 1987; David Ernst, "State Tax Chief Declares War," *Buffalo News*, Sept. 3, 1987.

4. Deborah Bachrach (N.Y.S. Department of Law) to Julia Kidd (chairperson, Museum of the American Indian-Heye Foundation), Dec. 5, 1986. The author thanks Dr. Robert W. Venables of the American Indian Community House in New York City for bringing this letter to his attention.

5. Stephen Moore, "Federal Indian Burial Policy—Historical Anachronism or Contemporary Reality?" *Native American Rights Fund Legal Review* 12 (Spring 1987), pp. 5–6.

6. Gerald C. Crotty to Rosemary Richmond, Feb. 24, 1987. Copy of letter in author's possession provided by Dr. Robert W. Venables.

7. Kallen M. Martin, "3rd Draft of A Statewide Native American Alcoholism Needs Assessment Study," Sept. 14, 1987 MSS., New York State Division of Alcoholism and Alcohol Abuse. I should like to thank Kallen M. Martin for bringing this important report to my attention.

8. "Japanese Developers Will Visit Reservation," *Olean Times-Herald* May 14, 1987; Dave Caryl, "Hoag Addresses Seminar for Minority Businesses," *Salamanca Press* June 5, 1987; Emily Campbell, "Hoag Woos High-tech Asian Investors," *Salamanca Press* May 19, 1987; "Seminars Tuned to Local Business: Minorities Emphasized, June 3," *Salamanca Press* May 13, 1987; Bob Maas, "Indians Learn of Opportunities for Starting Small Businesses," *Olean Times-Herald* June 4, 1987.

9. Ronald Patterson (Seneca Tribal Economic Development Specialist) quoted in Maas, "Indians Learn of Opportunities."

10. Bob Maas, " 'Town of Peace' Dedicated by Indian and State Leaders," *Olean Times-Herald* July 19, 1987; "Ceremony Designates Historic Iroquois Site," *Buffalo News* July 19, 1987.

11. Governor Mario M. Cuomo, "Message to the Legislature," Jan. 6, 1988, pp. 81–82.

Appendix I

Jurisdictional Acts, 1948 and 1950

Section 232. *Jurisdiction of New York State over offenses committed on reservations within State.*

The State of New York shall have jurisdiction over offenses committed by or against Indians on Indian reservations within the State of New York to the same extent as the courts of the State have jurisdiction over offenses committed elsewhere within the State as defined by the laws of the State: *Provided,* That nothing contained in this section shall be construed to deprive any Indian tribe, band, or community, or members thereof, hunting and fishing rights as guaranteed them by agreement, treaty, or custom, nor require them to obtain State fish and game licenses for the exercise of such rights.

(July 2, 1948, ch. 809, 62 Stat. 1224.)

Section 233. *Jurisdiction of New York State courts in civil actions.*

The courts of the State of New York under the laws of such State shall have jurisdiction in civil actions and proceedings between Indians or between one or more Indians and any other person or persons to the same extent as the courts of the State shall have jurisdiction in other civil actions and proceedings, as now or hereafter defined by the laws of such State: *Provided,* That the governing body of any recognized tribe of Indians in the State of New York shall have the right to declare, by appropriate enactment prior to September 13, 1952, those tribal laws and customs which they desire to preserve, which, on certification to the Secretary of the Interior by the governing body of such tribe shall be published in the Federal Register and thereafter shall govern in all civil cases involving reservation Indians when the subject matter of such tribal laws and customs is involved or at issue, but nothing herein contained shall be construed to prevent such courts from recognizing and giving effect to any tribal law or custom which may be proved to the satisfaction of such courts: *Provided further,* That nothing herein contained shall be construed as subjecting the lands within any Indian reservation in the State of New York to taxation for State or local purposes, nor as subjecting any such lands, or any Federal or State annuity in favor of Indians or Indian tribes, to execution on any judgment rendered in the State courts, except in the enforcement of a judgment in a suit by one tribal member against another in the matter of the use or possession of land: *And provided further*, That nothing herein contained shall be construed as authorizing the alienation from any Indian nation, tribe, or band of Indians of any lands within any Indian reservation in the State of New York: *Provided further*, That nothing herein contained shall be construed as conferring jurisdiction on the courts of the State of New York or making applicable the laws of the State of New York in civil actions involving Indian lands or claims with respect thereto which relate to transactions or events transpiring prior to September 13, 1952.

(Sept. 13, 1950, ch. 947, 64 Stat. 845.)

Effective Date

Section 2 of act Sept. 13, 1950, provided: "This Act [this section] shall take effect two years after the date of its passage [Sept. 13, 1950]."

Appendix II

American Indian Populations of New York State:
Federal Census

1900:	5,257
1910:	6,046
1920:	5,503
1930:	6,973
1940:	8,651
1950:	10,640
1960:	16,491
1970:	28,355
1980:	38,732

Appendix III

Counting American Indians?

The Statistics and footnotes below are reprinted verbatim from the New York State legislature, *Manual, 1984–1985* (Albany, N.Y.: New York Department of State). Please note that American Indian population estimates are quite unreliable and are largely based upon figures provided by the Indian tribal councils, several of whom do not cooperate in statistical gathering efforts. The figures for Mohawk tribal enrollment are for the socalled "American" side of reservation only and do not take into account Indians on the "Canadian side." Please also note that the footnote provided in the New York State legislative *Manual* about how the Oneidas and Cayugas lost their land is the official New York State government version of history, not the Indians' interpretation of events.

˙1980 amended figures in parenthesis provided by Dept. of Social Services, Office of Indian Services.

"The former Oneida Reservation was divided in severalty by Chapter 185, Laws of 1843. The Cayuga Nation has no reservation, having sold their lands as early as 1807. Members of the Cayuga Nation have intermarried with members of the other Iroquois tribes in New York and may reside on the reservation of their spouse."

⁺1980 figures revised by U.S. Census, Oct. 23, 1981.

Indian Reservations in New York

The Allegany Reservation, situated in Cattaraugus County, comprises 22,640 acres.

The Cattaraugus Reservation, situated in Erie, Cattaraugus, and Chautauqua Counties, comprises 21,680 acres.˙

The Oneida Reservation, situated in Madison County, comprises 35 acres.

The Onondaga Reservation, situated south of the city of Syracuse, comprises 7,300 acres.

The Poospatuck Reservation, situated near Mastic in Suffolk County, comprises 60 acres.

The St. Regis Reservation, situated in Franklin County, fronting on the St. Lawrence River, comprises 14,640 acres.

The Shinnecock Reservation, situated near Southampton in Suffolk County, comprises about 400 acres.

The Tonawanda Reservation, situated in the counties of Erie, Genessee, and Niagara, comprises 7,549 acres.

The Tuscarora Reservation, situated in Niagara County, comprises approximately 5,700 acres.

Population of Indian Reservations
FEDERAL ENUMERATIONS OF 1925-1980

Reservations	1925	1930	1940	1950	1960	1970	1980	1980*
Allegany	752	972	1151	1131	1059	1113	1243	(919)
Cattaraugus	1270	1392	1643	1649	1707	1384	1994	(2175)
Oil Spring	...	...	...	...	...	5	6	(...)
Oneida'	...	...	...	...	...	...	...	(45)
Onondaga	622	611	762	894	941	785	596+	(850)
Poospatuck	...	34	...	...	...	125	203	(88)
St. Regis	976	945	1262	1409	1774	1536	1802	(3100)
Shinnecock	177	160	156	183	234	174	297	(328)
Tonawanda	474	443	539	468	456	504	467	(600)
Tuscarora	395	402	462	634	1934	1134	921+	(725)
Total	4666	4959	5975	6368	8105	6635	7529	(8830)

Tribal Enrollment

Cayugas	396	Seneca Nation	5,427
Mohawks	3,100	Shinnecocks	1,900
Oneidas	623	Tonawanda Band of	
Onondagas	1,475	Senecas	1,025
Poospatucks	368	Tuscaroras	c.975

1986–87 New York State Indian Health Services Budget Summary

	Onon-daga	Tona-wanda	Tusca-rora	St. Regis	Seneca	Shin-necock	Total
Personal Service							
Regular	12,163	13,830	21,464				$ 47,457
Temporary		44,027	10,926				54,943
Non-Employee	6,250						6,250
Total	18,413	57,857	32,390	0	0	0	$108,660
Non-Personal Service							
Supplies	24,600	25,000	22,000				71,600
Travel		3,500	500				4,000
Contractual	16,740	2,500	1,000				20,240
Special Contracts	93,400			40,000	70,000	15,000	218,400
Total	134,740	31,000	23,500	40,000	70,000	15,000	$314,240
Grand Total	153,153	88,857	55,890	40,000	70,000	15,000	$422,900

Appendix V

State of New York Department of Transportation
Highway Maintenance Division

Center Lane Miles and Lane Miles of the Indian Reservation Roads, maintained as of January 1, 1983:

Region		Indian Reservation C.L. Miles	Indian Reservation Lane Miles
1	Albany	—	—
2	Utica	—	—
3	Syracuse	15.15	30.30
4	Rochester	21.20	37.47
5	Buffalo	96.52	193.04
6	Hornell	1.72	3.44
7	Watertown	27.55	55.10
8	Poughkeepsie	—	—
9	Binghamton	—	—
10	Hauppauge	8.58	16.75
	New York City	—	—
	STATE TOTAL	170.72	336.10

Appendix VI

Excerpts from New York State Museum's Draft Proposal:
UNMARKED HUMAN SKELETAL REMAINS, January 5, 1987

Enforcement Advantage

The use of the Health Law and the general prohibition against excavation of human remains is a more direct and understandable concept for the general public. It avoids the *perceived* debatable concepts of scientific value, historic preservation, ethics and cultural heritage. It also avoids the minority affiliation issue (Black remains, Indian remains, Irish remains, Chinese remains, etc.).

Administrative Concept

In order to provide effective field services and crisis management, a regionalized approach could be taken. Staff from Albany should not, and could not, be expected to provide on-site inspections statewide within the 24–48 hour turnaround expected.

Field Services Network

Expertise exists in several SUNY Anthropology Departments around the State in archeology and physical anthropology.

The State Museum's Cultural Resource Survey Program (C.R.S.P.) is in place (since 1963) to provide archeological field services to other state agencies, primarily the Department of Transportation and the Department of Correctional Services.

Several SUNY Anthropology Departments are already "on line" for emergency field operations via the State Museum's C.R.S.P. These persons are under annual contracts with the State Museum via the Research Foundation of SUNY, and their services are reimbursed by State Education department appropriations. These costs are later reimbursed to SED by the agency requesting the field activity.

Procedures for Burial

A contact person at the Department of Health would be established as a clearinghouse for issues relating to "historic" burials. ["Historic" means anything that requires an archeological evaluation.]

An interagency panel would be established to be convened as a consulting body when issues relating to "historic" human remains arise. This panel would also have a list of additional consulting members for special types of burial issues (prehistoric, historic, minority affiliation, military, etc.).

STEP 1: All actions involving unmarked human skeletal remains would be reported to the central clearinghouse at the Department of Health.

STEP 2: The Department of Health would screen these cases into three categories:

A. recent burials and corpses (less than 100 years).

B. "historic" burials and remains (over 100 years, but not "C" below).

C. Miscellaneous skeletal remains, such as medical skeletons, human bone not associated with any New York burials, etc.

STEP 3: If in category "B," the interagency panel would be convened (24 hour notice) to discuss the issue. If the issue involved a field inspection need, the State Archeologist's office would be contacted and arrangements made through the C.R.S.P. to dispatch a SUNY field team to inspect the site, collection or location.

STEP 4: Based on the field findings, if any, the interagency panel would develop a course of action and policy. [Where the curation of specimens is required, the Curator of Anthropology, New York State Museum, would provide consulting services. It is understood that the facilities of the New York State Museum would be available as needed for the curation of specimens resulting for cases involving human remains.]

STEP 5: The consulting field archeologists (SUNY, or under contract to SUNY) would submit a bill for their services to SED. At some later time, SED would bill the lead agency for reimbursement of costs incurred by the field team or associated with the curation of specimens. [If a non-SUNY consultant is needed, SED will pay that consultant on a purchase order basis.]

Advantages

This system requires no new law or regulations, although it does require a statement of policy on the part of the Department of Health.

This system requires no appropriation, since an existing appropriation for the SED C.R.S.P. should cover the level of costs anticipated for this service.

This system regionalizes the process of initial emergency field inspection, thus reducing time and utilizing existing expertise at the regional level.

This system provides for an interagency forum for the resolution of issues relating to unmarked human skeletal remains.

This system makes maximum use of existing networks, facilities and funding sources, while minimizing the delay in creating new procedures for dealing with the crisis.

BIBLIOGRAPHY

▼▼▼▼▼▼▼▼▼▼▼▼▼▼▼

Archives

Lyndon Baines Johnson Library, Austin, Texas. White House Central
Files, 1963–1968.

John Fitzgerald Kennedy Library, Boston.

1. White House Central Files, 1961–1963.
2. Senator Robert F. Kennedy MSS.
3. Lee White MSS.

National Archives, Washington, D.C.

1. Bureau of Indian Affairs, Central Classified Files, 1907–1956.
2. Records of the New York Agency, 1938–1949.

New York State Archives, Albany, N.Y.

Governor's Office.

1. Governor Hugh Carey Papers.
2. Governor Nelson A. Rockefeller Papers.
3. Governor Malcolm Wilson Papers.

New York State Department of Education.

1. Records of the Native American Indian Education Unit, 1968–
   1983 (records pre-exist unit).
2. Johnson O'Malley Act Project Files, 1971–1977.
3. Regents Position Paper on Native American Education, 1970–
   1975.
4. Office Files of Commissioner Ewald B. Nyquist, 1971–1977.

5. Records of the Assistant Commissioner for the New York State Museum, 1954–1971.

New York State Department of Environmental Conservation. Subject Files of the Commissioner.

1. Peter A. A. Berle.
2. Robert Flacke.

New York State Department of Health.

1. Subject Files of the Commissioner's Office (1974–1978).
2. Subject Files of the First Deputy Commissioner, 1974–1978.
3. Subject Files of the Executive Deputy Commissioner (1979–1986).

New York State Department of Social Services. Records of the Thomas Indian School (and Orphan Asylum).
New York State Department of State. Moss Lake Records, 1974–1978.
New York State Department of Transportation Records. Highway Development Planning and Progress Files, 1921–1975.
New York State Legislature. Legislative Bill Jackets, 1970–1984.
New York State Thruway Authority Records. Office of Public Information.
New York State, Board of Regents, Albany. Records of the Board of Regents, 1970–1984.
New York State, Governor's Office, Albany. Legislative Bill Jackets, 1985–1986.
Smithsonian Institution, National Anthropological Archives.

1. J. N. B. Hewitt Collection.
2. National Congress of American Indian Collection.

Manuscript Collections

American Philosophical Society, Philadelphia. William N. Fenton MSS.
Columbia University.

1. Herbert H. Lehman MSS.
2. Charles Poletti MSS.

Cornell University. Irving Ives MSS.
Georgetown University. Robert F. Wagner, Sr. MSS.

Hartwick College, Oneonta, N.Y. James Hanley MSS.
Historical Society of Pennsylvania, Philadelphia. Indian Rights Association MSS.
Library of Congress, Manuscript Division. Josephus Daniels MSS.
New York State Library, Manuscript Division.

　　1. William Beauchamp Collection.

　　2. Alfred E. Smith Personal Papers.

Princeton University.

　　1. American Civil Liberties Union Collection.

　　2. Association on American Indian Affairs Collection.

Syracuse University.

　　1. Governor Averell Harriman MSS.

　　2. Robert Moses MSS.

University of Rochester.

　　1. Governor Thomas E. Dewey MSS.

　　2. Kenneth B. Keating MSS.

Interviews (conducted by Laurence M. Hauptman)

Cornelius Abrams, Jr., September 29, 1984, March 21, 1986, Allegany Indian Reservation.
George Abrams, August 26, 1983, Allegany Indian Reservation.
Wint Aldrich, May 8, 1986, Albany, N.Y.
Colwyn Allen, June 3, 1986, Albany, N.Y.
Chief James Allen, August 17, 1979, Miami, Okla.; May 4–5, 1980, New Paltz, N.Y.
Marilyn Anderson, May 4–5, 1977, New Paltz, N.Y.
William Barnette, June 17, 1986, Albany, N.Y.
Robert Batson, January 15, March 6, 1986, Albany, N.Y.
Ernest Benedict, September 10–11, 1982, July 30, 1983, Akwesasne (St. Regis Mohawk) Indian Reservation.
Salli Benedict, September 11, 1982, Brasher Center, N.Y.
Roy Black, October 30-November 1, 1983, May 2–5, 1984, April 7, 1986, New Paltz, N.Y.
Louis R. Bruce, Jr., December 11, 1980, June 30, 1982, Washington, D.C.

William Carr, April 11, 1986, Albany, N.Y.

Rosa Castillo-Kesper, May 5, 1986, Albany, N.Y.

Ramona Charles, July 21, 1982, May 14, 1986, Tonawanda Indian Reservation.

Laura Chodos, February 24, 1986, Albany, N.Y.

Jeff Cohen, April 11, 1986, Albany, N.Y.

John Adrian Cook, February 24, 1986, Albany, N.Y.

Julius Cook, May 27-June 1, 1982, New Paltz, N.Y.; August 1, 1983, Akwesasne (St. Regis Mohawk) Indian Reservation.

Ann Cortese, May 27, 1986, Albany, N.Y.

Gerald C. Crotty, July 9, 1986, Albany, N.Y.

Michael Davis, June 17, 1986, Albany, N.Y.

Ray Elm, October 20, 1984, Rome, N.Y.; April 21, 1985, Syracuse, N.Y.

Hazel V. Dean-John, July 16, 1984, April 18, 1986, January 30, 1987, Albany, N.Y.

Vine Deloria, Jr., May 4, 1982, New Paltz, N.Y.

Ward DeWitt, April 7, 1986, Albany, N.Y.

Fernando DiMaggio, April 17, 1986, Albany, N.Y.

James Donovan, April 17, 1986, Albany, N.Y.

Henrik Dullea, April 18, 1986, Albany, N.Y.

John Fadden, September 11, 1982, Onchiota, N.Y.

Ray Fadden, September 11, 1982, July 14, 1985, Onchiota, N.Y.

James Feck, March 25, 1986, Albany, N.Y.

William N. Fenton, September 28, 1977, June 28, 1978, May 18, 1983, Albany, N.Y.

Gloria Tarbell Fogden, June 21, 1984, New Paltz, N.Y.

Bruce Fullem, May 12, 1986, Albany, N.Y.

Robert Funk, February 20, 1987, Albany, N.Y.

Jerry Gambill (Rarihokwats), August 22, 1984, Ottawa, Ont.

Fran Genovesi, April 18, 1986, Albany, N.Y.

James Gold, July 10, 1986, Peebles Island, N.Y.

Elmer Green, May 7, 1986, Albany, N.Y.

Elwood Green, April 11, 1985, Niagara Falls, N.Y.

Louis Grumet, March 24, 1986, Albany, N.Y.

Larry Hackman, May 28, 1986, Albany, N.Y.

Gloria Halbritter, April 21, 1985, Syracuse, N.Y.

Ray Halbritter, October 20, 1984, Rome, N.Y.

George Hamell, June 9, 1986, Albany, N.Y.

John Hennessy, May 15, 1986, Buffalo, N.Y.

William Hennessy, July 9, 1986, Albany, N.Y.

Selby Hickey, May 6, 1985, Old Westbury, N.Y.

Norbert Hill, Sr., October 17, 1978, July 28, 1982, Oneida, Wis.

Rick Hill, September 8, 1982, Syracuse, N.Y.; May 28, 1984, Six Nations Reserve.

Maurice Hinchey, February 25, 1986, Albany, N.Y.

John Hudacs, March 10, 1986, Albany, N.Y.

Paul Huey, July 10, 1986, Peebles Island, N.Y.

Leigh Hunt, May 7, 1986, Albany, N.Y.

T. Norman Hurd, February 26, 1986, Albany, N.Y.

Andrew Jackson, March 21, 1986, Buffalo, N.Y.

Roberta Jamieson, May 28–29, 1984, Six Nations Reserve.

G. Pete Jemison, May 15, 1986, Ganondagan State Park.

Jeanne Marie Jemison, August 26, 1977, Herndon, Va.; August 23, 1978, Tyson's Corners, Va.; May 2–4, 1978, New Paltz, N.Y.; July 14–17, 1982, September 8, 1984, March 21, September 13, 1986, Cattaraugus Indian Reservation.

Samuel Johnson, April 18, 1986, Albany, N.Y.

Nancy Johnson, May 27, 1986, Buffalo, N.Y.

Karen Kalaijian, May 7, 1986, Albany, N.Y.

John W. Kalas, June 12, 1985, Oneonta, N.Y.

Norma Kennedy, May 4–5, 1977, New Paltz, N.Y.

Donald Ketchum, May 15, 1986, Buffalo, N.Y.

Robert Kerker, May 20, 1986, Albany, N.Y.

Ben A. Kroup, May 20, 1986, Peebles Island, N.Y.

Jayantha Kumar, May 7, 1986, Albany, N.Y.

Chief Ron La France, October 30-November 1, 1983, New Paltz, N.Y.

Arthur Lazarus, Jr., July 17, 1982, Buffalo, N.Y.

Anna Lewis, June 10, 1983, Albany, N.Y.

F. Henry Lickers, June 10–13, 1986, Oneonta, N.Y.

Phil Lord, February 20, 1987, Albany, N.Y.

Chief Oren Lyons, September 8, 1984, Syracuse, N.Y.; May 6, 1985, Queens, N.Y.

Neil MacCormick, May 8, 1986, Albany, N.Y.

Gordie McLester, October 17–22, 1978, June 24, 1983, July 22–24, 1986, Oneida, Wis.

Kallen Martin, February 20, 1987, Albany, N.Y.

John Mladinov, February 26, 1986, Albany, N.Y.

Carol Moses, September 28, 1984, Allegany Indian Reservation.

Chief Edison Mt. Pleasant, October 20–21, 1984, Rome, N.Y.; November 30, 1984, Tuscarora Indian Reservation.

Ruth Mt. Pleasant, November 30, 1984, Tuscarora Indian Reservation.

Elma Patterson, November 30, 1984, Lewiston, N.Y.; April 15, 1972, New Paltz, N.Y.

Genevieve Plummer, July 28, 1977, Allegany Indian Reservation.

Tom Porter, May 5–6, 1982, New Paltz, N.Y.

Chief Irving Powless, Jr., October 21, 1984, Rome, N.Y.

Chief Irving Powless, Sr., May 15, 1979, Onondaga Indian Reservation.

Jess Present, March 12, 1986, Albany, N.Y.

Telisport Putsavage, May 8, 1986, Albany, N.Y.

Keith Reitz, May 2–4, 1982, New Paltz, N.Y.; July 21, 1982, June 8, 1984, Rochester, N.Y.

Michael Reynolds, June 12, 1985, Oneonta, N.Y.

Dave Richmond, March 22, 1985, Washington, Conn.

Howard Rowley, March 17, 1986, Rochester, N.Y.

Raymond Schuler, June 3, 1986, Albany, N.Y.

Pauline Seneca, June 4, 1978, July 15–17, 1982, September 13, 1986, Cattaraugus Indian Reservation.

George Shattuck, August 25, 1983, Syracuse, N.Y.

Chief Leon Shenandoah (Tadodaho), May 15, 1979, Onondaga Indian Reservation.

Leo Soucy, March 4, 1986, Albany, N.Y.

Cliff Spieler, December 10, 1984, Buchanan, N.Y.

Chief Corbett Sundown, May 22, 1980, Tonawanda Indian Reservation.

Chief Jake Swamp, April 25, 1985, New Paltz, N.Y.; May 6, 1985, Old Westbury, N.Y.

Philip Tarbell, December 7, 1981, New Paltz, N.Y.

Jacob Thompson, April 15, 1972, May 6, 1976, New Paltz, N.Y.

Daniel Walsh, March 13, 1986, Albany, N.Y.

Martin Wasser, April 11, 1986, New York, N.Y.

Lincoln White, July 1, 1982, Washington, D.C.

Duffy Wilson, April 11, 1985, Niagara Falls, N.Y.

Melvin Zimmer, March 11, 1986, Albany, N.Y.

Government Publications

American Indian Policy Review Commission. *Final Report.* 2 vols. Washington, D.C.: U.S.G.P.O., 1977.

American Indian Policy Review Commission. *Final Report: Report on Trust Responsibilities and the Federal Indian Relationship, Including Treaty Review* (Task Force 1). Washington, D.C.: U.S.G.P.O., 1976.

American Indian Policy Review Commission. *Final Report: Report on Tribal Government* (Task Force 2). Washington, D.C.: U.S.G.P.O., 1976.

American Indian Policy Review Commission. *Final Report: Report on*

Federal Administration and Structure of Indian Affairs (Task Force 3). Washington, D.C.: U.S.G.P.O., 1976.

American Indian Policy Review Commission. *Final Report: Report on Federal, State, and Tribal Jurisdiction* (Task Force 4). Washington, D.C.: U.S.G.P.O., 1976.

American Indian Policy Review Commission. *Final Report: Report on Indian Education* (Task Force 5). Washington, D.C.: U.S.G.P.O., 1976.

American Indian Policy Review Commission. *Final Report: Report on Indian Health* (Task Force 6). Washington, D.C.: U.S.G.P.O., 1976.

American Indian Policy Review Commission. *Final Report: Report on Reservation and Resource Development and Protection* (Task Force 7). Washington, D.C.: U.S.G.P.O., 1976.

American Indian Policy Review Commission. *Final Report: Report on Urban and Rural Non-Reservation Indians* (Task Force 8). Washington, D.C.: U.S.G.P.O., 1976.

American Indian Policy Review Commission. *Final Report: Law Consolidation, Revision, and Codification* (Task Force 9). 2 vols. Washington, D.C.: U.S.G.P.O., 1977.

American Indian Policy Review Commission. *Final Report: Report on Terminated and Nonfederally Recognized Indians* (Task Force 10). Washington, D.C.: U.S.G.P.O., 1976.

American Indian Policy Review Commission. *Final Report: Report on Alcohol and Drug Abuse* (Task Force 11). Washington, D.C.: U.S.G.P.O., 1976.

Cohen, Felix S. *Handbook of Federal Indian Law.* Washington, D.C.: U.S. Department of the Interior, 1942; Reprint, Albuquerque, N.M.: University of New Mexico Press, 1971.

Donaldson, Thomas, comp. *The Six Nations of New York.* Special Supplement Prepared by the Interior Department for the Eleventh Census, 1890. Washington, D.C., 1892.

Hough, Franklin B., comp. *Proceedings of the Commissioners of Indian Affairs Appointed by Law for the Extinguishment of Indian Titles in the State of New York.* 2 vols. Albany, N.Y.: Munsell, 1861.

Kappler, Charles J., comp. *Indian Affairs: Laws and Treaties.* 5 vols. Washington, D.C. 1904–1941. (Vol. 2 has been reprinted as *Indian Treaties, 1778–1883,* New York, 1972.)

Mohawk, John. *The War Against the Seneca: The French Expedition of 1687.* Victor, N.Y.: Ganondagan State Historic Site, New York State Office of Parks, Recreation, and Historic Preservation, 1986.

New York *Red Book*, 1969–1970–1985–1986. Albany, N.Y.: Williams Press, 1970–1986.

New York State Board of Charities. *Annual Reports, 1868–1929*. Albany, N.Y., 1868–1929.

New York State Board of Regents. *Official Minutes, 1968–1983*. Albany, N.Y., 1968–1983.

New York State Board of Social Welfare. *Annual Reports, 1929–1936*. Albany, N.Y., 1929–1936.

New York State Council on State Priorities. *Report to the Governor*. Albany, N.Y., 1982.

New York State Department of Civil Service. *Ethnic Survey of New York State Agency Work Force, 1982*. Albany, N.Y., 1985.

New York State Department of Commerce. *Annual Report, 1981*. Albany, N.Y., 1981.

New York State Department of Commerce. *Directory of Minority and Women-Owned Business Enterprises*. Albany, N.Y., 1986.

New York State Department of Education. *Annual Reports, 1970–1985*. Albany, N.Y., 1971–1986.

New York State Department of Education. Bureau of Curriculum Development. *Social Studies 7 and 8: United States and New York History. Field Test Edition for Discussion Only 1986*. Albany, N.Y., 1986.

New York State Department of Education. Native American Indian Education Unit. *Indian Education in New York State*. Albany, N.Y., undated.

New York State Department of Environmental Conservation. *Annual Reports, 1974–1985*. Albany, N.Y., 1975–1986.

New York State Department of Health. *Annual Reports, 1970–1985*. Albany, N.Y., 1971–1986.

New York State Department of Law. *Opinions of the Attorney General, 1970–1985*. Albany, N.Y., 1971–1986.

New York State Department of Public Instruction. *Annual Reports, 1854–1904*. Albany, N.Y., 1855–1905.

New York State Department of State. *Annual Report, 1984*. Albany, N.Y., 1985.

New York State Department of Social Services. *Annual Reports, 1970–1985*. Albany, N.Y., 1971–1986.

New York State Department of State. *Annual Reports, 1980–1985*. Albany, N.Y., 1981–1986.

New York State Department of Social Welfare. *Manual of Indian Affairs and Procedures (Including Historical Data)*. Albany, N.Y., 1954.

New York State Department of Social Welfare. *Annual Reports, 1936–1945.* Albany, N.Y., 1937–1946.

New York State Division of Alcoholism and Alcohol Abuse. *Five Year Comprehensive Plan for Alcoholism Services in New York State 1984–1989: Focus on Research, Planning and Professional Development Final 1987 Update.* Albany, N.Y., 1986.

New York State Division of the Budget (Robert Kerker). *The Executive Budget in New York State: A Half Century Perspective.* Albany, N.Y., 1981.

New York State Division of State Police. *New York State Police Manual, 1986.* Albany, N.Y., 1986.

New York State Governor. *Executive Budget, 1969–1970–1986–1987.* Albany, N.Y., 1969–1986.

New York State Governor. Mario M. Cuomo. *Messages to the Legislature, 1983–1987.* Albany, N.Y., 1983–1987.

New York State Governor. Mario M. Cuomo. *Three-Year Report.* Albany, N.Y., 1986.

New York State Governor. *Public Papers of George Clinton.* Hugh Hastings and J. A. Holden, eds. Albany, N.Y., 1899–1914.

New York State Governor. *Public Papers of Thomas E. Dewey.* 12 vols. Albany, N.Y., 1944–1957.

New York State Governor. *Public Papers of Hugh L. Carey.* New York, N.Y., 1982.

New York State Governor. *Public Papers of Averell Harriman.* 4 vols. Albany, N.Y., 1958–1961.

New York State Governor. *Public Papers of Nelson A. Rockefeller.* 13 vols. Albany, N.Y., 1959–1972.

New York State Governor. *Public Papers of Malcolm Wilson.* Albany, N.Y., 1977.

New York State Interdepartmental Committee on Indian Affairs. *Annual Reports, 1960–1975.* Albany, N.Y., 1961–1976.

New York State Legislature. *Classification of Appropriations, 1970–1976.* Albany, N.Y., 1970–1986.

New York State Legislature. *Report to the Legislature of the State of New York Concerning the Condition of the Onondaga Indians.* Albany, N.Y., 1883.

New York State Legislature. *Assembly Doc. No. 51: Report of the Special Committee to Investigate the Indian Problem* (Whipple Report). Albany, N.Y., 1889.

New York State Legislature. *Assembly Doc. No. 40: Report of the Special Committee to Investigate and Ascertain the Extent of the Powers Possessed by the State to Regulate and Control the Affairs and Property Rights of the Indians.* Albany, N.Y., 1906.

New York State Legislature. Joint Legislative Committee on Indian Affairs. *Public Hearings, 1943.* Buffalo, N.Y., 1943.

New York State Legislature. Joint Legislative Committee on Indian Affairs. *Reports, 194–1962.* Albany, N.Y., 1944–1962.

New York State Legislature. Joint Legislative Committee on Indian Affairs. *Minutes of Public Hearing. . . November 9, 1963 at Tonawanda Indian (Akron, N.Y.) Community House.* Albany, N.Y., 1963.

New York State Legislature. Subcommittee on Indian Affairs of the Committee on Governmental Operations. Public Hearings, 1970–1971. Albany, N.Y., 1970–1971.

New York State Legislature. Subcommittee on Indian Affairs of the Committee on Governmental Operations. *Final Report.* Albany, N.Y., 1971.

New York State Legislature. Assembly Standing Committee on Governmental Operations. *Annual Reports, 1973–1980.* Albany, N.Y., 1973–1980.

New York State Legislative Commission on State-Local Relations. *New York's Police Service: Perspectives on the Issues.* Albany, N.Y., 1985.

New York State Museum and Science Service. *Annual Reports, 1957–1966.* Albany, 1958–1967.

New York State Office for the Aging. *Annual Report, 1983–1984.* Albany, N.Y., 1985.

New York State Office of Mental Health. *Five Year Comprehensive Plan for Mental Health Services, 1985–1990.* Albany, N.Y., 1986.

New York State Office of Parks, Recreation, and Historic Preservation. Bureau of Historic Sites. *Art from Ganondagan: "The Village of Peace."* Albany, N.Y., 1986.

New York State Office of Parks, Recreation, and Historic Preservation. Bureau of Historic Sites. *Granary Trail at Fort Hill.* Albany, N.Y., 1986.

New York State Office of Parks, Recreation, and Historic Preservation. *People, Resources, Recreation, 1983: New York Statewide Comprehensive Recreation Plan, March 1983.* Albany, N.Y., 1983.

New York State Office of Parks, Recreation, and Historic Preservation. Bureau of Historic Sites (Ben A. Kroup). *Master Plan for Gannagaro State Historic Site.* Albany, N.Y., 1985.

New York State Office of Parks, Recreation, and Historic Preservation. Bureau of Historic Sites. *Ethnological Trail Boughton Hill.* Albany, N.Y., 1986.

New York State Office of Planning Services. *Final Report of the Pilot Planning Program for the Indians in New York State.* (Indian Needs Planning Project.) Albany, N.Y., 1974.

New York (State) Power Authority. *Annual Reports, 1952–1986.* New York, N.Y., 1952–1986.

New York (State) Power Authority. *Robert Moses' Open Letter to the Tuscarora Indian Nation, February 11, 1958. New York, N.Y., 1958.*

New York State Regents of the University of the State of New York. Journal, 1970–1982. Albany, N.Y., 1971–1983.

New York State Regents of the University of the State of New York. *Position Paper No. 22: Native American Education.* Albany, N.Y., 1975.

(New York) State University of New York. *College Bulletins, 1975–1986.*

1. SUNY/Albany.
2. SUNY/Binghamton.
3. SUNY College at Brockport.
4. SUNY/Buffalo.
5. SUNY College at Buffalo.
6. SUNY College at Cortland.
7. SUNY College at Fredonia.
8. SUNY College at Geneseo.
9. SUNY College at New Paltz.
10. SUNY College at Oneonta.
11. SUNY College at Oswego.
12. SUNY College at Plattsburgh.
13. SUNY College at Potsdam.
14. SUNY College at Purchase.
15. SUNY/Stony Brook.

(New York) State University of New York (Michael Reynolds). *Report on Native American Studies.* Albany, N.Y.: SUNY Office of Academic Programs, Policy and Planning, January, 1984.

Surles, Kathryn B. *Update on the Health Status of American Indians in North Carolina: A Special Report Prepared for North Carolina Com-*

mission of Indian Affairs, June, 1985. Raleigh, N.C.: North Carolina State Center for Health Statistics, 1985.

Taylor, Theodore W. *The States and Their Indian Citizens.* Washington, D.C.: U.S. Bureau of Indian Affairs, 1972.

Tyler, S. Lyman. *A History of Indian Policy.* Washington, D.C.: U.S. Department of the Interior, 1973.

Thomas Indian School (and Orphan Asylum). *Annual Reports, 1856–1956.* Iroquois, N.Y., 1857–1957.

United States Commission on Civil Rights. *Indian Tribes: A Continuing Quest for Survival.* Washington, D.C., 1981.

United States Congress. *Congressional Record, 1970–1986.*

United States Congress. House Committee on Indian Affairs. *Hearings on H.R. 9720: Indians of New York.* 71st Congress, 2d session. Washington, D.C.: U.S.G.P.O., 1930.

United States Congress. House. *Conference Report No. 1821: Seneca Indian Nation.* Washington, D.C.: U.S.G.P.O., 1964.

United States Congress. House Committee on Interior and Insular Affairs. *Report No. 1128: Authorizing Acquisition of and Payment for Flowage Easement and Rights-of-Way within Allegany Indian Reservation.* Washington, D.C., 1964.

United States Congress. House Committee on Interior and Insular Affairs. *Hearings on H.R. 6631: Settlement of the Cayuga Indian Nation Land Claims in the State of New York.* March 3, 1980. 96th Congress, 2d session. Washington, D.C., 1980.

United States Congress. *House Document No. 300: Hearings: Allegheny River, N.Y. and Pennsylvania, Allegheny Reservoir.* 76th Congress, 1st session. Washington, D.C.: U.S.G.P.O., 1939.

United States Congress. House Subcommittee on Indian Affairs. *Hearings on H.R. 1794, H.R. 3343 and H.R. 7354: Kinzua Dam (Seneca Indian Relocation).* 88th Congress, 1st session. Washington, D.C.: U.S.G.P.O., 1964.

United States Congress. House Committee on Public Lands. *Report No. 2355: Conferring Jurisdiction on State of New York with Respect to Offenses Committed on Indian Reservations within Such State.* Washington, D.C., 1948.

United States Congress. House Committee on Public Lands. *Report No. 2720: Conferring Jurisdiction on Court of New York with Respect to Civil Actions between Indians or to Which Indians Are Parties.* Washington, D.C., 1950.

United States Senate. Committee on Indian Affairs. *Hearings on S. 5302: Fish and Game within the Allegany, Cattaraugus, and Oil Spring Reservations.* 72nd Congress, 2d session. Washington, D.C., 1933.

United States Congress. Senate Committee on Interior and Insular Affairs. *Report No. 969: Authorizing Acquisition and Payment for Flowage Easement and Rights-of-Way Over Lands within Allegany Indian Reservation. . .* Washington, D.C., 1964.

United States Senate. Subcommittee of the Committee on Indian Affairs. *Hearings on S. Res. 79: Survey of Conditions of the Indians in the United States.* 43 parts. 70th–76th Congress. Washington, D.C., 1928–1943.

United States Congress. Senate Subcommittee of the Committee on Interior and Insular Affairs. *Hearings on S. 1683, S. 1686, S. 1687: New York Indians.* Washington, D.C., 1948.

United States Congress. Senate Committee on Interior and Insular Affairs. *Report No. 1139: Commuting Annuities, Seneca and Six Nations of New York.* Washington, D.C., 1948.

United States Congress. Senate Committee on Interior and Insular Affairs. *Report No. 1489: Conferring Jurisdiction on Courts of New York over Offenses Committed by Indians.* Washington, D.C., 1948.

United States Congress. Senate Committee on Interior and Insular Affairs. *Report No. 1836: Conferring Jurisdiction on Courts of New York with Respect to Civil Actions between Indians or to Which Indians Are Parties.* Washington, D.C., 1950.

United States Congress. Senate Subcommittee on Indian Affairs of the Committee on Interior and Insular Affairs. *Hearings on S. 1836 and H.R. 1794: Kinzua Dam (Seneca Indian Relocation).* 88th Congress, 2d session. Washington, D.C.: U.S.G.P.O., 1964.

United States Congress. Senate Select Committee on Indian Affairs. *Hearings on S. 2829: Proposed Settlement of Maine Indian Land Claims, July 1–2, 1980.* 2 vols. 96th Congress, 2d session. Washington, D.C.: U.S.G.P.O., 1980.

United States Congress. Senate Select Committee on Indian Affairs. *Hearings on S. 1181, S. 1722 and S. 2832: Jurisdiction on Indian Reservations, March 17–19, 1980.* Washington, D.C.; U.S.G.P.O., 1980.

United States Congress. Senate Select Committee on Indian Affairs. *Hearings on S. 2084: Ancient Indian Land Claims.* 97th Congress, 2d session. Washington, D.C., 1982.

United States Congress. Senate Special Subcommittee on Indian Education. *Report No. 501: Indian Education: A National Tragedy—A Na-*

tional Challenge. 91st Congress, 1st session. Washington, D.C.: U.S.G.P.O., 1969.

United States Department of Commerce. Bureau of the Census. *U.S. Census of Population: 1970. Subject Report: American Indians.* Washington, D.C.: U.S.G.P.O., 1973.

United States Department of Commerce. Bureau of the Census. *1980 Census of Population, Supplementary Reports: Race of the Population by States, 1980.* Washington, D.C.: U.S.G.P.O., 1981.

United States Department of Commerce. Bureau of the Census. *Subject Reports: American Indians. . . 1980.* Washington, D.C.: U.S.G.P.O., 1985.

United States Department of Health, Education and Welfare. Indian Health Service. *The Indian Health Program.* Washington, D.C.: U.S.G.P.O., 1978.

United States Department of Health, Education and Welfare. Indian Health Service. *Indian Health Program, 1955–1980.* Washington, D.C.; U.S.G.P.O., 1980.

United States Department of the Interior. *Annual Report of the Commissioner of Indian Affairs, 1941–1973.* Washington, D.C.: U.S.G.P.O., 1941–1973.

United States Department of the Interior. Secretary of the Interior. *Annual Reports, 1940–1986.* Washington, D.C.: U.S.G.P.O., 1940–1986.

United States Indian Claims Commission (August 13, 1946–September 30, 1978). *Final Report.* Washington, D.C.: U.S.G.P.O., 1979.

Unpublished Reports, Agency Memoranda, Speeches or Tribal Documents

Agreement Between the Seneca Nation of Indians and the People of the State of New York for the Southern Tier Expressway, Cattaraugus County, June 28, 1976.

Ambach, Gordon M. "The Education of Indians." Speech before the Third Annual Conference on Indian Education. January 14, 1971, Massena, N.Y.

Birdseye, Ruth A. *Indian Education in New York State, 1846–1953–1954.* Albany, N.Y.: New York State Department of Education, 1954.

Hauptman, Laurence M. "Formulating American Indian Policies in New York State, 1970–1986: A Public Policy Study." Study prepared for the

Nelson A. Rockefeller Institute of Government, Albany, N.Y., and submitted to the Governor's Office and American Indian Nations, September 1986.

John, Randy. *Annual Implementation Plan (Older Americans Act) for the Seneca Nation of Indians Area Office for the Aging, October 1, 1986-September 20, 1987 (III–B), January 1, 1986 to December 31, 1986 (III–C).*

Kalaijian, Karen. *Indian Health Services in Western New York State: Past, Present and Future.* Albany: New York State Department of Health, 1976.

Kaplan, D. W. (in cooperation with the Seneca Nation of Indians). *Seneca Nation of Indians: Indian Health Proposal,* March 1, 1975. Boston, 1975.

Lewis, Anna M. and Lillian T. Samuelson. *"We Shall Live Again": A Positive Approach for Survival of a People, Proposal for Indian Education in New York State, March 1971.* Albany, N.Y.: New York State Department of Education, 1971.

New York State Department of Education. Division of Historical and Anthropological Services. *Draft Proposal: Unmarked Human Skeletal Remains, January 5, 1987.*

New York State Legislature. (Everett Report) Assembly. *Report of the Indian Commission to Investigate the Status of the American Indian Residing in the State of New York. . . March 17, 1922* (unpublished).

Martin, Kallen M. "3rd Draft: a Statewide Native American Alcoholism Needs Assessment Study," September 14, 1987. New York State Division of Alcoholism and Alcohol Abuse.

Memorandum of Understanding Between New York State Department of Transportation and Seneca Nation of Indians, July 28, 1976 (unpublished).

Selikoff, Irving, E. Cuyler Hammond, and Stephen Levin. *Environmental Contaminants and the Health of the People of the St. Regis Reserve: A Report Submitted to the Minister of Health and Welfare of Canada.* 2 vols. New York: Mount Sinai School of Medicine, 1984–1985.

Seneca Nation of Indians. Council Minutes, June 28, 1976. (MSS in author's possession.)

Seneca Nation of Indians. Area Office for the Aging. *Four Year Plan for Older Americans Act and New York State Community Services for the Elderly Programs, April 1, 1984-March 31, 1988.*

Starna, William A. "Indian Land Claims in New York State: A Policy

Analysis." Study prepared for the Nelson A. Rockefeller Institute of Government, Albany, N.Y., and submitted to the Governor's Office and American Indian Nations, August 1987. [Published by Rockefeller Institute, Fall, 1987].

Stone, Ward. "Progress Report RAGTW Project No.: W–4, April 1, 1985-March 31, 1986." New York State Department of Environmental Conservation, Bureau of Wildlife Pathology.

Court Cases

Federal Power Commission v. Tuscarora Indian Nation; Power Authority of (the State of) New York v. Tuscarora Nation. 80 S.Ct. 543 (1960).

County of Oneida, New York, et al. v. Oneida Indian Nation of New York State et al.; New York v. Oneida Indian Nation of New York State, et al. U.S. Sup.Ct.—83–1065; 83–1240—opinion (March 4, 1985).

Oneida Indian Nation of New York, et al. v. County of Oneida, New York, et al. 94 S.Ct. 772 (1974).

People v. Redeye. 358 NYS 2d 632 (1974).

St. Regis Tribe v. State of New York. 4 Misc. 2d 110 (1956); 168 NYS 2d 894 (1957); 177 NYS 2d 289 (1958).

Seneca Nation of Indians v. Wilbur M. Brucker, et al. 360 U.S. 909 (1959); 262 F.2d 27 (1958); 162 F.Supp. 580 (1958).

United States v. Boylan. 265 F. 165 (1920).

Newspapers and Periodicals

Akwesasne Notes.
Albany [N.Y.] Knickerbocker News.
Albany [N.Y.] Times-Union.
American Indian Journal.
Batavia [N.Y.] News.
Buffalo [N.Y.] Courier-Express.
Buffalo [N.Y.] Evening News.
Bradford [Pa.] Era.
Capital Region.
The Conservationist (issue, January-February, 1976: *The Iroquois of New York — Their Past and Present*).
Cornwall (Cornwall, Ont.) Standard-Freeholder.

Empire State Reports.
Indian Historian.
Indian Time.
Indian Truth.
Inside Education.
Kingston [N.Y.] Daily Freeman.
Lake Placid [N.Y.] News.
Massena [N.Y.] Observer.
Native American Rights Fund Announcements.
Newsday.
Newsweek.
New York Daily News.
New York State Education (April 1971 issue devoted to American Indian education.
New York Teacher.
New York Times.
Niagara Falls [N.Y.] Gazette.
Northeast Indian Quarterly (formerly *Indian Studies*).
Plattsburgh [N.Y.] Press-Republican.
O-HI-YOH-NOH (Allegany Indian Reservation).
Olean [N.Y.] Times Herald.
Poughkeepsie [N.Y.] Journal.
Rochester [N.Y.] Democrat and Chronicle.
Rochester [N.Y.] Times-Union.
Salamanca [N.Y.] Republican-Press. [Salamanca-Press]
Si Wong Geh (Cattaraugus Indian Reservation).
Syracuse [N.Y.] Herald-American.
Syracuse [N.Y.] Herald-Journal.
Syracuse [N.Y.] Post-Standard.
Tekawennake (Six Nations Reserve, Ohsweken, Ont.).
Time.
Turtle Quarterly.
Utica [N.Y.] Daily Press.
Washington [D.C.] Post.
Wassaja (San Francisco).
Watertown [N.Y.] Daily Times.

Books

Abbot, Frank. *Government Policy and Higher Education: A Study of the Regents of the University of the State of New York, 1784–1949.* Ithaca, N.Y.: Cornell University Press, 1958.

Abrams, George. *The Seneca People.* Phoenix, Ariz.: Indian Tribal Series, 1976.

Akwesasne Notes. Basic Call to Consciousness. Rooseveltown, N.Y.: Akwesasne Notes, 1978.

Akwesasne Notes. BIA: I'm Not Your Indian Anymore. Rooseveltown, N.Y.: Akwesasne Notes, 1974.

Akwesasne Notes, comp. *Voices from Wounded Knee: The People Are Standing Up.* Rooseveltown, N.Y.: Akwesasne Notes, 1974.

American Indian Studies Center, UCLA. *New Directions in Federal Indian Policy: A Review of the American Indian Policy Review Commission.* Los Angeles, Calif.: American Indian Studies Center, UCLA, 1979.

Auletta, Ken. *The Streets Were Paved with Gold.* New York: Random House, 1979.

Austin, Alberta, ed. & comp. *NE HO NIYO DE: No, That's What It was Like.* Irving, N.Y.: Seneca Nation of Indians Curriculum Development Project, 1984.

Axtell, James. *The Invasion Within: The Contest of Cultures in Colonial North America.* New York: Oxford University Press, 1985.

Balhl, Roy W. *The New York State Economy: 1960–1978 and the Outlook.* Syracuse, N.Y.: Metropolitan Studies Program. Syracuse University, 1979.

Barsh, Russel L., and James Y. Henderson. *The Road: Indian Tribes and Political Liberty.* Berkeley, Calif.: University of California Press, 1980.

Beauchamp, William M. *A History of the New York Iroquois.* New York State Museum Bulletin 78. Albany, N.Y.: University of the State of New York, 1905.

Bee, Robert L. *The Politics of American Indian Policy.* Cambridge, Mass.: Schenkan Publishing Co., 1982.

Benjamin, Gerald, and Robert H. Connery. *Rockefeller of New York: Executive Power in the Statehouse.* Ithaca, N.Y.: Cornell University Press, 1979.

Benjamin, Gerald, and T. Norman Hurd, eds. *Making Experience Count: Managing Modern New York in the Carey Era.* Albany, N.Y.: Nelson A. Rockefeller Institute of Government, 1985.

Benjamin, Gerald, and T. Norman Hurd, eds. *Rockefeller in Retrospect: The Governor's New York Legacy.* Albany, N.Y.: Nelson A. Rockefeller Institute of Government, 1984.

Berkhofer, Robert F., Jr. *The White Man's Indian.* New York: Alfred A. Knopf, 1978.

Berle, Peter A. A. *Does the Citizen Stand a Chance? Politics of a State Legislature: New York.* Woodbury, N.Y.: Barron's Educational Series, 1974.

Blanchard, David S. *Seven Generations.* Caughnawaga: Kanien'kehaka Raotitiohkwa Press, 1980.

Bonvillain, Nancy, ed. *Studies on Iroquoian Culture.* Occasional Publications in Northeastern Anthropology, No. 6. Rindge, N.H.: *Man in the Northeast,* 1980.

Brodeur, Paul. *Restitution: The Land Claims of the Mashpee, Passamaquoddy and Penobscot Indians of New England.* Boston, Mass.: Northeastern University Press, 1985.

Brasser, Ted J. C. *Riding on the Frontier's Crest: Mahican Indian Culture and Culture Change.* Ottawa, Ont.: National Museum of Man, Ethnology Division. Mercury Series No. 13, 1974.

Burnette, Robert, and John Koster. *The Road to Wounded Knee.* New York: Bantam, 1974.

Cadwalader, Sandra L., and Vine Deloria, Jr. *The Aggressions of Civilization: Federal Indian Policy Since the 1880s.* Philadelphia, Pa.: Temple University Press, 1984.

Caldwell, Lynton K. *The Government and Administration of New York.* New York: Thomas Y. Crowell, 1954.

Caro, Robert A. *The Power Broker: Robert Moses and the Fall of New York.* New York: Alfred A. Knopf, 1974.

The Case of the Seneca Nation in the State of New York. Printed for the Information of the Society of Friends (Hicksite), 1840 Also including A Further Illustration of the Case of the Seneca Indians in the State of New York, 1841 and A Brief Statement of the Rights of the Seneca Indians in the State of New York to Their Lands in That State. Stanfordville, N.Y.: Earl Coleman Publisher, 1979.

Chazenoff, William. *Joseph Ellicott and the Holland Land Company: The Opening Up of Western New York.* Syracuse, N.Y.: Syracuse University Press, 1970.

Colby, Peter W., ed. *New York State Today: Politics, Government, Public Policy.* Albany, N.Y.: SUNY Press, 1985.

Congdon, Charles E. *Allegany Oxbow: A History of Allegany State Park and the Allegany Reserve of the Seneca Nation.* Little Valley, N.Y.: Straight Publishing, 1967.

Connery, Robert H., and Gerald Benjamin, eds. *Governing New York State: The Rockefeller Years.* New York: *Proceedings* of the Academy of Political Science, vol. 31, 1974.

Cuomo, Mario M. *Diaries of Mario M. Cuomo.* New York: Random House, 1984.

Cuomo, Mario. *Forest Hills Diary: The Crisis of Low Income Housing.* New York: Random House, 1974.

Deardorff, Merle. *The Religion of Handsome Lake: Its Origin and Development.* Bureau of American Ethnology. Bulletin 149. Washington, D.C.: U.S.G.P.O., 1951.

Deloria, Vine, Jr., ed. *American Indian Policy in the Twentieth Century.* Norman, Okla.: University of Oklahoma Press, 1985.

Deloria, Vine, Jr., and Clifford M. Lytle. *American Indians, American Justice.* Austin, Tex.: University of Texas Press, 1983.

Deloria, Vine, Jr. *Custer Died for Your Sins: An Indian Manifesto.* New York: Macmillan, 1969.

Deloria, Vine, Jr. *God Is Red.* New York: Dell, 1973.

Deloria, Vine, Jr., and Clifford M. Lytle. *The Nations Within: The Past and Future of American Indian Sovereignty.* New York: Pantheon, 1984.

Deloria, Vine, Jr. *We Talk, You Listen: New Tribes, New Turf.* New York: Macmillan, 1970.

Diamond, Sigmund, ed. *Modernizing State Government: The New York Constitutional Convention of 1967.* New York: The Academy of Political Science, January 1967.

Doty, William J., et al., eds. *The Historic Annals of Southwestern New York.* New York: Lewis Historical Publishing Co., 1940.

Ebbot, Elizabeth, and Judith Rosenblatt, eds. *Indians in Minnesota.* 4th ed. Minneapolis, Minn.: University of Minnesota, 1985.

Ellis, David M. *New York: State and City.* Ithaca, N.Y.: Cornell University Press, 1979.

Evans, Paul D. *The Holland Land Company.* Buffalo, N.Y.: Buffalo Historical Society, 1924.

Fenton, William N., ed. *Symposium on Local Diversity in Iroquois Culture*. Bureau of American Ethnology. Bulletin 149. Washington, D.C.: U.S.G.P.O., 1951.

Fleischmann Report on the Quality, Cost and Financing of Elementary and Secondary Education in New York State. New York: Viking Press, 1973.

Forbes, Jack D. *Native Americans and Nixon: Presidential Politics and Minority Self-Determination, 1969–1972*. Los Angeles, Calif.: UCLA American Indian Studies Center, 1981.

Foster, Michael K., Jack Campisi, and Marianne Mithun, eds. *Extending the Rafters: Interdisciplinary Approaches to Iroquoian Studies*. Albany, N.Y.: SUNY Press, 1984.

Fuchs, Estelle, and Robert J. Havighurst. *To Live on This Earth: American Indian Education*. Garden City, N.Y.: Doubleday, 1972.

Getches, David H., et al. *Cases and Materials on Federal Indian Law*. St. Paul, Minn.: West Publishing Co., 1979.

Gervasi, Frank. *The Real Rockefeller*. New York: Atheneum, 1964.

Gibson, Arrel Morgan, ed. *Between Two Worlds: The Survival of Twentieth Century Indians*. Oklahoma City, Okla.: Oklahoma Historical Society, 1986.

Graham, Frank, Jr. *The Adirondack Park: A Political History*. New York: Alfred A. Knopf, Inc., 1978.

Graymont, Barbara, ed. *Fighting Tuscarora: The Autobiography of Chief Clinton Rickard*. Syracuse, N.Y.: Syracuse University Press, 1973.

Graymont, Barbara. *The Iroquois in the American Revolution*. Syracuse, N.Y.: Syracuse University Press, 1972.

Hagan, William T. *American Indians*. 2nd ed. Chicago, Ill.: University of Chicago Press, 1979.

Hale, Horatio. *The Iroquois Book of Rites*. ed. by William N. Fenton. Toronto, Ont.: University of Toronto Press, 1963.

Hammil, Jan, and Larry J. Zimmerman, eds. *Reburial of Human Skeletal Remains: Perspectives from Lakota Holy Men and Elders*. Indianapolis, Ind.: American Indians Against Desecration, 1983.

Hauptman, Laurence M. *The Iroquois and the New Deal*. Syracuse, N.Y.: Syracuse University Press, 1981.

Hauptman, Laurence M. *The Iroquois Struggle for Survival: World War II to Red Power*. Syracuse, N.Y.: Syracuse University Press, 1986.

Hauptman, Laurence M., and Jack Campisi, eds. *An Ethnohistorical Exploration of the Indians of Hudson's River*. Ottawa, Ont.: National

Museum of Man, Canadian Ethnology Service Mercury Series, Paper No. 39, 1978.

Heth, Charlotte, and Suzanne Guyette. *Issues for the Future of American Indian Studies.* Los Angeles, Calif.: UCLA American Indian Studies Center, 1986.

Hertzberg, Hazel W. *The Great Tree and the Longhouse: The Culture of the Iroquois.* New York: Macmillan Co. in cooperation with the American Anthropological Association, 1966.

Hertzberg, Hazel W. *The Search for an American Indian Identity: Modern Pan-American Movements.* Syracuse, N.Y.: Syracuse University Press, 1973.

Hevesi, Alan G. *Legislative Politics in New York State: A Comparative Analysis.* New York: Praeger Publishers, 1975.

Hewitt, J. N. B. *Iroquoian Cosmology.* Part I, 21st Annual Report of the Bureau of American Ethnology. Washington, D.C.: U.S.G.P.O., 1928.

Hoxie, Frederick E. *A Final Promise: The Campaign to Assimilate the Indians, 1880–1920.* Lincoln, Neb.: University of Nebraska Press, 1984.

Ismaelillo and Robin Wright, eds. *Native Peoples in Struggle: Cases from the Fourth Russell Tribunal and Other International Forums.* Bombay, N.Y.: *Akwesasne Notes,* 1982.

Javits, Jacob K. *The Autobiography of a Public Man.* Boston, Mass.: Houghton, Mifflin, 1981.

Jennings, Francis. *The Ambiguous Iroquois Empire: The Covenant Chain Confederation of Indian Tribes With English Colonies From Its Beginnings to the Lancaster Treaty of 1744.* New York: W. W. Norton & Co., 1984.

Jennings, Francis, William N. Fenton, et al. *The History and Culture of Iroquois Diplomacy.* Syracuse, N.Y.: Syracuse University Press, 1985.

Johannsen, Christina B., and John P. Ferguson, eds. *Iroquois Arts: A Directory of a People and Their Work.* Warnerville, N.Y.: Association for the Advancement of Native North American Arts and Crafts, 1983.

Josephy, Alvin M., Jr. *Now That the Buffalo's Gone: A Study of Today's American Indians.* New York: Alfred A. Knopf, 1982.

Josephy, Alvin M., Jr., ed. *Red Power: The American Indians Fight for Freedom.* New York: American Heritage Press, 1971.

Kelsay, Isabel Thompson. *Joseph Brant, 1743–1807: Man of Two Worlds.* Syracuse, N.Y.: Syracuse University Press, 1984.

Kickingbird, Kirke, et al. *Indian Sovereignty.* Washington, D.C.: Institute for the Development of Indian Law, 1977.

Kickingbird, Kirke, and Karen Ducheneaux. *One Hundred Million Acres.* New York: Macmillan, 1973.

Kvasnicka, Robert, and Herman Viola, eds. *The Commissioners of Indian Affairs, 1824–1977.* Lincoln, Neb.: University of Nebraska Press, 1979.

Leder, Lawrence H., ed. *The Livingston Indian Records, 1666–1723.* Gettysburg, Pa.: Pennsylvania Historical Association 1956.

Lurie, Nancy O., and Stuart Levine, eds. *The American Indian Today.* Rev. ed. Baltimore, Md.: Penguin, 1968.

Mabee, Carleton. *The Seaway Story.* New York: Macmillan, 1961.

McClelland, Peter D., and Alan L. Magdovitz. *Crisis in the Making: The Political Economy of New York State Since 1945.* New York: Cambridge University Press, 1981.

McKinney's Consolidated Laws of New York State. Annotated. St. Paul, Minn.: West Publishing Co., 1987.

McNickle, D'Arcy. *Native American Tribalism: Indian Survivals and Renewals.* Rev. ed. New York: Oxford University Press, 1973.

McNickle, D'Arcy. *They Came Here First.* Rev. ed. New York: Octagon, 1975.

Manley, Henry S. *Treaty of Ft. Stanwix, 1784.* Rome, N.Y.: Rome Sentinel Co., 1932.

Matthiesson, Peter. *Indian Country.* New York: Viking Press, 1984.

Matthiesson, Peter. *In the Spirit of Crazy Horse.* New York: Viking Press, 1983.

Miringoff, Lee M., and Barbara L. Carvalho. *The Cuomo Factor: Assessing the Political Appeal of New York's Governor.* Poughkeepsie, N.Y.: Marist College, Institute for Public Opinion, 1986.

Morgan, Lewis Henry. *The League of the Ho-de-no-sau-nee or Iroquois.* Rochester, 1851; reprint, New York: Corinth Books, 1962.

Moscow, Warren. *Politics in the Empire State.* New York: Alfred A. Knopf, 1948.

Moses, Robert. *Working for the People: Promise and Performance in Public Service.* New York: Harper, 1956.

Munger, Frank J., and Ralph A. Straetz. *New York Politics.* New York: New York University Press, 1960.

National Lawyers Guild Committee on Native American Struggles, comp. and ed. *Rethinking Indian Law.* New Haven, Conn.: Advocate Press, 1982.

O'Callaghan, Edmund B., ed. *Documentary History of the State of New York.* 4 vols. Albany, N.Y.: Weed, Parsons and Co., 1849–1851.

O'Callaghan, Edmund B., and Berthold Fernow, eds. *Documents Relative to the Colonial History of the State of New York.* 15 vols. Albany, N.Y.: Weed, Parsons, 1856–1887.

Newfield, Jack, and Paul De Brul. *The Abuse of Power: The Permanent Government and the Fall of New York.* New York: Viking Press, 1979.

Noon, John A. *Law and Government of the Grand River Iroquois.* New York: Viking Fund Publications in Anthropology, 12, 1949.

Parker, Arthur C. *Parker on the Iroquois.* ed. by William N. Fenton. Syracuse, N.Y.: Syracuse University Press, 1968.

Pevar, Stephen L. *The Rights of Indians and Tribes.* New York: American Civil Liberties Union and Bantam Books, 1983.

Philip, Kenneth R., ed. *Indian Self-Rule: First-Hand Accounts of Indian-White Relations from Roosevelt to Reagan.* Salt Lake City, Utah: Institute of the American West, 1986.

Porter, Frank W., III, ed. *Strategies for Survival: American Indians in the Eastern United States.* Westport, Conn.: Greenwood Press, 1986.

Price, Monroe E. *Law and the American Indian: Readings, Notes, and Cases.* Indianapolis, Ind.: Bobbs-Merrill Co., 1973.

Prucha, Francis Paul. *American Indian Policy in the Formative Years: The Indian Trade and Intercourse Acts, 1790–1834.* Cambridge, Mass.: Harvard University Press, 1962.

Prucha, Francis Paul. *The Great Father: The United States Government and the American Indians.* 2 vols. Lincoln, Neb.: University of Nebraska Press, 1984.

Prucha, Francis Paul. *Indian Policy in the United States: Historical Essays.* Lincoln, Neb.: University of Nebraska Press, 1981.

Prucha, Francis Paul. *The Indians in American Society: From the Revolutionary War to the Present.* Berkeley, Calif.: University of California, 1985.

Quick, Polly McW., ed. *Proceedings: Conference on Reburial Issues.* Washington, D.C.: Society for American Archaeology, 1986.

Rockefeller, Nelson A. *The Future of Federalism.* Cambridge, Mass.: Harvard University Press, 1962.

Nelson A. Rockefeller Institute of Government. 1984–1985 *New York State Statistical Yearbook*. 11th edition. Albany, N.Y., 1985.

Rose, Mark. *Interstate*. Lawrence, Kan.: University Press of Kansas, 1979.

Sandstrom, Roy H., ed. *Educating the Educators: A Report of the Institute on "The American Indian Student in Higher Education," St. Lawrence University, July 12–30, 1971*. Canton, N.Y.: St. Lawrence University, 1971.

Scarrow, Howard. *Parties, Elections and Representation in the State of New York*. New York: New York University Press, 1983.

(Smithsonian) *Handbook of North American Indians*. Vol. 15. ed. by Bruce G. Trigger and William C. Sturtevant. Washington, D.C.: U.S.G.P.O., 1978.

Sorkin, Alan L. *American Indians and Federal Aid*. Washington, D.C.: Brookings Institution, 1971.

Shimony, Annemarie. *Conservatism Among the Iroquois at the Six Nations Reserve*. Publications in Anthropology, 65. New Haven, Conn.: Yale University, 1961.

Smith, Richard Norton. *Thomas E. Dewey and His Times*. New York: W. W. Norton, 1982.

Stone, Graynell, ed. *The Shinnecock Indians: A Culture History*. Readings in Long Island Archaeology and Ethnohistory. Vol. VI. Lexington, Mass.: Ginn Custom Publishing, 1983.

Strickland, Rennard, et al., eds. *Felix S. Cohen's Handbook of Federal Indian Law, 1982 Edition*. Charlottesville, Va.: Michie, Bobbs-Merrill, 1982.

Stuart, Paul. *The Indian Office: Growth and Development of an American Institution, 1865–1900*. Ann Arbor, Mich.: UMI Research Press, 1978.

Sufrin, Sidney C., and Edward E. Palmer. *The New St. Lawrence Frontier: A Survey of the Economic Potential in the St. Lawrence Area of New York State*. Syracuse, N.Y.: Syracuse University Press, 1956.

Sullivan, James, et al., eds. *The Papers of Sir William Johnson*. 14 vols. Albany, N.Y.: University of the State of New York, 1921–1965.

Sutton, Imre, ed. *Irredeemable America: The Indians' Estate and Land Claims*. Albuquerque, N.M.: University of New Mexico Press, 1985.

Swagerty, William, ed. *Indian Sovereignty, Proceedings of the Second Annual Conference on Problems and Issues Concerning American In-*

dians Today. Chicago, Ill.: Newberry Library Center for the History of the American Indian. Occasional Papers, II, 1979.

Swagerty, W. R., ed. *Scholars and the Indian Experience: Critical Reviews of Recent Writing in the Social Sciences.* Bloomington, Ind.: Indiana University Press, 1984.

Szasz, Margaret C. *Education and the American Indian: The Road to Self-Determination, 1928–1973.* Albuquerque, N.M.: University of New Mexico Press, 1974.

Taylor, Theodore W. *American Indian Policy.* Mt. Airy, Md.: Lomond, 1984.

Taylor, Theodore W. *The Bureau of Indian Affairs.* Boulder, Colo.: Westview Press, 1984.

Thompson, John. H., ed. *Geography of New York State.* Syracuse, N.Y.: Syracuse University Press, 1966.

Tooker, Elisabeth, ed. *Iroquois Culture, History and Prehistory: Proceedings of the 1965 Conference on Iroquois Research.* Albany, N.Y.: New York State Museum and Science Center, 1967.

Trelease, Allen W. *Indian Affairs in Colonial New York: The Seventeenth Century.* Ithaca, N.Y.: Cornell University Press, 1960.

Underwood, James E., and William Daniels. *Governor Rockefeller in New York: The Apex of Pragmatic Liberalism in the United States.* Westport, Conn.: Greenwood Press, 1982.

Upton, Helen. *The Everett Report in Historical Perspective.* Albany, N.Y.: American Revolution Bicentennial Commission, 1980.

Vecsey, Christopher, and Robert W. Venables, eds. *American Indian Environments: Ecological Issues in Native American History.* Syracuse, N.Y.: Syracuse University Press, 1980.

Wallace, Anthony F. C. *The Death and Rebirth of the Seneca.* New York: Alfred A. Knopf, 1970.

Washburn, Wilcomb E. *The Indian in America.* New York: Harper and Row, 1975.

Weaver, Sally. *Making Canadian Indian Policy: The Hidden Agenda.* Toronto, Ont.: University of Toronto Press, 1981.

Weaver, Sally. *Medicine and Politics Among the Grand River Iroquois: A Study of the Non-Conservatives.* Ottawa, Ont.: National Museum of Man, Mercury Series, 1972.

Weyler, Rex. *Blood of the Land: The Government and Corporate War Against the American Indian Movement.* New York: Everest House Publishers, 1982.

Williams, Ted C. *The Reservation*. Syracuse, N.Y.: Syracuse University Press, 1976.

Willoughby, William R. *The St. Lawrence Waterway: A Study in Politics and Diplomacy*. Madison, Wis.: University of Wisconsin Press, 1961.

Wilson, Edmund. *Apologies to the Iroquois*. New York: Random House, 1959.

Zimmerman, Joseph G. *The Government and Politics of New York State*. New York: New York University, 1981.

Articles

Anderson, Duane C. "Reburial: Is It Reasonable?" *Archaeology*, 33 (1985): 48–51.

Antos, Susan C. "Indian Land Claims Under the Nonintercourse Act." *Albany Law Review* 44 (October 1979): 110–138.

Apple, R. W. "The Question of Mario Cuomo." *New York Times Magazine* (September 1986): 44–50, 87.

Bee, Robert L. "To Get Something for the People: The Predicament of the American Indian Leader." *Human Organization* 38 (Fall 1979): 239–247.

Bennett, Robert L. "Indian-State Relations in Their Historical Perspective." *Journal of the Wisconsin Indians Research Institute* 3 (September 1967): i–iv.

Bishop, Bruce. "The States and Indian Jurisdiction: Another Approach." *State Government* 51 (Autumn 1978): 230–234.

Blanchard, David S. "High Steel! The Kahnawake Mohawk and the High Construction Trade." *Journal of Ethnic Studies* 11 (Summer 1983): 32–60.

Brasser, Ted J. C. "The Coastal Algonkians: People of the First Frontiers." In: *North American Indians in Historical Perspective*. Eleanor B. Leacock and Nancy O. Lurie, eds. New York: Random House, 1971.

Brown, Judith K. "Economic Organization and the Position of Women Among the Iroquois." *Ethnohistory* 17 (1970): 151–167.

Campisi, Jack. "New York-Oneida Treaty of 1795: A Finding of Fact." *American Indian Law Review* 4 (Summer 1976): 71–82.

Campisi, Jack. "The Trade and Intercourse Acts: Land Claims on the Eastern Seaboard." In: *Irredeemable America: The Indians' Estate and Land Claims*. Imre Sutton, ed. Albuquerque, N.M.: University of New Mexico Press, 1985.

Clarke, Noah T. "The Wampum Belt Collection of the New York State Museum." *New York State Museum Bulletin* 288 (July 1931): 85–124.

Clinton, Robert N., and Margaret Tobey Hotopp. "Judicial Enforcement of the Federal Restraints on Alienation of Indian Land: The Origins of the Eastern Land Claims." *Maine Law Review* 31 (1979): 17–90.

Clute, James W. "The New York Indians' Rights to Self-Determination." *Buffalo Law Review* 22 (Spring 1973): 985–1019.

Decker, George. "Treaty Making with the Indians." New York State Archaeological Association, *Researches and Transactions* 2 (1920): 44–65.

Dincauze, Dena F. "Report on the Conference on Reburial Issues." *Bulletin of the Society for American Archaeology* 3 (1985): 1–2.

Doherty, Matthew F. "Toward a Better Tomorrow." *New York State Education* 58 (April 1971): 16–17.

Elm, Lloyd. "Needed: A Philosophy of Education for American Indians." *American Indian Journal* 1 (November 1975): 2–5.

Fadden, John, and Louis Mofsie. "Student Reactions to Indian Teachers of Non-Indian Children." *Social Education* 36 (May 1972): 507–511.

Fadden, Stephen. "Indian Burial Sites—Protection an Issue for New York But Questions Remain." *Indian Studies* 2 (Winter 1985): 4–7.

Fenton, William N. "A Day on the Allegheny Ox-Bow." *The Living Wilderness* 10 (1945): 1–8.

Fenton, William N. "The Iroquois in History." In: *North American Indians in Historical Perspective*. Eleanor Burke Leacock and Nancy Oestrich Lurie, eds. New York: Random House, 1971.

Fenton, William N. "The New York State Wampum Collection: The Case for the Integrity of Cultural Treasures." *Proceedings* of the American Philosophical Society 115 (1971): 431–461.

Fenton, William N. "The Lore of the Longhouse: Myth, Ritual and Red Power." *Anthropological Quarterly* 48 (1975): 131–147.

Fenton, William N. "Problems Arising From the Historic Northeastern Position of the Iroquois." In: *Essays in Historical Anthropology of North America*. Smithsonian Miscellaneous Collections, 100. Washington, D.C., 1940.

Fenton, William N. "Seth Newhouse's Traditional History and Constitution of the Iroquois Confederacy." *Proceedings* of the American Philosophical Society 93 (1949): 141–158.

Fenton, William N. "Some Social Customs of the Modern Senecas." New York State Department of Social Welfare *Bulletin* 7 (1936): 4–7.

Fenton, William N. "This Island, the World on the Turtle's Back." *Journal of American Folklore* 75 (October-December 1962): 283-300.

Fenton, William N. "The Tonawanda Indian Community Library." *Indians at Work* 3 (1935): 46-48.

Fenton, William N. "Toward the Gradual Civilization of the Indian Natives: The Missionary and Linguistic Work of Asher Wright [1803-1875] Among the Senecas of Western New York." *Proceedings* of the American Philosophical Society 100 (1956): 567-581.

Freilich, Morris. "Cultural Persistence Among the Modern Iroquois." *Anthropos* 53 (1958): 473-483.

Gillette, Charles H. "Wampum Beads and Belts." *Indian Historian* 3 (Fall 1970): 33-38.

Goldberg, Carol E. "Public Law 280: The Limits of State Jurisdiction Over Reservation Indians." *UCLA Law Review* 22 (1975): 535-594.

Graymont, Barbara. "New York State Indian Policy After the Revolution." *New York History* 57 (October 1976): 439-474.

Grimes, Ronald L. "Desecration of the Dead: An Inter-Religious Controversy." *American Indian Quarterly* 10 (Fall 1986): 305-309.

Gunther, Gerald. "Governmental Power and New York Indian Lands—A Reassessment of a Persistent Problem of Federal-State Relations." *Buffalo Law Review* 8 (Fall 1958): 1-14

Hagan, William T. "Archival Captive—The American Indian." *American Archivist* 41 (April 1978): 135-142.

Hagan, William T. "Tribalism Rejuvenated: The Native American Since the Era of Termination." *Western Historical Quarterly* 12 (January 1981): 5-16.

Harris, LaDonna. "Indian Education in New York State Education: Hope for the Future." *New York State Education* 58 (April 1971): 18-21.

Hauptman, Laurence M. [N. Y. State v. The Indians] "Circle the Wagons." *Capital Region* 2 (February 1987): 29-31, 52-53.

Hauptman, Laurence M. "Designing Woman: Minnie Kellogg, Iroquois Leader." In: *Indian Lives: Essays on Nineteenth- and Twentieth-Century Native American Leaders*. L. George Moses and Raymond Wilson, eds. Albuquerque, N.Y.: University of New Mexico Press, 1985.

Hauptman, Laurence M. "General John S. Bragdon, the Office of Public Works Planning, and the Decision to Build Pennsylvania's Kinzua Dam." *Pennsylvania History* 53 (July 1986): 181-200.

Hauptman, Laurence M. "Governor Theodore Roosevelt and the Indians of New York State." *Proceedings* of the American Philosophical Society 119 (February 1975): 1–7.

Hauptman, Laurence M. "The Historical Background to the Present Day Seneca Nation-Salamanca Lease Controversy: The First Hundred Years, 1851–1951." Rockefeller Institute of Government, *Working Paper No. 20* (Fall 1985).

Hauptman, Laurence M. "Senecas and Subdividers: Resistance to Allotment of Indian Lands in New York, 1875–1906." *Prologue* 9 (Summer 1977): 105–116.

Henry, Jeanette. "A Rebuttal to the Five Anthropologists on the Issue of Wampum Return." *Indian Historian* 3 (Spring 1970): 15–18.

Hogan, Thomas E. "City in a Quandary: Salamanca and the Allegany Leases." *New York History* 55 (January 1974): 79–101.

Hill, Rick, and Jim Wake. "The Native American Center for the Living Arts." *American Indian Art*, V (Summer 1980): 22–25.

"The Iroquois Wampum Controversy." *Indian Historian* 3 (Spring 1970): 4–14. [Includes several articles and statements.]

"Issues in Archaeology: The Questions of Reburial: Archaeologists Debate the Handling of Prehistoric Human Skeletal Remains." *Early Man Magazine* (Autumn 1981): 25–27.

Jemison, G. Pete. "Ganondagan Lives On." *Turtle Quarterly* 1 (1986): 2–3.

Krook, Lennart, and G. A. Maylin. "Industrial Fluoride Pollution: Chronic Fluoride Poisoning in Cornwall Island Cattle." *Cornell Veterinarian* 69, Suppl. 8 (1979): 1–70.

Kroup, Ben A. "A Step Forward." *Turtle Quarterly* 1 (1986): 13–16, 24.

Kwartler, Richard. " 'This Is Our Land': The Mohawk Indians v. The State of New York." In: *Roundtable Justice: Case Studies in Conflict Resolution: Reports to the Ford Foundation.* R. B. Goldman, ed. Boulder, Colo.: Westview Press, Inc., 1980.

Landsman, Gail. "Ganienkeh: Symbol and Politics in an Indian/White Conflict." *American Anthropologist* 87 (December 1985): 826–839.

Landy, David. "Tuscarora Tribalism and National Identity." *Ethnohistory* 5 (1958): 250–284.

Lytle, Clifford M. "The Supreme Court, Tribal Sovereignty and Continuing Problems of State Encroachment into Indian Country." *American Indian Law Review* 8 (1979): 65–77.

Manley, Henry S. "Buying Buffalo from the Indians." *New York History* 28 (July 1947): 313–329.

Manley, Henry S. "Indian Reservation Ownership in New York." *New York State Bar Bulletin* 32 (April 1960): 134–138.

Manley, Henry S. "No Man's Land, Southampton." *Long Island Forum* 16 (October 1953): 183–194.

Meighan, Clement W. "Archaeology: Science or Sacrilege?" In: *Ethics and Values in Archaeology*, Ernestine L. Greene, ed. New York: Free Press, 1984.

Mohawk, John. "Gannagaro: Walking Ancestor Trails." *Indian Studies* 2 (Winter 1985): 10–13.

Parker, Arthur C. "The Status of New York Indians." New York State Museum *Bulletin* 253 (1924): 67–82.

Pound, Cuthbert W. "Nationals Without a Nation: The New York State Tribal Indians." *Columbia Law Review* 22 (February 1922):97–102.

Prucha, Francis Paul. "American Indian Policy in the Twentieth Century." *Western Historical Quarterly* 15 (January 1984): 5–18.

Pyke, Beverly J., Beatrice White, and Charles Heerman. "Akwesasne QRQ, ABE, GED and College Extension." *Journal of American Indian Education* XIV (May 1975): 1–4.

Rebich, Theodore, Jr., Jayanth Kumar, et al. "Dental Caries and Tetracycline-Stained Dentition in an American Indian Population." *Journal of Dental Research* 64 (March 1985): 462–464.

Rebich, Theodore, Jr., Jayanth Kumar, et al. "The St. Regis Environmental Health Issue: Assessment of Dental Defects." *Journal of the American Dental Association* 106 (May 1983): 630–633.

Rosen, Lawrence. "The Excavation of American Indian Burial Sites: A Problem in Law and Professional Responsibility." *American Anthropologist* 82 (1980): 5–23.

Russell, Charles. "Centralizing New York Indian Schools: Report of a Survey." *American Indian* 7 (1955): 45–54.

St. Clair, James D., and William F. Lee. "Defense of Nonintercourse Act Claims: The Requirement of Tribal Existence." *Maine Law Review* 31 (1979): 91–113.

Staub, Henry P. "Health Supervision of Infants on the Cattaraugus Indian Reservation, New York: The Record Is No Better than in Big City Slum Areas." *Clinical Pediatrics* 15 (January 1976): 44–52.

Treuer, Margaret. "Ganienkeh: An Alternative to the Reservation System and the Federal Trust." *American Indian Journal* 5 (1979): 22–26.

Vernon, Howard. "The Cayuga Claims: A Background Study." *American Indian Culture and Research Journal* 4 (Fall 1980): 21–35.

Vizenor, Gerald. "Bone Courts: The Rights and Narrative Representation of Human Bones." *American Indian Quarterly* 10 (Fall 1986): 319–332.

Vollman, Tim. "A Survey of Eastern Indian Claims: 1970–1979." *Maine Law Review* 31 (1979): 5–16.

Wallace, Harry B. "Indian Sovereignty and Eastern Indian Land Claims." *New York Law School Review* 27 (1982): 921–950.

Wasser, Martin. "The Six Nations and the State." *Conservationist* 30 (January-February 1976): 36–37.

Wasser, Martin B. "Sovereign New York and Sovereign Mohawks." *North Country Life* (Summer 1977): 4–5, 16.

Wasser, Martin B., and Louis Grumet. "Indian Rights—The Reality of Symbolism." *New York State Bar Journal* 50 (October 1978):483–485, 514–518.

Wells, Robert, and Minerva White. "Operation Kanyengehaga: An American Cross Cultural Program." *American Indian Culture and Research Journal* 1 (1975): 22–28.

Wilkinson, Charles F., and John M. Volkman. "As Long as Water Flows or Grass Grows Upon the Earth—How Long a Time Is That?" *California Law Review* 63 (1975): 601–666.

Zimmerman, Larry J. " 'Tell Them About the Suicide': A Review of Recent Materials on the Reburial of Prehistoric Native American Skeletons." *American Indian Quarterly* 10 (Fall 1986): 333–343.

Dissertations

Abler, Thomas S. "Factional Dispute and Party Conflict in the Political System of the Seneca Nation (1845–1895): An Ethnohistorical Analysis." Unpublished Ph.D. dissertation, Toronto, Ont.: University of Toronto, 1969.

Campisi, Jack. "Ethnic Identity and Boundary Maintenance in Three Oneida Communities." Unpublished Ph.D. dissertation, Albany, N.Y.: State University of New York, Albany, 1974.

Dullea, Henrik Norman. "Chapter Revision in the Empire State: The Politics of New York's 1967 Constitutional Convention." Unpublished Ph.D. dissertation, Syracuse, N.Y.: Syracuse University, 1982.

Flad, Harvey. "The City and the Longhouse: A Social Geography of American Indians in Syracuse, N.Y." Unpublished Ph.D. dissertation, Syracuse, N.Y.: Syracuse University, 1973.

Flannery, Thomas P., Jr. "The Indian Self-Determination Act: An Analysis of Federal Policy." Unpublished Ph.D. dissertation, Evanston, Ill.: University of Illinois, 1980.

Geier, Philip Otto. "A Peculiar Status: A History of Oneida Indian Treaties and Claims: Jurisdictional Conflict Within the American Government." Unpublished Ph.D. dissertation, Syracuse, N.Y.: Syracuse University, 1980.

Frisch, Jack A. "Revitalization, Nativism and Tribalism Among the St. Regis Mohawks." Unpublished Ph.D. dissertation, Bloomington, Ind.: Indiana University, 1970.

Huff, Henry M., Jr. "Thomas Indian School: An Account of the Death of an Institution." Unpublished M.A. thesis, Pennsylvania State University, 1977.

Johannsen, Christina. "Efflorescence and Identity in Iroquois Art." Unpublished Ph.D. dissertation, Providence, R.I.: Brown University, 1984.

Landsman, Gail Heidi. "Ganienkeh: Symbol and Politics in an Indian/White Land Dispute." Unpublished Ph.D. dissertation, Washington, D.C.: Catholic University of America, 1982.

Rosenthal, Harvey D. "Their Day in Court: A History of the Indian Claims Commission." Unpublished Ph.D. dissertation, Kent, Ohio: Kent State University, 1976.

INDEX

▼ ▼ ▼ ▼ ▼

1909
1910